WOMEN IN GERMAN YEARBOOK

Volume Twenty-two

2006

EDITORIAL BOARD

Friederike Eigler, Georgetown University, 2004–07
eiglerf@georgetown.edu

Marjorie Gelus, California State University, 2006–09
gelus@csus.edu

Katharina Gerstenberger, University of Cincinnati, 2004–07
gerstek@email.uc.edu

Julia Hell, University of Michigan, 2004–07
hell@umich.edu

Patricia Herminghouse, University of Rochester, 2006–09
pahe@troi.cc.rochester.edu

Ruth-Ellen Boetcher Joeres, University of Minnesota, 2004–09
joere001@tc.umn.edu

Ruth Kluger, University of California, Irvine, 2006–09
rkluger@uci.edu

Dagmar C.G. Lorenz, University of Illinois at Chicago, 2006–09
dlorenz@uic.edu

Elizabeth R. Mittman, Michigan State University, 2004–08
mittman@msu.edu

Leslie Morris, University of Minnesota, 2004–08
morri074@umn.edu

Tanja Nusser, Ernst-Moritz-Arndt Universität, 2004–08
nusser@uni-greifswald.de

Monika Shafi, University of Delaware, 2006–09
mshafi@udel.edu

Lora Wildenthal, Rice University, 2004–08
wildenth@rice.edu

PAST EDITORS

Marianne Burkhard, 1984–88
Edith Waldstein, 1984–87
Jeanette Clausen, 1987–94
Helen Cafferty, 1988–90
Sara Friedrichsmeyer, 1990–98
Susanne Zantop, 1998–2001
Patricia Herminghouse, 1994–2002
Ruth-Ellen Boetcher Joeres, 2002–04
Marjorie Gelus, 2003–05

WOMEN IN

Feminist Studies in German Literature & Culture

GERMAN

Edited by Helga Kraft and Maggie McCarthy

YEARBOOK

Volume Twenty-two

2006

University of Nebraska Press, Lincoln and London

Excerpts from the novel *Entfernung.*, S. Fischer Verlag GmbH, 2006, are reprinted and translated here by the generous permission of the publisher.
© 2007 by the Board of Regents of the University of Nebraska. All rights reserved. Manufactured in the United States of America. ∞
Published by arrangement with the Coalition of Women in German.
ISBN-13: 978-0-8032-1113-1 (Cloth)
ISBN-10: 0-8032-1113-9 (Cloth)
ISBN-13: 978-0-8032-5972-0 (Paper)
ISBN-10: 0-8032-5972-7 (Paper)
ISSN: 1058-7446

CONTENTS

Acknowledgments vii
Preface ix

Focus: Film

**Liebe Perla, Memento Mori:
On Filming Disability and Holocaust History** 1
Sara Eigen

**Re-Producing the Class and Gender Divide:
Fritz Lang's *Metropolis*** 21
Gabriela Stoicea

**"She's Got Her Own Way of Asserting Herself":
Interview with Seyhan Derin** 43
Angelica Fenner

* * *

Focus: Writers

**Ruth Angress Kluger:
To the Writer and Scholar on Her 75th Birthday** 62
Helga Kraft and Dagmar C.G. Lorenz

**"Language Is Not an Instrument for Me but Existence":
Interview with Marlene Streeruwitz** 74
Helga Kraft

Excerpt from the Novel *Entfernung*. 88
Marlene Streeruwitz

Focus: Teaching

Feels Like Teen Spirit: Teaching Cultural Difference through Bodies, Gender, and Affect 94
Richard Langston

* * *

The Making of Transnational Textual Communities: German Women Translators, 1800–1850 119
Andrew Piper

"Weil ich der raschen Lippe Herr nicht bin": Oral Transgression as Enlightenment Disavowal in Kleist's *Penthesilea* 145
Heather Merle Benbow

The Photographic Enactment of the Early New Woman in 1890s German Women's Bicycling Magazines 167
Beth Muellner

Artist for Art's Sake or Artist for Sale: Lulu's and Else's Failed Attempts at Aesthetic Self-Fashioning 189
Kelly Comfort

Marital Status and the Rhetoric of the Women's Movement in World War I Germany 211
Catherine Dollard

Cooking up Memories: The Role of Food, Recipes, and Relationships in Jeannette Lander's *Überbleibsel* 236
Heike Henderson

About the Contributors 258
Notice to Contributors 262

ACKNOWLEDGMENTS

The coeditors would like to thank the current Editorial Board for their welcome assistance in reviewing manuscripts, their participation in our on-line discussions, and their general support and encouragement. We also gratefully acknowledge the assistance and advice of the following individuals in reviewing manuscripts submitted for publication in the *Women in German Yearbook*.

Vanessa Agnew, University of Michigan
Nora Alter, University of Florida
Susan Anderson, University of Oregon
Wendy Arons, University of Notre Dame
Hester Baer, University of Oklahoma
Erika Berroth, Minnesota State University, Mankato
Claudia Breger, Indiana University
Gisela Brinker-Gabler, Binghamton University
Kathleen Canning, University of Michigan
Tom Cheesman, University of Wales
Susan Cocalis, University of Massachusetts, Amherst
Sarah Colvin, University of Edinburgh
John Davidson, Ohio State University
Friederike Edmonds, University of Toledo
Stefani Engelstein, University of Missouri, Columbia
Rachel Freudenburg, Boston College
Sara Friedrichsmeyer, University of Cincinnati
Marjanne Goozé, University of Georgia
Sara Hall, University of Illinois at Chicago
Katharina von Hammerstein, University of Connecticut
Gail Hart, University of California, Irvine
Jonathan Hess, University of North Carolina, Chapel Hill
Peter Hess, University of Texas, Austin
John Hoberman, University of Texas, Austin
Shawn Jarvis, Saint Cloud State University
Regina Kecht, Rice University
Ruth Kluger, University of California, Irvine
Kathleen Komar, University of California
Susanne Kord, University College London
Barbara Kosta, University of Arizona

Sara Lennox, University of Massachusetts, Amherst
Waltraud Maierhofer, University of Iowa
Tracie Matysik, University of Texas, Austin
Rick McCormick, University of Minnesota
Helga Meise, Les Universités à Aix en Provence
Barbara Mennel, University of Florida
Sabine Moedersheim, University of Wisconsin, Madison
Tanja Nusser, Universität Greifswald
Diana Orendi, Cleveland State University
Nicholas Rennie, Rutgers University
Susanne Rott, University of Illinois at Chicago
Richard Schade, University of Cincinnati
Elmar Schenkel, Universität Leipzig
Stephan Schindler, Washington University, St. Louis
Monika Shafi, University of Delaware
Lorna Sopcak, Ripon College
Inge Stephan, Humboldt-Universität
Eva Szalay, Weber State University
Astrida Tantillo, University of Illinois at Chicago

Special thanks to Victoria Hoelzer-Maddox
for manuscript preparation,
to Elizabeth Frye for editorial assistance,
and to Don Maddox for computer assistance.

PREFACE

Last fall Maggie McCarthy joined Helga Kraft as co-editor of the *Yearbook*. Together, they combine the skills of a native German and native English speaker, a "SWIGGIE" or senior WIG member, to borrow a 2005 Cabaret coinage, and the next generation. Our yin/yang energy has fueled some intense summer months as we pulled the current volume together. Maggie would also like to emphasize that many of her editing maxims are a direct legacy from Patricia Herminghouse, her *Doktormutter*. She's grateful for all the mentoring that supported her own early efforts to produce publishable prose and glad to sustain the momentum with the young scholars whose work appears here.

Volume 22 of the *Yearbook* saw considerable changes in the production process as it transitioned to paperless editing. Manuscript reviewers worked by and large with e-mail attachments, and our instructions for retaining the anonymity of authors and readers were cited in the *Chronicle of Higher Education* in an article on editing in the virtual age. Thanks to Adobe® Acrobat® 7.0 Professional, the essays that appear in this volume zinged back and forth this summer between Helga in Berlin, Maggie in North Carolina, editorial assistant Liz Frye in Chicago, and our intrepid formatter Victoria in Michigan. Despite some inevitable glitches, in general we're feeling very modern. The discussion continues about just how virtual the *Yearbook* should be, but for the moment you can still count on our sprightly colored volumes arriving in your mailbox once a year.

This volume features some already familiar characters, like women warriors and machine vamps, but also entirely new kinds of voices, issuing from Turkish filmmaker Seyhan Derin, bicycling feminists of the 1890s, and the handicapped female dwarves of Shahar Rozen's documentary *Liebe Perla*. Spanning three centuries and media as diverse as literature, film, magazines, and photography, this volume has strong breadth and diversity. A variety of feminist scholarly imperatives underpin all of these essays.

Good Germanists of all stripes, of course, have long paid hard attention to the insistent cultural and historical particulars informing real, literary, or filmic lives, and feminist scholars in particular have examined their concrete imprint on female bodies, souls, and psyches.

The result is not always oppression pure and simple, as Heather Benbow's essay surmises, given the way Kleist's Penthesilea reacts to Enlightenment discourses of female oral modesty, namely by literally feasting on her lover. Less wantonly, Jeannette Lander's autobiographical protagonist in her novel *Überbleibsel* struggles as well with issues of eating and control. Orchestrating lavish dinners while bemoaning their effects on her waistline, she performs an age-old female service, but also, as Heike Henderson argues, maintains a power dynamic over her family that feeds her own agency. Mining oppressive circumstances for hidden, double-edged forms of agency has also prompted much feminist scholarship, and Kelly Comfort contributes to this strain in her examination of Frank Wedekind's Lulu and Arthur Schnitzler's Fräulein Else. Although ultimately commodified out of existence, both women out-Madonna Madonna in the process, reveling in the power and pleasure of performance and aesthetic self-fashioning. Beth Muellner examines issues of representational propriety in 1890s photographs of bicycling feminists in pantaloons and the textual captions that tamed their visual shock value. Less visible in the subterranean spaces of Fritz Lang's *Metropolis* are the links between work, gender, and sexuality that Gabriela Stoicea examines in her essay, including the female workers' part in challenging the status quo.

A basic feminist concern to uncover hidden female voices informs Sara Eigen's reading of *Liebe Perla*. What a female dwarf displayed naked in a film made by Josef Mengele has to say, however, again reveals not only horrific oppression, but also implicitly suggests that some hidden Holocaust artifacts should perhaps be covered up again. Filming the lives of her Turkish mother and grandmother, Seyhan Derin worked around a patriarch intent on keeping their lives shrouded rather than documented. Less challenging and with their own surprising artistic upside were the episodes of the teen soap *Good Times / Bad Times* that Seyhan has directed on the side. Andrew Piper charts another form of veiled, artistic production among women, but two centuries earlier by female translators of the early nineteenth century. Their imprint and aesthetic choices remain unmistakably entwined with the canonical voices they translated. To what extent we shouldn't translate into our own cultural reference points and instead simply let alterity resound in our classrooms informs Richard Langston's essay on teaching Benjamin Lebert's autobiographical novel, *Crazy*. He offers very useful pedagogical strategies for teaching the story of a handicapped German teen and his adventures at a posh German boarding school.

This volume also includes the textual stamp of last year's invited speaker at the WIG conference—Austrian playwright and author, Marlene Streeruwitz. We include Helga's interview with her, as well as an excerpt from her most recent novel, *Entfernung*. Both contributions manifest Streeruwitz's experimental style, theory-savvy reflections on globalization, and unapologetic feminist stance.

Finally, and with great pleasure, we include Helga's and Dagmar Lorenz's tribute to Ruth Kluger in celebration of her 75th birthday. We hope their reflections not only do justice to the magnitude of Ruth's intellectual achievements, but also reveal how these achievements are equally matched by her extraordinarily generous spirit.

We close our preface then on the same note we opened with—recognition of an older generation's achievements and their impact on the new ranks. We hope that good, old-fashioned mentoring among women remains a feminist imperative that never goes out of style.

Helga Kraft
Maggie McCarthy
August 2006

Liebe Perla, Memento Mori:
On Filming Disability and Holocaust History

Sara Eigen

The documentary film *Liebe Perla* (1999), a German-Israeli co-production directed by Shahar Rozen, is a rumination on the life of Perla Ovici. It is a film that, due to the unfortunately limited circulation suffered by most documentaries, few are likely to see. Yet its narrative and cinematographic excellence offer surprisingly novel treatment of issues that include the treatment of the disabled during the Holocaust, the function of film as documentary record, and the potential conflict between personal and political claims upon the archives of history. (SE)

Liebe Perla begins with two credits appearing in silent succession on a black screen: "Keshet Broadcasting" and "Eden Productions." A brief text follows, accompanied by a restrained and unobtrusive musical score consisting of a short sequence of notes in a Kletzmer key. The text reads, "Several years ago German researcher Hannelore Witkofski read about the Jewish Lilliput Troupe from Hungary. / She contacted Perla, the last surviving member of the family, and asked if she could interview her at her home in Israel." And then, on another screen, "Perla and Hannelore became close friends. / On her third visit to Haifa, accompanied by friends and assistants, Hannelore was presented with an unusual request...[.]"[1] This text then fades to black, and moving pictures begin: a man in a living room quietly arranges a low table for a dinner party. Several shots of various individuals follow, including close-ups of hands at work cutting tomatoes and applying lipstick.[2] A woman is led into the living room—a dwarf with extremely limited eyesight who moves with difficulty. Another older and startlingly small woman, Perla, enters, pushed on a chair. As Hannelore (identified by context rather than by name) and Perla begin to talk, the film cuts between them and three men of average height who prepare a meal in the kitchen. The unidentified men join in to share champagne over a birthday cake, and while they celebrate, Perla suddenly speaks of Josef Mengele. She speaks of him familiarly, recalling that she and her siblings were favorite subjects for his genetic research in Auschwitz: they were his "seven dwarves." As Perla insists that she can say nothing negative about the man whose interest saved her life, Hannelore protests, prompting Perla's denial that Mengele ever killed little people in the camp. The women's voices blend, the image cuts to a stack of letters addressed to Perla from Hannelore, and the title of the film finally appears on screen, punctuated as an address, the beginning of another letter: *Liebe Perla*.

So begins this 54–minute-long documentary film, a German/Israeli co-production made for Israeli television in 1999 and shot on video in German and Hebrew. As is typical of documentaries, the film's availability is limited, despite its having won numerous awards around the world.[3] Although few readers will ever see it, I will analyze *Liebe Perla* through five problems around its highly sophisticated use of the evidentiary, ethical, and poetic potential of documentary film images.

Problem 1: The Introductory Frame

Like the beginning of a poem, the sights and sounds of the film's introductory frame provide formal and semantic guidelines for what follows. Thus a re-viewing is crucial to appreciate the film's richness, to an awareness of stylistic elements that move both with and indifferently against the temporality of the medium. As with many rereadings, parsing the rhetorical effect of the film's beginning is useful, specifically in how information unfolds in time and sights and sounds are employed. Since the first two production-credits merely signal the social networks in and by which the film was produced, I will move to the introductory text with its sparse information. What kind of preliminary and contextualizing facts does it offer to guide the viewer's interpretation of the film? On the first screen, we read of two women, Hannelore and Perla, a German and a Hungarian-Israeli, a researcher and a surviving member of a "Jewish Lilliput Troupe," an interviewer and a subject. We learn of multiple nationalities and of a scholarly agenda. The second screen provides facts of a different kind: here we learn that the two women "became close friends," thereby translating the asymmetry of the scholar/ subject relationship into mutual regard, and it is within this friendship that Perla made an "unusual request." The punctuation of the final sentence, an ellipsis marking the omission of an end, helps connect this text with the pictures and sound to come. The possibilities begin unfolding in the subsequent image and its ambient sounds—a man setting a table in a living room, which fades prematurely to prompt our speculations about its source. The two-directional enjambment of punctuation and sound, as each moves against and across the edit that separates their visual location, is a typical metrical device of this film. Once we have seen *Liebe Perla* in its entirety and begin to reread, we will understand that the elision points to what comes after, not the sentence's completion, but its extended irresolution.

The textual introduction does not identify either woman as being short-statured or otherwise disabled. The first few minutes of the film reveal this information visually in the dinner preparation segment, without any situating dialogue or voiceover. These few minutes operate as a second frame, ending with the film's title on the screen. This second, visual frame provides different information via another medium: it is here that the audience learns of Hannelore's and Perla's dwarfism and Perla's imprisonment at Auschwitz. For audiences who see the film without prior knowledge of its subject, the unexpected sight of the two women with their non-standard bodies is startling. This constitutes an aesthetic gesture, a calculated shock via the image of a non-normal body, appearing without warning or comment. The sight of people entering a living room for a birthday celebration, which is easy to comprehend via conventional visual cues, plus the ordinariness of the scenario, underscored by long cuts further slowed by conversational pauses, triggers a semantic shock alongside of the visual discovery. This introduction insists upon the normalcy of what most viewers initially experience as abnormal. It effectively manipulates and prepares the viewer for the film's project, becoming as well a psychological conditioning exercise in understanding disability not as an individual's medical problem deserving of compassion or revulsion, but rather as a particular aspect of human experience similar to race, class, gender, or sexuality, as academics and activists are beginning to argue.[4]

In order to hear and see the film's concerns, we have to consider the possibility of disability as normal. In most cases, the viewer has to have been caught, made self-conscious at least for a moment by incorrectly assuming that disability ought to be depicted as a problem, one that is justifiably—and filmically—spectacular. Only by effectively refuting this assumption on the surface of the film can *Liebe Perla*'s task begin.

Contrary to this significant opening set of choices, publicity for screenings of *Liebe Perla* stresses Auschwitz survival, Nazi medical atrocities, and some variant on the friendship between two women of short stature. Such advertising effectively re-edits the beginning of the documentary by highlighting these facts and contexts for the viewer's subsequent experience of the film. It hardly surprises that these elements are used to attract an audience, particularly since the film is often screened in the context of either disability advocacy or Holocaust study.[5]

Yet viewers poised to consider Nazi experiments, contemporary bioethics debates, and the persisting need to reconfigure cultural notions of abled/disabled will see the film in bluntly overwhelming terms that occlude the subtle work of the film itself. *Liebe Perla*'s introduction is deliberate and spare: it focuses neither on the Nazi past per se nor on the women's physical condition. Instead it provides only what is necessary for us to read the "unusual request" in the doubled context of scholarship and friendship. The visual frame then adds depth and particular complications. Since the "unusual request" is where the prefatory text ends and the video footage begins, we can assume that either the request itself, the making of the request, or the attempt to fulfill the request will constitute the substance of the movie.

If one attempts to recount the story told by the film, it runs something like this: Perla requests that Hannelore find a lost film; Hannelore tries to find it; Hannelore cannot find it but finds other things instead. A slightly longer version of this story might look as follows: Perla requests that Hannelore find a lost film that Mengele made of her, naked with her siblings, in Auschwitz; Perla wants to recover it so that no one else will ever see it again. Hannelore, who researches the fate of little people during the era of National Socialism, tries to find the film in archives throughout Germany and at Auschwitz; she cannot find it but finds other things instead, and in the process sharply criticizes attitudes toward the disabled in contemporary Germany, drawing lines of continuity from the Nazi past to the democratic present.

The film itself, however, is not structured along so simple a narrative line. On the contrary, it resists easy viewing. Visually, the film contains two types of footage: one of the women (either together in dialogue or alone, pursuing independent but interrelated tasks), another of their local environment (portraits on Perla's wall, construction sites in Haifa, exteriors of various institutes and archives, Auschwitz). The soundtrack consists of live, captured dialogue as well as of a voiceover rereading letters—the latter an epistolary dialogue between Hannelore and Perla that reflects on the search for the film and on Perla's memories of the camp. There is no explication, no voiceover that establishes the identities of participants, no précis providing background either for Perla or for Hannelore, no director's overt presence to represent a central perspective. The frame offers a sampling of ensuing difficulties: we watch people who remain unidentified (the men, in particular) as they discuss and witness unreliable information, whether in small mistakes like misremembering the name of Mengele's son, or on a large scale, such as whether or not Mengele killed his subjects. The frame already tells us not to approach a film about disability and the Holocaust as if it were about disability and the Holocaust. From the beginning, we are off-center, invited to share partially in a correspondence between friends, both of whom remain for the most part enigmatic. It is within these conditions, which require the viewer's acknowledgment of his or her own incomprehension of and exclusion from Perla and Hannelore's shared knowledge and experiences, that we are invited to share the film's insights into a larger problem of looking and being looked at.

Like a poem, this film is sustained by a tension between its metrics—the editing rhythm and juxtapositions of pictures and sounds—and its semantics. A montage of constantly changing sites and subjects, as well as the encroachment of intimate live and epistolary dialogues onto public sites (enjambment), ultimately generates the film's meanings. In particular, commemoration and politics are collapsed, and an irreconcilable tension between personal claims of friendship and the collective claims of history emerges. These meanings are filmic artifacts insofar as they are the products of special effects.

Problem 2: Perla's Request

Must one comply with a request to honor it? Perla's request, which catalyzes the actions within the film and the making of the documentary itself, is not merely "unusual" but potentially impossible. She asks that a lost film be found, one directed by Mengele in Auschwitz as he himself stood before the camera and presented the naked bodies of Perla and her siblings to a group of medical and SS colleagues. It is a film for which no public post-war record exists. Were it available, it would have attracted considerable historical attention, providing unique evidence of Nazi medical practice and the treatment of subjects in the camp. As things stand currently, there is no extant film footage of Auschwitz whatsoever.

Perla insists that, unless Mengele took the film with him to South America, it is likely in an archive waiting to be found. This possibility weighs upon her, and she wants Hannelore to find the film so that she, Perla, can destroy it. This is an extraordinary request, made not only of Hannelore, but of the documentary director, Rozen, and of every viewer: we are all asked to search as long as we promise never to look at what we find. We are informed of an artifact's existence and of the basic conditions of its production; we participate in a search for this artifact, the historical evidentiary power of which might be unparalleled. As

Susan Sontag has noted, "the very notion of atrocity, of war crime, is associated with the expectation of photographic evidence. Such evidence is, usually, of something posthumous; the remains, as it were" (83). In this case, the images offered for (non)contemplation are remarkable for offering an authentic and uniquely doubled view of Auschwitz: the film would provide visual evidence of the camp in operation, as well as of the viewing tactics of camp authorities. However, such speculation and anticipation marks the limit of our approach: we can only contemplate the film's existence. We cannot share in an experience of it. Nor will we witness what it is. Further complicating this lost, unwatchable film is its location within the context of the "Final Solution"—a context that is wrenching and simultaneously all too well-known and never adequately known, one that demands unceasing publicity and that is already saturated with familiarly horrifying images.[6]

How do we read this film about a lost film, particularly a film sought precisely so that it will not be seen? Not even Perla saw the film and can only recount the process of making it. It is a lost object with many meanings, all different for its forced subjects, its director, and its past or future viewers. For us, it embodies the simultaneous loss and burden to the world that is the Final Solution. The power of the lost film, as long as we never see it, is the anticipation of its discovery and display. This recovery evokes shadowy possibilities that we cannot help but imagine, ghostly images that are present as a palimpsest beneath the inscribed images of the video. It is impossible not to wonder whether, if viewed, the images would be either too horrifying, or not horrifying enough. Yet for Perla, the film she seeks is, as long as it remains missing, an artifact embodying the loss of dignity and of the possibility of happiness. It is Perla's memory preserved on a lost screen that she wishes to reclaim—for destruction.

Perla's desire is to contain the artifact and the action and recollection, past and present, it would unleash, a desire to serve selective forgetting rather than public remembering. Perla's words, "Find the film but don't look at it," request a restoration of violated privacy. She also requests control over the image of her own and her siblings' naked bodies, which, if actually found, would constitute the only surviving artifact of her experience at Auschwitz, one of utter powerlessness. Her request thus goes deeper than simply requiring that the film not be screened.

An additional problem emerges as well: that of our imagining the film. We do not have to screen the film to violate Perla's wishes, those of the Holocaust survivor to both witness and to look away, because her descriptions alone prompt us to imagine the film. In Old Testament terms, we have already on some level violated the law of "look not upon the nakedness of." This was Ham's crime—to look upon the undignified and vulnerable nakedness of Noah, his father, a crime that resulted in his expulsion from the family and exile from the covenantal new beginning after devastation. For Perla, the surviving subject, a screening of Mengele's lost film would make her yet again the victim of a crime, a crime of looking with curiosity (medical, historical, aesthetic, or otherwise) rather than with compassion upon nakedness, a crime that would compromise the human-scripted covenant "never again."[7]

We should not imagine what the lost film looks like, but we are required to imagine what it means. *Liebe Perla* tests a strategy for compliance with Perla's request that can both discourage our uncontrollable projections of what those lost images might be, and yet pursue the existence and the significance of the film itself. Responding to the ethical requirement to react to a survivor's testifying will, *Liebe Perla* films around the missing artifact such that the documentary's multiple visual layers, narrative threads, and ethical demands are each reflected and refracted off the imagined screen of the lost film.

Problem 3: *Liebe Perla, Sur Place* the Lost Film

Liebe Perla is the only extant document attesting to the existence of the lost film. As such it substitutes for and signifies the lost film. Even as we seek, hoping not to see images of Mengele's Perla, it is *Liebe Perla* that we do see, with its images of the living, independent woman Perla replacing the missing pictures she herself has invoked. *Liebe Perla* offers itself as a placeholder for the missing film, and at the same time it also replaces or refigures the process and intention of representing Perla at all.

Mengele's film directed the scientifically curious eye, one not aesthetically, politically, or ethically engaged, to consider a collection of sibling bodies as instances of patterned abnormality. His film was made without the consent of its subjects. *Liebe Perla* operates as a corrective lens insofar as it frames itself as the product of and filmic witness to Perla's will. It shows willing subjects who place themselves—their bodies, their speech, their written words—comfortably before the camera.

We do well to recall here that the lost object of our search and our discourse is a film of naked bodies, in particular Perla's. The naked female form has always been a favored subject for image-making, usually presented to incite desire and conjure an idealized norm. Of course, this norm is far from natural, as Rosemarie Garland-Thomson points out: "The beautiful woman of the twenty-first century is sculpted surgically from top to bottom, generically neutral, all irregularities regularized, all particularities expunged" (12).[8] By contrast, the bodies that we would confront in the lost film are not only unmodified, but unmistakably unmodifiable and, as such, stimulate the scientific gaze. Here the scientifically and the erotically aroused gaze converge uncomfortably: both identify physiological conditions for an appropriate sexual object. The premise of Perla's film is its representation of bodies precisely as inappropriate objects of erotic desire, since the subjects were objects of eugenic research, exemplifying forms that should not reproduce themselves further.

Liebe Perla inserts itself between oppositions of female beauty and ugliness, between the normal and the monstrous, between science and pornography, between Mengele's film and the glamour-driven film industry. This film insists upon the bodies of its subjects, Perla and Hannelore, as neither ideal nor as monstrous, but as another version of the normal. This strategy also makes them extremely vulnerable.[9] As Levinas writes in his engagement with an embodied ethics: "The body is neither an obstacle opposed to the soul, nor a tomb that imprisons it, but that by which the self is susceptibility itself. Incarnation is an extreme passivity; to be exposed to sickness, suffering, death; to be exposed to compassion [...]" (195, n. 12). Such a description of the body as susceptible offers a productive reconfiguration of the mind/body convergence offered by Kantian tradition whereby ideals of human (physical) beauty correlate directly with ethical ideals of equilibrium and strength. Lennard Davis formulates a similar, if less poetic alternative both to Enlightenment embodiment and its postmodernist legacy of identity positions, a theory of embodiment he calls "dismodernist." He clarifies:

> In a dismodernist mode, the ideal is not a hypostatization of the normal (that is, dominant) subject, but aims to create a new category based on the partial, incomplete subject whose realization is not autonomy and independence but dependency and interdependence. This is a very different notion from subjectivity organized around wounded identities: rather, *all* humans are seen as wounded. (30)

Like Perla's lost film, *Liebe Perla* exposes non-standard bodies to a curious eye: it both shows and shows off the bodies of these two women, stressing their physicality in simple, particular, minute detail. Perla had been a professional performer, and she seems to enjoy this late opportunity to practice her trade. We watch Perla sew a dress for Hannelore;

we see the two women in wheelchairs in a fabric store in Haifa; we see them laugh together as Perla tries to persuade Hannelore to wear makeup. We see how Hannelore and her assistants cope with her limited movement and eyesight on their journey. One might ask how Shahar Rozen, in making *Liebe Perla,* could avoid a charge of voyeurism in a film that constantly reminds us of short-statured people's long history of being regarded as abnormal and freakish, with lives potentially not worth living. Yet the answer lies in Rozen's manner of iterating critical checks through Hannelore's labors. Following her patient but stressful search across Germany and Poland, we do not simply witness a disabled person at work, given the challenge implicit in the nature of her work. Hannelore's research and advocacy focus on how the disabled are seen and represented, or more accurately misapprehended and misrepresented. In a sense Hannelore and Perla's friendship also requires room in their exchange for Hannelore's own concerns.

The lost film was for Mengele a scientific instrument. For Perla, it is a document of suffering. For us, it critically documents an indifference to this suffering, the indifference of Mengele and his immediate medical community, who were interested in examining depersonalized bodies that might be used for experiments, including torture and death. For the historian, the missing film represents the technological coordination of science and war, since it shows the controlled examination of select objects by an audience of experts who practiced the ideologically driven destruction of life.

Because this film remains lost, its power is confined to the threat of resurfacing, its presence is limited to the level of anecdote within survival testimony, and it cannot serve as material evidence of events in the camp. At the same time, it cannot be dismissed because it could be found. The combination of keeping the lost film in mind, yet not knowing what it shows, operates as a potent invitation to expand what we do know: the film's story of science colluding with destruction. As a lost object, the film's moral claims operate like a nagging conscience upon *Liebe Perla* and prove easily transferable to the present. This transfer is, in part, Hannelore's agenda for the documentary: her story is not only the search for Perla's film (the action of a friend), but also the expression of anger at the continued indifference, pity, and disgust in the presence of disability.

Evoking current bioethics debates like selective infanticide and midterm abortion of "defective" fetuses, an option some disability activists view as a "coercive form of genocide against the disabled,"[10] as well as research into surgical and genetic improvement of bodies that are thereby reduced to "cultural plastic" (Bordo 246), Hannelore remarks with bitter calm that despite Germany's "history," many Germans think that she and others like her would be better off dead. Hannelore stresses a blurring of the Nazi past and FRG present that defies the post-war new beginning and its awareness of "history." This continuity, spoken within the context of her search for Perla's lost film and edited effectively into the "road trip to the archives" segment of the documentary, embeds the bioethics debates to which she refers within a Nazi ethos. This manner of representation attests to Hannelore's rhetorical skill as an activist, as well as the director's and editor's support thereof. Were she to come out and accuse particular geneticists or bioethicists of Nazi-like or fascist research agendas, her words would be dismissed as exploitative and ahistorical. On the other hand, by beginning her argument with evidence of criminal medical experimentation connected to Nazi eugenics research and then drawing comparisons with the present, Hannelore moves rhetorically from a stable position (Nazis were bad when they did x) to the present (today we do x). The logical demonstration of similarity between the past and the present is hard to resist.

Reinforcing this connection between past and present, the film's focus expands if one considers its possibilities: much of what we see of Hannelore's quest is devoted to archival evidence not of Perla's film, but of the careers of Nazi medical scientists after the war. Garland-Thomson has noted that "there has been no archive, no template for understanding disability as a category of analysis and knowledge, as a cultural trope, and an historical community" (2). We can understand Hannelore's efforts as the founding efforts of such an archive. The evidence she uncovers verifies continuity between the present and research that presumably ended with the Nazi regime.[11] Specifically, in a Berlin archive—once the Kaiser-Wilhelm-Institut, now the Max-Planck-Gesellschaft—Hannelore attempts to trace Mengele's communication and shared research with his mentor, collaborator, and the war-time director of the Institute for Anthropology, Human Hereditary Teaching and Genetics, Otmar Freiherr von Verschuer. This leads to an investigation of missing evidence (here too, lost documentation is what is at stake) that allowed Verschuer, despite indications that he collaborated with Mengele in some of the latter's most grisly research, to avoid prosecution for warcrimes. Verschuer instead went on to become the head of the Institute for Human Genetic Research at the University of Münster. Hannelore reads aloud from his obituary in the German press of 1969, in which he was celebrated for his contributions toward humanistic eugenic research.[12]

The film juxtaposes Hannelore's documentation of past atrocities with her own testimony, via letters to Perla, of the current prejudice that she encounters. The rhetorical power of the film's editing manifests its sympathy with her efforts as a disability rights activist. However, this gesture attempts to reframe *Liebe Perla* to serve an agenda that is very much not Perla's. Perla herself, whose request launches the film, has no interest in disability-rights or the continuities of history's horror; she simply wants to possess and destroy the film she should not have had to make. *Liebe Perla* seems to understand this and to incorporate the conflicting needs into the film's temporal structure: while the intercutting between Hannelore's research and Perla at home suggests parallel time, the differences are subtle but significant. As Hannelore's search unfolds we have no idea how quickly she works since there are no dates given, no sense of precise time. Yet her work directs and advances the film. Her research trips are regularly interrupted by shots of Perla's ongoing life in Haifa, quiet scenes in which she sits or moves slowly through her house, or sews. Unlike Hannelore's pursuit, however, these scenes function quite differently. While Hannelore moves through time on a quest toward a goal, Perla seems suspended in time. And this difference in the temporal rhythm of their representation speaks to the differences in their desire for the lost film. Hannelore wishes to acquire, to help a friend, to learn, to contribute historical evidence, to argue, to provoke change over time. Perla wishes to end something that hovers over her life, to gather memories and privacy, to foreclose possibilities.

With such different needs in mind, we have no choice but to search for a film we hope never to find. As long as we cannot find the film, it remains with us on some level. But how, precisely? We are simultaneously excused by the past's irretrievability and accused by the limited reach of our reconstructions. This instability, however, proves productive for ethical contemplation. It may be more useful lost, with its ontological status as a real thing intact. As a real object, it was the product of technology, of laws of optics and physics and chemistry. As a project it was the product of the social networks of science and war. As a real, lost object, it is the missing screen upon which old and new ideas of "Auschwitz" are projected. Thus its potential value as evidence for the "unimaginable" that we imagine, the unthinkable that we contemplate, the inhuman that was quite matter-of-factly human becomes clear. Perla's film remains discursively rich as long as it remains imprecise, hovering mid-translation between past and present, lost and found.

Problem 4: A Third Film

Disrupting the absence/presence relationship between Perla's missing film and *Liebe Perla* is a third movie offered by an archivist to

Hannelore as visual evidence of eugenics programs in the Third Reich. This is the Nazi documentary *Opfer der Vergangenheit* (Victim of the Past), a short film produced by the Propaganda Ministry in 1937 for screening in every movie theater in Germany. This third film, combining documentary footage with fictional scenarios and a melodramatic score, claims to present statistics and medical facts about the incurably ill and hereditarily insane in Germany. It offers a rational framework for mandatory sterilization policies, marriage restrictions, and ultimately euthanasia through an alliance of science, technology, and law.

The clips shown are depicted both on a television monitor and at an angle—a double-framing that inserts a critical distance between it and *Liebe Perla*. This framing also echoes our relationship—non-identical, but akin—to the lost film: our given view is askew, displayed but with deliberate distortion, conveying ambivalence about whether we should look or not. And yet the *Opfer* clip, as an "authentic" Nazi documentary about the disabled, operates as another substitute for the film we are not allowed to see, offering evidence of Nazi image-making that supplants the evidence we will not be able to view.

As the *Opfer* clip begins, we hear Hannelore's voice telling Perla in a letter of her unwillingness to watch this documentary that she has seen already too many times. Its function as the exemplar of Nazi eugenics propaganda has not diminished its power, yet the particular historical use to which the film was always put has restricted our capacity to see its range of possible meanings. Extending her criticism somewhat, one could argue that the gothic-horror aesthetic tactics evident in the grainy, slightly damaged film are easily assigned to screen history. Yet the voiceover subdues its histrionic tone, and the film is all too easily filed in the archive as Nazi propaganda to be discussed, remembered, and analyzed as such by well-intentioned scholars, theater owners, and documentary filmmakers, among others. Such collective efforts unintentionally render any of the film's potential resonance, beyond its direct relationship to the Nazi euthanasia project and the Final Solution, almost unthinkable. And thus Hannelore's frustration: when we see these film clips, they effectively translate the entire problem represented—the devaluation of the lives of the disabled—to a clearly labeled past. From our viewing position, tempered by time and reconstructed political views, we can look at the film as evidence confirming what is known rather than as evidence of issues requiring engagement.

The fate of *Opfer der Vergangenheit* is its reduction to evidence that speaks only of the past it is now employed to prosecute, a fate to which Perla's film might succumb should it be found. For, if found, its discovery might well "amount to disposal, settlement of the case, which can then be placed in the files of history," as survivor Jean Améry wrote of the precarious status of Holocaust testimony (xxi).

Problem 5: The Files of History

A final problem emerges, that of the archive and its preserved documents. Perla's claim to her film—her asserting the right to possess and destroy it—directly challenges what Giorgio Agamben has called the "archive's constitution." The archive, he writes, is "founded on the subject's disappearance into the anonymous murmur of statements" (*Remnants of Auschwitz* 145). It is this archive of the Nazi past—an archive that would subordinate Perla to the film that was made of her, making her depersonalized image once again an object of historically minded study—that Perla challenges in sending Hannelore, Rozen, and all viewers to locate and destroy its contents. It is *Liebe Perla* that develops and sustains an irreconcilable tension between the archive (an essential resource, as Hannelore effectively demonstrates) and the subject who makes a singular and institutionally impossible claim upon it. It becomes an ethical contest between, on the one hand, an individual's claim to privacy and dignity, to the simultaneous repair and guarantee of no further damage that the lost film's recovery would threaten, and, on the other hand, potential claims by those interested in furthering collective history and representability. Such groups might include other Holocaust survivors, people of short stature, or the variously disabled. Others might make institutional claims serving fields of knowledge, whether academic, scientific, or legal. Other issues may also arise in confronting the history of National Socialists, who were notoriously careful in destroying evidence of the Final Solution. If we do not expose all crimes as fully and as publicly as possible, yet honor Perla's claim to her lost film, do we not perversely support the Nazi resolve to destroy all records, to conceal all activities, and to erase all evidence of camp activities?

These questions all involve socially constructed claims to access. Other possible problems could arise if the film were found, specifically legal claims over the film as a form of property. *Liebe Perla* never raises the question of who might legally own the film or which individuals, institutions, or countries might have legal claims to handle, view, store, copy, study, display, transcribe, or destroy it. Had Hannelore found it, it is unlikely she would have been allowed to walk away with it and deliver it into Perla's hands. Which legal forum would ultimately decide where property rights should lie? Given what we know of dispersal patterns, the film—if it still exists—could be in Germany in an unmarked canister in an archive. It could be stored at the Universität Münster with other, publicly unavailable papers of Otmar von Verschuer from the 1940s. It might be somewhere in the former Soviet Union, where a mass of Auschwitz material disappeared from Western sight after the war. It might lie with other materials of Mengele's somewhere in South America or in Germany. The possibilities open question of national jurisdiction, institutional discretion, and personal estate law, all of which might conflict with Perla's claim.

As long as the film remains lost, no claims will be made. Near the end of *Liebe Perla,* we hear Hannelore rereading a letter she sent to Perla: "Today is our last day in Auschwitz. We did not find the film. Often I hoped that if I do find it, as soon as I open the box, it would crumble into dust. I'm afraid that someone in some archive or other or in some attic would find it and show it." And she continues, "The film belongs to you, and you alone." This statement, written as private correspondence between friends, is captured on film and thereby translated from the discursive level of intimate opinion to that of public imperative. In some ways, it is hard not to agree with Hannelore. *Liebe Perla* itself manages much of the work that would be demanded of the lost film, if found. It deftly manages and creatively plays with archival exposure to serve history and to re-open the case against the Nazi-era and post-war German medical communities, all without exploiting the lost film's actual images as historical evidence.[13] Hannelore's assertion of Perla's rights seem right and good; history has been served by *Liebe Perla,* and historians should return the favor by allowing the film to remain lost.

Hannelore's recorded words run over visual edits to link Auschwitz as archive (Hannelore exits, not having found the film) to Auschwitz as tourist site, populated with visitors photographing each other. A pause follows, filled only by ambient sound, as Hannelore in her wheelchair is pushed across the nearly deserted remains of the Auschwitz barracks, where she leaves flowers at the site where Perla lived and suffered.

This is a sentimental moment, familiar as a gesture that ends a dramatic arc, as if flowers and a promise to remember the life of a friend—as complex as that might be—were sufficient to resolve all of the demands of the film. It demonstrates eloquently the desire to commemorate and finally put to rest the disturbing interruptions of artifacts and memories. This is not the end of the film, though. Like any good poem, its ending is hard-won. We might say of this film what Giorgio Agamben writes of the "end of the poem": namely, that the work of balancing conflicting meanings wrought from the chafing of form against content, "looks for shelter in suspending its own end in a declaration, so to speak, of the state of poetic emergency" (113). This poetic emergency is initiated by the over-simplified finality of flowers at a memorial site, a gesture that threatens to silence, to mark as dead, as better-left-alone not just Perla's film but all of the open questions of testimony, evidence, suffering, and looking that the film has raised.

Over the course of about fifty minutes, *Liebe Perla* has done a remarkable job both in probing and trying to answer by example just what the relationship between Perla and film should be. We hear of a missing film, and we see scenes from a misread film, but in the end *Liebe Perla* offers itself as the corrective for both, as that which replaces—by refilming—a relationship between Perla and film, between dis/ability and film, between Holocaust remembrance and film. This is the film about Perla—and about the fate of the disabled during the Holocaust—that we should and can see. And yet, much of *Liebe Perla*'s artistry lies in its nuanced acknowledgment of its own limitations, brought on as much by filmic form as by content. The flowers-on-the-monument ending is a failure, both poetically and ethically, and as such it necessitates what feels like a filmic coda.

Like the poetic emergency, *Liebe Perla* returns us to the urgency of the lost-and-found tension, offering as substitution for the still-lost film a different set of objects and images. Perla learns that Yad Vashem has located musical instruments and photographs that belonged to her family. The film ends in a storage room at Yad Vashem as Perla, Hannelore, and the assistant examine the artifacts. Not all of the instruments are there and the violin is missing its strings. When Perla sees posters covered with photographs of her siblings performing, she cries bitterly and hides her face. The camera waits for an uncomfortable moment, forcing us to see that she both needs to look and cannot, that she needs to recover herself and her lost past and cannot. We look, wondering if we should or not. The camera cuts away to another worker in the room who averts his eyes. It then quietly traverses the collected objects as if to provide Perla a moment of privacy in real time. Finally we return to Perla, smiling now and increasingly animated as she points to the severely damaged photographs, replacing her siblings one by one: "This is Mickey. That's Franziska, with the violin. This is Frieda with the cymbal. That's me...." Pointing to a white space where the image has been worn away entirely, she reads the erasure quietly, seeing what no one else could, and slipping from German into Hebrew for a moment: "This is where Avram should be." Here we might hear the "declaration of poetic emergency" with which the film could end, illustrating the impossibility of doing justice to history with images.

Perla evokes the missing image, illegible except to one who was there. The image that she reinserts onto the poster belongs to her memory. However, her shared and filmed recollection—the alchemical elixir of life that returns Avram to the image such that the image brings her siblings back—is now an event that belongs to us. This is a strong poetic moment in which hover echoes of nearly all of the major issues of loss, images, and understanding that shape the film. This moment registers the endless series of substitutions for loss and longing of which *Liebe Perla* itself is a part.

But we do well to recall that the film shapes itself, by its title and through its voiceovers, as a letter to a friend. A letter is not a poem with an ending, but is part of an ongoing exchange. It is therefore somehow appropriate that another few lines follow, a fond exchange among Perla, Hannelore, and the assistant. This exchange transforms the intensity of an aesthetically and emotionally over-determined moment to the conversational level of discourse with which the film begins. Life goes on in its way. Perla points to an image that we do not see, noting that she played an alarming "angel among men." Hearing this, Hannelore's assistant places his arm around her and says, "That is appropriate." Perla laughs into the camera, and the film ends.

Perla Ovici, the last of her immediate family and the only known remaining witness to the film that she hoped to locate and destroy, died in 2001.

Notes

I learned of *Liebe Perla* when helping to plan the Vanderbilt Holocaust Lecture Series for the fall of 2003 with my friend and colleague Gregg Horowitz. Sara Ezell, who works with Vanderbilt's Opportunity Development Center, had a copy of the film and urged us to consider adding it to the schedule. I began to think seriously about the film after discussing it with Gregg, whose initial response was far more nuanced than mine. I no longer remember precisely what was said and thus cannot credit him properly; however, I would like to note that credit is due.

[1] All citations are taken directly from the video copy owned by Vanderbilt University. Where I cite dialogue, I use the translations from German or Hebrew that appear as English subtitles.

[2] Over these images, the following credits appear: A Film by Shahar Rozen; Producer Edna Kowarsky; Camera Sharon De Mayo; Editing Rebecca Yogev.

[3] *Liebe Perla* has received numerous awards, including Best Script at the Haifa Film Festival 1999; Best Documentary in the Tursak Festival in Istanbul 2000; the Magnolia prize for Best Documentary in Humanitites, Festival Shanghai 2000; and the "Masua" Award for Best Documentary dealing with the Holocaust. It has been broadcast on Israeli, German (NDR), and French (ARTE) television. Copies are available through Cinephil Distribution and Coproductions <http://www.cinephil.co.il>.

[4] See Longmore; Davis; Garland-Thomson. Paul Longmore writes in the introduction to his influential collection of essays, *Why I Burned My Book,* the following reconceptualization of disability: "The new mode of analysis challenges the medical paradigm that has generally shaped modern social practices. The medical model assumes that pathological physiological conditions are the primary obstacle to disabled people's social integration. [...] It renders disability as a series of physiological, psychological, and functional pathologies originating within the bodies of individuals" (1).

[5] It is worth questioning whether such advertising is ultimately detrimental not only as an aesthetic compromise, but as a skewing of the entire perspective that the film offers of lives that include disability. It perpetuates the bifurcated imagery that David Hevey has so sharply critiqued (1992), which either denigrates the disabled as "creatures" or "positively" depicts them as the "happy handicapped." While this film clearly condemns the Nazi reduction of the disabled to "creatures" unworthy of life, advertising *Liebe Perla* as an uplifting story of women transcending their deformities serves to confirm an ableist perspective of disability as a personally compromising medical misfortune, as something that only extraordinary individuals might "overcome."

[6] While my concern is the film's balance of form and content rather than a historical documentation of the disabled during the Holocaust, some readers may profit from a basic contextual orientation. In 1933, the Nazi government issued the "Law for the Prevention of Progeny with Hereditary Diseases," subjecting all those "afflicted with a hereditary disease" to potential forcible sterilization. Medically overseen euthanasia of the disabled began officially in 1939 under the code-name "Operation T4." Between 1940 and 1941, approximately 70,000 people were killed under the T4 program. Despite the official end of the program in 1941, killings continued until 1945. It is estimated that nearly 300,000 disabled people were murdered. While the fate of the disabled in the camps has not yet received the scholarly attention it deserves, the following studies are noteworthy: Suzanne Evans's *Forgotten Crimes*; and Sandy O'Neill's dissertation entitled, *First*

They Killed the "Crazies" and "Cripples": The Ableist Persecution and Murders of People with Disabilities by Nazi Germany 1933–45. Also relevant is Aly et al., *Cleansing the Fatherland*; and finally Michael Burleigh's *Death and Deliverance: "Euthanasia" in Germany c. 1900–1945.* One controversial book—praised in the mainstream press, condemned in disability forums—focusing on Perla Ovici and her family, entitled *In Our Hearts We Were Giants,* was published by Yehuda Koren and Eilat Negev, 2004.

[7] Here many potential issues arise, involving ethical considerations that are far from clear when dealing with life-writing involving subjects of trauma. These issues are further complicated when the subjects are disabled. Thomas Couser observes rightly that, "people with disadvantaging or stigmatizing conditions are increasingly visible in life writing, and those who represent them must take care not to override their interests or over-write their stories" (14).

[8] Consider Sander L. Gilman's analysis of "aesthetic surgery" (1998), Rosemarie Garland Thomson's study of the "normate" (1997), the consumerism created by a societal beauty system written about by Elizabeth Haiken (1997). An aggressively avant-garde alternative, however, might be the model Aimee Mullins, whose fashion shoots consistently include her artificial legs. As Garland-Thomson notes, "Mullins uses her conformity with beauty standards to assert her disability's violation of those very standards. As legless and beautiful, she is an embodied paradox, invoking an inherently disruptive potential" (27).

[9] Feminist disability studies provide a productive arena in which to address the cultural presumptions that deny eroticism, sexuality, and reproductive rights to women with disabilities (see, for example, Fine and Asch [1988] and Finger [1990]).

[10] This comment was made by Garland-Thomson, who goes on to cite "a more nuanced argument against selective abortion" made by Adrienne Asch and Gail Geller: "Asch and Geller counter the quality-of-life and prevention-of-suffering arguments so readily invoked to justify selective abortion, as well as physician-assisted suicide, by pointing out that we cannot predict or, more precisely, control in advance such equivocal human states as happiness, suffering, or success" (15–16). See also Kittay.

[11] Paul Julian Weindling writes, "The eugenicists received lighter treatment, as its criminality appeared less certain and of marginal value to the prosecution of the Nazi leadership at Nuremberg" (41). Weindling notes further: "The German state prosecutors were loath to investigate, or as the Mengele case shows, to apprehend even notorious war criminals. How Mengele was able to leave Germany in 1948 and keep in touch with his family showed continued failings in the legal and police authorities' will to prosecute medical crimes. The Auschwitz survivor Hermann Langbein found

Mengele's Argentinian address on divorce papers brazenly filed in Freiburg in 1954" (318).

[12] Raphael Falk writes of how "biologists of the Swastika were smoothly reintegrated into the scientific community and acquired university posts, many becoming leading and honored members of the German, or even international scientific community." He identifies Verschuer as a "most striking" case, as he was "a virulent anti-Semite, who was already active as an instructor of the Hitler-Jugend in the 1930s" (55). Gerald Posner and John Ware write that, during the war, Verschuer was among other things the editor of *Der Erbarzt* (The Physician for Genetics), a racist medical journal, and that he and Mengele worked together, "writing judicial reports for specially convened courts which sat in judgment over Jews caught cohabiting with German Aryans" (12).

[13] See Weindling for an account of how the Nuremberg Trials failed to prosecute fully the medical crimes. He elucidates the staunch British and American support of ongoing research.

Works Cited

Agamben, Giorgio. *Remnants of Auschwitz: The Witness and the Archive*. Trans. Daniel Heller-Roazen. New York: Zone Books, 2000.

———. *The End of the Poem: Studies in Poetics*. Trans. Daniel Heller-Roazen. Stanford UP, 1999.

Aly, Götz, Peter Chroust, and Christian Pross, *Cleansing the Fatherland: Nazi Medicine and Racial Hygiene*. Baltimore: Johns Hopkins UP, 1994.

Améry, Jean. *At the Mind's Limits: Contemplations by a Survivor on Auschwitz and its Realities*. Trans. Sidney and Stella P. Rosenfeld. New York: Schocken Books, 1990.

Asch, Adrienne, and Gail Geller. "Feminism, Bioethics and Genetics." *Feminism, Bioethics: Beyond Reproduction*. Ed. S.M. Wolf. Oxford: Oxford UP, 1996. 318-50.

Bordo, Susan. *Unbearable Weight: Feminism, Western Culture and the Body*. Berkeley: U of California P, 1993.

Burleigh, Michael. *Death and Deliverance: "Euthanasia" in Germany c. 1900-1945*. Cambridge: Cambridge UP, 1994

Couser, G. Thomas. *Vulnerable Subjects: Ethics and Life Writing*. Ithaca: Cornell UP, 2004.

Davis, Lennard J. *Bending over Backwards: Disability, Dismodernism & Other Difficult Positions*. New York: New York UP, 2002.

Evans, Suzanne. *Forgotten Crimes: The Holocaust and People with Disabilities*. Chicago: Ivan R. Dee, 2004.

Falk, Raphael. "The Emergence of German Geneticists from the Swastika." *Bioethical and Ethical Issues Surrounding the Trials and Code of Nuremberg*. Ed. Jacques J. Rozenberg. Lewiston, UK: Edwin Mellen, 2003. 49–68.

Fine, Michelle, and Adrienne Asch, eds. *Women with Disabilities: Essays in Psychology, Culture, and Politics*. Philadelphia: Temple UP, 1988.

Finger, Anne. *Past Due: A Story of Disability, Pregnancy, and Birth*. Seattle: Seal P, 1990.

Garland-Thomson, Rosemarie. "Integrating Disability, Transforming Feminist Theory." *NWSA Journal* 14.3 (2002): 1–32.

Garland Thomson, Rosemarie. "Extraordinary Bodies: Figuring Physical Disability." *American Culture and Literature*. New York: Columbia UP, 1997.

Gilman, Sander L. *Creating Beauty to Cure the Soul*. Durham: Duke UP, 1998.

Haiken, Elizabeth. *Venus Envy: A History of Cosmetic Surgery*. Baltimore: Johns Hopkins UP, 1997.

Hevey, David. *The Creatures Time Forgot: Photography and Disability Imagery*. London: Routledge, 1992.

Koren, Yehuda, and Eilat Negev. *In Our Hearts We Were Giants: The Remarkable Story of the Lilliput Troupe—A Dwarf Family's Survival of the Holocaust*. New York: Carroll & Graf, 2004.

Levinas, Emmanuel. *Otherwise than Being or Beyond Essence*. Trans. Alphonso Lingis. Boston: Martinus Nijhoff, 1981.

Liebe Perla. Dir. Shahar Rozen. Israel, 1999.

Longmore, Paul K. *Why I Burned My Book and Other Essays on Disability*. Philadelphia: Temple UP, 2003.

O'Neill, Sandy. *First They Killed the "Crazies" and "Cripples": The Ableist Persecution and Murders of People with Disabilities by Nazi Germany 1933–45: An Anthropological Perspective*. Diss. California Institute of Integral Studies, 2000.

Posner, Gerald L., and John Ware. *Mengele: The Complete Story*. New York: McGraw-Hill, 1986.

Sontag, Susan. *Regarding the Pain of Others*. New York: Ferrar, Straus and Giroux, 2003.

Weindling, Paul Julian. *Nazi Medicine and the Nuremberg Trials: From Medical War Crimes to Informed Consent*. New York: Palgrave, 2004.

Re-Producing the Class and Gender Divide: Fritz Lang's *Metropolis*

Gabriela Stoicea

The following article outlines the economy of gender relations in Fritz Lang's *Metropolis* (1927). I approach the topic of gender relations from a previously neglected perspective that examines connections between gender, sexuality, and work as conceptualized by Marx and the early Socialists who preceded him. Close analyses of several key sequences will demonstrate that *Metropolis* translates cinematically the inversion of causality between work and sexuality that Marx introduced after the Saint-Simonians, from whom he otherwise distanced himself. By keeping women either completely outside the cinematic space or relegating them to certain strategic roles within the narrative, Harbou and Lang move towards their own understanding of the relationship between work, gender, and sexuality, suggesting that cinema not only reflects, but actively participates in the creation and maintenance of the status quo. (GS)

Commenting on the line "The debauchees returned, broken by their business"[1] (Baudelaire 85) from "Morning Twilight"[2]—the same poem in which Charles Baudelaire compares Paris to an "aged workman" (85; "vieillard laborieux")—Walter Benjamin notes, "With the Saint-Simonians, industrial labor is seen in the light of sexual intercourse; the idea of the joy of working is patterned after an image of the pleasure of procreation. Two decades later, the relation has been revised: the sex act itself is marked by the joylessness which oppresses the industrial worker" (367). As Saskia Poldervaart has shown, sex and sexuality were issues of central concern for Charles Fourier, Saint Simon, Robert Owen, and their proponents, all of whom, taken together, represent the first socialists of the early to mid-nineteenth century. Although Saint-Simonians explicitly rejected utopianism as a doctrine that promotes a static image of society (Poldervaart 61), they are known, to this day, as "utopian socialists"—a derogatory name given to them by Marx and Engels, who dismissed the work of their predecessors due to the latter's rejection of violent class struggle (Poldervaart 41–42). Granted, Fourier, Simon, and Owen did not see eye-to-eye with Marx on the precise means whereby economic and social reform were to come about. Utopian socialists invested sexuality with a strong potential for revolution. They believed in "changing the relationships of production as well as relations between the sexes by problematizing sexuality, the family and the public/private distinction" (Poldervaart 42). Marx, on the other hand, was intent first and foremost on emphasizing the absolute necessity of political struggle for the collapse of an economic system of large-scale oppression such as capitalism—so much so that, in theory at least, he diminished the importance of gender, sexuality, and family issues, absorbing them indiscriminately into the larger goal of class struggle. He did so, for instance, by inverting the relationship of causality between sexuality and work, by appropriating a term such as "reproduction" into the economic vocabulary, and by introducing a major change in the qualitative nature of sexuality. If Saint Simonians still talked about the "pleasure of procreation" (Benjamin 367), Marx introduced a radical disjuncture between the sexual instinct of pleasure (Sexus) and the life instinct of procreation (Eros). His emphasis on the instinctual nature of biological reproduction in proletarian workers provides an example: "The maintenance and reproduction of the working-class is, and must ever be, a necessary condition to the reproduction of capital. But the capitalist may safely leave its fulfillment to the laborer's instincts of self-preservation and of propagation" (Marx, *Simple Reproduction*). The sense of assurance that emanates from this sentence is misleading when it comes to capitalists' and Marx's own attitude toward sexuality. As my analysis of Fritz Lang's celebrated film *Metropolis*[3] will suggest, elites and governments have always sought to regulate gender and sexuality, sometimes precisely by keeping them outside the official political and economic discourse. Subsequently, for all their differences of opinion and doctrine, Marx and his followers did have a lot in common with the early socialists. Of particular interest to me is how they all helped to construct and refine a discourse of direct causality between work and sexuality in the nineteenth and early twentieth centuries. For all of the above-mentioned theoreticians, work and sexuality were key discursive categories, even if, as Benjamin makes clear, Marx and the Saint Simonians produced different and sometimes radically opposite evaluations regarding which of the two categories most influenced the other and with what qualitative difference(s). In line with this argument, I intend not so much to demonstrate which of these two sides Lang and Harbou's film ultimately supports—if it does so at all—but to trace the dynamic between work and sexuality specific to *Metropolis* and relate it more generally to the historical discourse initiated by Saint Simonians and continued by Marx.

For a very brief moment, the beginning of Fritz Lang's *Metropolis* captures in brilliant visual terms the transition from Saint Simonism to a Marxist critique of capitalism. The film commences with a series of orchestrated shots that suggest a layered structure not only of signification but, as will become apparent later in the film, also of spatial, primarily vertical, organization. The progression from one shot to the next proceeds in less a horizontal, i.e., linear, consequential manner, than top-down, following an associative logic that exposes and deconstructs the palimpsestic texture of Joh Fredersen's capitalist empire and of the film itself. The opening shots of *Metropolis* vaguely recall Walter Ruttman's interest in the possibilities of abstract animated film, which he began exploring in 1921 with the first abstract film the world had ever seen, *Lichtspiel Opus I* (Cinema Opus I). In *Metropolis* we first see the mechanism whereby the illusion of geometric shapes is created on-screen through a controlled projection of lights and shadows. The resulting collage of intersecting shapes and lines then brings forth the word *Metropolis,* from which an intensely radiating light grows to inundate the screen and literally starts to dissolve the image. Revealed beneath it are the painted contours of a monumental city panorama, more precisely a mountainous formation of urban architecture envisioned by set designers Erich Kettelhut, Otto Hunte, and Carl Vollbrecht. The word *Metropolis* itself remains intact. Its cropped appearance becomes a bridge to the next shot of skyscrapers, onto which it remains grafted for a few seconds before it finally fades out. A direct visual link is thus established between the first two shots of the film. Here Lang reveals the significance of *Metropolis* for the first time in its entirety: as visualized on the screen, this name not only conjures the title of the film, but also refers specifically to the eponymous city around which the narrative revolves. The impression of animation and the passage of time, evident in the rising sun over Metropolis, derive in this shot from an ingenious lighting effect achieved, in turn, through frame-by-frame shooting.

This trick photography sequence gradually dissolves into a montage of individual documentary-like shots in which movement becomes the key element, possibly as an echo of Marx's understanding that economic reproduction is concerned not with a static, but with the dynamic motion of an economy. Vertical phallic-like pistons combine with endlessly spinning wheels and other rotating devices to create the impression of a pulsating rhythm with clear sexual overtones, underscored toward the end of the sequence also by the dramatic cadence of a clock, which grows to dominate the musical score.[4] At first glance, the message conveyed by this montage seems to tie in perfectly with the parallel that Saint Simonians drew between industrial labor and sexual intercourse, although the idea appears here not for the utopian socialist goal of "rehabilitating the flesh by valuing its pleasure and incentives" (Poldervaart 41). Upon closer inspection, the visual depiction of technology in this particular sequence conforms only partially to the utopian socialist idea of patterning the joy of working "after an image of the pleasure of procreation" (Benjamin 367). To be sure, pleasure plays an important role in the almost fetishistic visualization of the technical apparatus. The idea of procreation, on the other hand, is also of some consequence in this scene, but only at the level of the film text itself, not its diegesis. Significantly, in the entire film we never see what the machines actually produce, an approach that diametrically opposes Walter Benjamin's in his *Arcades Project*. At most one could say that the images of machines simply produce more images of machines, whether identical or different. Multiple exposures convey this idea cinematically, evident in the superimposition of two or more shots of the same or similar rotating devices in the film's opening montage sequence. Replacing commodities with film images in the production process highlights the self-reflexive dimension of Lang's cinematography. But the visual ban on physical commodities in *Metropolis* also comments on the sterile environment of technology. This sterility is hardly compatible with the "pleasure of procreation" about which Saint Simonians talked. Instead it provides a point of entry into Marx, more specifically the separation between Sexus and Eros that the German theorist introduced when he transposed the concept of "reproduction" into economic terms.

Marx's understanding of sexuality becomes apparent in the sequence that portrays the daily lives of the oppressed workers, who are as plagued by the separation between Sexus and Eros as technology itself. The most obvious instance of the proletarian workers' sublimating desire appears in the striking contrast between the energy emanating from automated machines and the following shot of exhausted human laborers returning home at the end of a working day. The compelling visual and acoustic tempo of the previous sequence gives way to the slow-moving rhythm of a mass of overworked men with whom the camera never identifies, perhaps an implicit acknowledgment on Lang's part of cinema's debt to technology. In order to visually translate the rotation of factory shifts, Lang creates the perfect synchronization of one group of workers arriving while another departs. This shift creates the impression of regimented repetition without the possibility of escape, which is sustained visually by the numerous iron bars demarcating the various spaces that contain the workers. Day after day, at the end of their shift, laborers descend into the depths of Metropolis, slowly and unenthusiastically making their way to the lifeless, uninhabited, and uninviting tenements that retain nothing of the glamour of the upper city. As the camera follows the workers' downward trajectory, Lang unveils yet another level of spatial organization, but also reveals for the first time the vertical arrangement of the city. This sequence stands in stark contrast to the subsequent depiction of the privileged class and its carefree life, but it prompts no further action on the level of the narrative. This representation suggests, on the one hand, that the workers' city represents the lowest level of Metropolis—a hypothesis that will be revised in the course of the film—and, on the other, that the sequence itself was designed primarily to comment on the catatonic state of the workers.

One of the most striking elements in this sequence is the complete absence of women and children, as male workers return to a seemingly deserted city. Historically, massive layoffs of women and children from factories exiled them within the private sphere of the household after they had constituted the bulk of the industrial proletariat.[5] By all rules of logic, the so-called worker's city in *Metropolis* should therefore be a space inhabited mostly by women and children. Visually, however, there are next to no traces of their existence, except perhaps for the dim lights irradiating from some of the apartments to which the workers return. This minimalist visual representation of the domestic space marks it as a potential sphere of resistance because it escapes the capitalists' visual perimeter and our own, and it is where the women and children reside. This interpretation, however, loses much of its subversive potential because the rest of the film fails to corroborate it conclusively. Additionally, Marx himself refused to acknowledge the importance of women's domestic labor for the daily reproduction of workers' labor power since it was not remunerated financially. More subtly still, by de-emphasizing the reproduction of the working class, since it comes about of its own accord (Marx, *Simple Reproduction*), Marx purges the term "reproduction" of any connotations of desire and pleasure that might have carried over from the sexual realm. At the same time, however, he holds onto the instinctual implications of the term and mobilizes them to dismiss the tasks that comprise a woman's daily activity and maintain the workers.

I will return later to a more detailed discussion about women's distribution across various spaces in *Metropolis* and their link to a complex discourse about work and sexuality. Remaining for now in the thematic sphere of industrial labor and reproduction, I will focus on the portrayal of children in Fritz Lang's film. Our first glance of the workers' city initiates many covert visual references to proletarian children.

Straightforward cinematic representations of children in *Metropolis* generally show them in large groups, separated both spatially and visually from their parents. The process of capital-induced familial alienation decried by some Socialist Feminists finds its literal translation in *Metropolis* on the level of plot and cinematography: "The passage from serfdom to free labor power separated the male from the female proletarian and both of them from their children" (Dalla Costa and James 42). Despite the general invisibility of children in *Metropolis,* the film abounds with implicit visual and/or symbolic cues to their importance. A case in point is the ten-hour clock that appears several times throughout the film. It probably refers to the nineteenth-century struggle for a more humane regulation of children's work schedule and for the improvement of working conditions at a time when women and children represented the primary work force in English factories. Freder's first hallucinatory vision immediately following the tragic accident in the machine room also alludes to the centrality of children and reproduction to capitalist ideology. Moloch, the terrifying man-eating monster into which the M-machine transforms, takes its name from a bull-headed Phoenician god to whom parents sacrificed their children. This transformation plunges viewers back in time to a moment when children were the most likely and the most vulnerable victims of capitalist aggression. Marx himself insists in the first volume of *Das Kapital* (*Capital*) on "the physical deterioration [...] of the children and young persons as of the women, whom machinery [...] subjects to the exploitation of capital." Further on Marx notes "the enormous mortality, during the first few years of their life, of the children of the workers" ("Machinery and Modern Industry"). But the machine's metamorphosis into Moloch also raises interesting questions about the relation between mythology and technology, which many years after the release of *Metropolis* still preoccupied critics as famous as Theodor Adorno and Marx Horkheimer. Thirdly, as Andreas Huyssen has argued very convincingly in "The Vamp and the Machine," the entire film, and this sequence in particular, testifies to the significance of sexuality in negotiating male fears of technology in Weimar Germany. I would like to suggest one way of supplementing Huyssen's reading of the Moloch machine as a projection of "the male fear of uncontrolled female potency displaced to technology" ("Vamp and Machine" 235). As he recovers from the explosion, Freder sees the killer machine come to life. Ropes haul a group of half-naked men, presumably slaves, up the long flight of stairs that leads straight into the monster's gaping mouth. The ascent progresses with great difficulty, primarily because the slaves resist. The camera closes in on the men several times to capture their futile struggle. After the entire group of slaves succumbs to the machine's unquenchable, murderous desire, subsequent groups emerge at intervals as if on a conveyor belt. The upward trajectory remains the same throughout, but slaves are now no longer the ones on whose flesh the machine feeds. Proletarian workers take their place, recognizable as such by their constraining factory uniforms and perfectly coordinated movements. Unlike the slaves, the workers are neither subjected to coercive physical measures nor reluctant to jump into the abyss. This portion of the Moloch sequence consists of a single, extreme long shot that prevents us from getting close to the victims. Once again, identification with the workers is strongly discouraged. The wave-like distorting effect that traverses the image from left to right at the end of the scene suggests a point-of-view shot, confirmed then by a cut to Freder as he reaches out to the chimerical tableau in a futile attempt to touch what he sees. It is thus through Freder's eyes that Lang has us observe the workers as they rhythmically march up the stairs. The sequential arrangement of the shots linking slaves and workers comments on the affinity between slavery and capitalism. Workers may lack shackles on their feet but, since they also fall prey to Moloch, one could hardly consider them free. Throwing oneself into the mouth of a monster no longer represents a noble act of sacrifice. But it does not proceed from an exertion of will either. If anything, the implacable movement of the workers testifies to a complete erasure of individual will. This reading challenges Marx's belief in the link between freedom of employment and the freedom of workers to rule over their own lives as they see fit: "[As against slavery,] the capitalistic form presupposes, from first to last, the free wage-laborer, who sells his labor-power to capital" (Marx, *Co-operation*). What then compels the workers to renounce their own lives? Here the children once again become significant. By conjuring Moloch as the locus of absolute terror in Metropolis, especially so soon after proletarian children have made their first on-screen appearance in the Eternal Gardens, Harbou and Lang suggest that male fear of technology not only demonizes female sexuality, as Huyssen has argued, but articulates workers' fear of losing their offspring to the same capitalist machinery that necessitates individual *and* generational reproduction and that reduces human laborers to productive and reproductive abilities. According to Lloyd Spencer, the word "proletariat" itself comes from the Greek *proles,* or offspring, thus denoting quite fittingly those "who have nought to offer but their offspring" (66). While children remain invisible in the Moloch sequence, adult male workers take over their role as victims. This switch suggests the way men have historically replaced women and children on the assembly line. Beyond this, by stepping into the shoes of their children, the workers of Metropolis have, theoretically at least, the chance to break the chain of destruction in which their offspring would be caught otherwise. They could thus follow through with a revolutionary sense of empowerment released through the love for one's children. Yet the workers' automated movements suggest the impenetrability of an unrelenting mechanism that will eventually devour the children as well as the adults. What remains clear is that reproduction and workers' sexuality play a crucial role in the negotiation, whether in the form of mobilization or restraint, of illicit political energies.

Women's part in this process is significant. Judging by the large cast of men and the minimal intervention of proletarian women in the plot, one might conclude that the separation between Sexus and Eros affects primarily men, or that women's exclusion from the sphere of paid work signals their insignificance in the eyes of the state. These are both erroneous conclusions that reinforce the patriarchal tradition described by Kate Millett: "Since the Enlightenment, the West has undergone a number of cataclysmic changes: industrial, economic, and political revolution. But each *appeared* to operate, to a large extent, without much visible or direct reference to one half of humanity" (64; my emphasis), i.e., to women. In actual fact, however, women's lives *were* impacted, even if in ways which critics have only recently begun to uncover, by men's choices and by the constantly changing ideological investment in human sexuality. Furthermore, as I will demonstrate using specific examples from Lang's film, women's bodies, with their unique reproductive ability, often became indispensable vehicles throughout history for implementing official discourses on sexuality and politics. Being outside a normative category such as that of wage laborers does not exclude women from other less visible categories and hierarchies with which the state keeps its subjects in check. It is precisely these unseen norms and categories that interest me, as well as the ways in which they operate in *Metropolis*.

By activating the Sexus/Eros divide, certain categories of sexual relations were legitimated and others criminalized in order to establish specific economic and political doctrines and maintain desired structures of domination. Reproduction provides a case in point. Historically, it became the single most important criterion by which human interaction among members of the proletariat was evaluated in the nineteenth century. Drawing on Gunnar Heinsohn and Rolf Knieper's seminal work *Theorie des Familienrechts: Geschlechtsrollenaufhebung, Kindervernachlässigung, Geburtenrückgang* (1976, Theory of Family Law: Abolishment of Gender Roles, Neglect of Children, Decline in the Birth Rate), Maria Mies explores some of the reasons why the German state intervened in the "production" of people. For the early industrial proletariat, "the family, as we understand it today, was much less the norm than is usually believed" (Mies 183). The propertyless proletariat had even less material interest in the production of children than in marriage, because children provided no insurance in old age, unlike the sons of the bourgeoisie. Farmers also tended to have large families because they needed as much help as possible to work the land. So in order to inspire the proletarians to produce enough children for the next generation of workers, it became imperative to find ways of channeling their sexual energies "into the straightjacket of the bourgeois family" (Mies 184). The colonization of workers by the bourgeois morality was carried out through concrete state legislation and police measures, as well as ideological campaigns, many of which were aimed at curbing sexuality "in such a way that it took place within the confines of the family" (Mies 184). As a consequence, sexual intercourse before and outside of marriage was criminalized. Aside from ensuring a future generation of workers, the legal provisions and ideological campaigns designed by the German state to boost reproduction among the proletariat also provided an effective way of keeping in check the growing threat posed by women both at home, via the sexual liberation characteristic of the Weimar period, and outside the home in the labor market. Women's presence in the labor market and within the sexual revolution was deemed so dangerous to patriarchy as to necessitate "getting women out of the factory altogether and back into the safety of the 'home'" (Millett 87). Possible reasons for this drastic measure were, according to Kate Millett, the disruption of the family structure, including the authority of the father as provider and head of household, and the fact that women worked too hard in the factory to serve in the home (87).

One of the more concrete historical measures implemented in Germany during the early industrial period was the so-called "housewifization campaign" whose origins can be traced back to the bourgeois ideal of the domestic woman and which quickly caught on among male workers. This campaign reinforced patriarchy at a moment in German history when women were supposed to throw off their sexual inhibitions and make way for the "emanzipierte Frau." On a more abstract ideological level, patriarchy could be sustained through a tight control over female sexual desire and by sanctioning certain forms of sexuality in various types of women. Carol Diethe, for instance, argues that more often than not in Weimar Germany the pervasive but unseen control of female sexuality revolved around an idealization of the mother's role (120). This argument applies only partially to *Metropolis*. The elaborate religious symbolism surrounding Fritz Lang and Thea von Harbou's

Maria suggests that she is meant to embody the idealized form of motherhood perpetuated to this day by the Christian doctrine. Yet Maria's role is not always entirely straightforward, and neither is that of the proletarian women in *Metropolis*. Visually, they are hardly ever portrayed as mothers. The presence of children does imply that workers' wives have given birth, but we never see them with the children performing their maternal role. Moreover, on the rare occasions when proletarian women take center stage, they form a "flowing mass of female aggression" (Ruppert 7) that evokes anything but maternal feelings. The de-individualized female figures that participate in the workers' rebellion lack Maria's maternal nurturing and care, and she in turn lacks any biological ties to the workers' children. Arguably this latter detail links Maria to the figure of the Virgin Mother, but on a non-symbolic level it suggests a multiply deficient motherhood.

In an attempt to untangle the symbolic ramifications of the "raging femininity" in *Metropolis,* Andreas Huyssen has suggested that the timing of the proletarian women's first appearance on screen is anything but arbitrary.[6] According to him, this moment signals women's threat, which challenges both the machines and the men, replacing the threat of technology (Huyssen, "Vamp and Machine" 232). In *After the Great Divide* (1986) Huyssen offers a more detailed explanation for the nineteenth-century gendering of mass culture and rebellious crowds. Beginning with the negative feminine characteristics normally associated with mass culture toward the end of the nineteenth century ("serialized feuilleton novels, popular and family magazines, the stuff of lending libraries, fictional bestsellers, [...] not, however, working-class culture or residual forms of older popular or folk cultures" [49]), Huyssen then traces the gendering of masses in general back to the gendering of mass culture: "In the age of socialism *and* the first women's movement in Europe, the masses knocking at the gate were also women, knocking at the gate of a male-dominated culture" (47). This kind of genealogy applies very well to *Metropolis,* especially if we bear in mind that Thea von Harbou's novel was first serialized in a magazine before being published as a book and eventually turned into a screenplay. It also helps complete the picture of what exactly fueled male fears of femininity in the industrial era and why proletarian women make their first major appearance in *Metropolis* as a raging mob. Just as the gendering of angry mobs in modernity is not accidental, so too is the fact that proletarian women have children not fortuitous. Despite its puzzling absence in the first half of *Metropolis,* the maternal instinct becomes a decisive factor in the outcome of the workers' rebellion. Attention to the dynamic of this rebellion can help deconstruct the mechanism that undermines the rule of capital, which is then restored by a cosmeticized and highly problematic reconciliation at the end of the film. Understanding this dynamic requires first off an analysis of class and sexuality in Joh Fredersen's empire.

The same Sexus/Eros divide that characterizes both technology and the workers can be applied more generally to the two social classes that are locked in a dialectical relationship of opposition and mutual dependency. Sexuality in *Metropolis* splits into two apparently incompatible categories. Each category comes with its own set of prescribed sexual practices and enacts a boundary that divides the rich from the poor. The capitalist thinkers enjoy a virtual monopoly over a hedonistic type of sexuality that underemphasizes biology and usurps the female procreative role. The most resonant scene in this regard takes place in the Eternal Gardens and focuses on the freedom of capitalists' sons in pursuing the gratification of their wildest sexual desires and fantasies. The film offers no corresponding exploration of the domestic/erotic spaces inhabited by the workers, implying that the proletariat is confined by a reproduction-oriented sexuality that tends to overemphasize biology.

Except for Hel and Maria, all of the women in Lang's film are either prostitutes or proletarian mothers/housewives. Whether or not one female character has access to the world of the thinkers or that of the workers depends solely on her bodily experiences and the category in which these experiences situate her. This kind of categorization in women is directly proportional to the two class-based types of sexuality discussed previously. The reason for this is that the Sexus/Eros divide, as well as masculine identities themselves, are constantly negotiated in the film over the bodies of women. Separating reproductive and non-reproductive sexuality in *Metropolis* depends largely on a functionalization of women's bodies, i.e., on efforts to graft their bodily experiences onto their class affiliation. In turn, this process dictates the specific intra-diegetic spaces to which women can gain access, as well as the extent to which they can literally lay claim to visibility in Lang's film.

If, following Walter Benjamin, the separation between pleasure and procreation has its origins in the introduction of industrial labor, one would expect it to affect men only, since they dominated the labor market after the gradual but steady elimination of women and children from factories. Given women's exile from wage-paying industrial labor to the private, wageless sphere of domestic labor, why does the female body in Lang's film become the perfect ground for negotiating and implementing the Sexus/Eros divide? Huyssen offers one possible answer when he underscores male fears of errant female sexuality in both the film and Weimar culture in general. Yet one must question the expectation that people not directly involved in the reproduction of capital are not influenced by this sphere, or that capitalism offers the only means for neutralizing women's bodies through objectification and marginalization. Both of these latter points seem evident in *Metropolis*, especially if one considers the events that allow women to become visible and how this impacts the other social actors.

The prostitutes in the Eternal Gardens are the first women to appear on screen, at least according to the most recently restored but still incomplete version of *Metropolis*. They also become the largest female presence overall in the world of the thinkers.[7] At no point in the narrative does it become unequivocally clear to which class the prostitutes belong and whether they feel the pleasure they deliver to the rich. All we can infer is that the presence of prostitutes in the Eternal Gardens derives primarily from their ability to produce pleasure without children. According to Walter Benjamin, "the depraved woman stays clear of fertility" (556). Prostitutes embody a sexuality apart from pregnancy and family, relieving their clients temporarily of the burdensome prospect of parenthood. With their attire and demeanor, the prostitutes blend into the décor of the Eternal Gardens. We first see them summoned by an odd-looking man, presumably the master of ceremonies, under a cavernous canopy that resembles the sculptural shape of the prostitutes' skirts. This canopy invokes both *Jugendstil* (Art Nouveau) and the works of Antoni Gaudi, a famous Spanish architect who died one year before the release of *Metropolis* but whose sculptures can still be admired in present-day Barcelona. One of Gaudi's most notable merits was developing a uniquely organic style influenced by shapes and structures from the natural world—sinuous curves, stylized creatures, and floral motifs that betray an aversion to straight lines and symmetry. Later on in the same sequence, Freder prompts a panning shot of the Eternal Gardens in which all architecture disappears, giving way to various exotic plants and trees. One could argue that the canopy suggests an architectural style designed to reconcile human, in this case female, and natural shapes. The women themselves stand out, first through their provocative clothes, which nevertheless blend in with the decorative style of the set. The camera also insists on the prostitutes' theatrical movements and gestures as they compete with each other to entertain Joh Fredersen's son. By having the actresses look straight into the camera as they bow and turn, Lang allows the spectator to choose a prostitute for Freder. Eventually the main hero chooses one himself, which suggests the illusory nature of spectators' agency. Linking viewers with the subject of the gendered cinematic gaze is nevertheless important insofar as it contributes to a fetishization of the female body in its performance of femininity.

By the very nature of their work, prostitutes qualify as ideal mouthpieces for the separation between sex and the desire to procreate, an idea to which the affluent people of Metropolis generally subscribe. But prostitutes also protect the boundaries of the Eternal Gardens from potential intrusions by gratifying the sexual needs of the rich young men within the walls of Joh's empire. The Eternal Gardens thus function as a pressure valve that thwarts the pursuit of sexual pleasure beyond its gates among the lower class. But the forbidden fruit inevitably emerges to challenge the legitimacy and haunt the permeable boundaries of this sanctioned outlet. The actual breach takes place in the sequence in which Maria enters the Gardens surrounded by a large group of children. Paradoxically, such a vigilantly guarded space dedicated exclusively to the enjoyment of physical pleasures proves highly vulnerable to the lower levels of the city. Like the introduction of prostitutes in the beginning of the sequence, the intrusion of uninvited onlookers is framed in a theatrical manner. First we see the doors open, as if a curtain had gone up to allow eye contact between actors and members of the audience. Long shots alternate with medium ones, some from Freder's perspective, to show Maria and the children advancing on a stage-like platform until they come into full view. A series of point-of-view shots associated successively with Freder and Maria follows, although it remains unclear who watches. Prostitutes gather slowly around Freder in disbelief, projecting their inquisitive gaze onto Maria who, in turn, registers the artificial quality of the frozen tableau unfolding before her eyes and the children's. Maria's assertive gaze, which the camera holds and with which it identifies on more than one occasion, suggests an actress who refuses to pretend that she does not see the audience watching her. By Maria's own admission, her presence in the Eternal Gardens is motivated by an intention to show the workers' children how their richer "brothers" live. Of course, this makes little sense if we bear in mind the activities that go on inside. But the presence of children is crucial in establishing the main female character as a would-be mother figure from the very beginning. The transition to the second class-specific understanding of sexuality evident in *Metropolis* is thereby completed.

When Freder, surrounded by prostitutes and holding one of them in his arms, meets Maria in the Eternal Gardens, we witness the first of several head-to-head confrontations between sexuality as physical enjoyment and motherhood as biological procreation designed to perpetuate capitalism by replenishing the workforce with ever new labor power. Presented with the alternative model of sexuality embodied by Maria, Freder starts to oscillate. He becomes unsure about how to respond to Maria—as a lover, as a would-be father figure to the children, or as a son. All of these roles suggest that Freder now longs for integration into Maria's maternal tableau. Physically, however, he remains frozen until Maria leaves the Eternal Gardens, and he continues clutching the prostitute he had previously chased. Spatially and ideologically, Maria occupies a diametrically opposed position, which explains why Lang never films them all in the same frame, preferring instead a series of point-of-view shots that suggest some kind of interaction.

The opposition implied in this sequence between the good mother and the prostitutes anticipates the subsequent split between the good and the bad Maria. But Kate Millett's argument that "one of the chief effects of class within patriarchy is to set one woman against another" (38) should make us wary of such antagonisms and suspicious of systems of domination that try to cover up the precarious situation of all women. Even mothers and prostitutes turn out to have things in common, starting with the way they disappear from the screen as imperceptibly as they appeared on it. Emma Goldman, writing to her English countrywomen in 1910, addressed the incredible openness of nineteenth-century Britain toward prostitution by citing academic sources that link industrial labor with vast masses of people in a competitive market that drove many working girls and married, working-class women into prostitution, mostly due to sheer need (121). In addition to this direct historical link between these two categories of women, *Metropolis* suggests that what prostitutes share with the wives of factory workers is a rather curious and paradoxical double standard. Although wageless women do not count for much in the eyes of the state, unofficially a lot of ideological work goes into promoting certain roles that are then imposed on women to keep the status quo in place. Strangely enough, this gesture suggests a silent recognition of women's potential for subversive action, even if capitalism quickly finds solutions for neutralizing any shred of resistance among those who fall between the cracks of state-sanctioned categories.

In light of the confrontation between reproductive and non-reproductive sexuality that takes place in the Eternal Gardens, the instant chemistry between Freder and Maria can be interpreted as the attraction of two opposing individuals for what the other represents. Predictably, a series of transgressions follows, replete with Biblical associations. Unable to put the encounter with Maria behind him and on the verge of venturing into her unfamiliar space, Freder takes a good long look at what he would leave behind. The camera pans horizontally from right to left, revealing the wondrous vegetation and visual pleasures that Freder is about to renounce. According to sources that cite Günther Rittau, one of Lang's two cinematographers in *Metropolis,* this panoramic shot was taken with a Debrie camera that could not be moved. Hence, the relief painting of the landscape representing the Eternal Gardens had to be moved manually in front of the camera. The resulting dream-like appearance of the painted backdrop may reflect Freder's exhilaration, but it also suggests that whatever the Eternal Gardens once offered him can no longer hold him back. As Freder dashes with resolve through the swinging doors of the Eternal Gardens, we realize that the panning shot did not deter him from pursuing his dreams. If anything, it precipitated his final decision. By moving beyond the walls of the Eternal Gardens, Freder breaks some of the unwritten rules of his father's dominion. He casts his descent into the workers' city as an unruly act by lying to Joh Fredersen about his reason for visiting the machine halls: "I wanted to look into the faces of the people whose little children are my brothers, my sisters." The threat that Freder and Maria's escapade poses to the capitalist empire derives from the ease with which Freder escapes his father's rule in precisely the space over which Joh should have ultimate control: the machine halls and the workers' city.

Like Freder, Maria strives to exceed the type of sexuality she embodies at the beginning. As I argued previously, she emerges in the Eternal Gardens via an assertive gaze, even as she becomes an object of the male gaze in the same scene. This dynamic alerts Maria to her sexual potential much earlier and in a much less violent form than in the chase/rape scene with Rotwang's light in the catacombs. To be sure, Freder's gaze upon Maria in the gardens of pleasure differs from the gaze of the capitalists' sons during the robot Maria's erotic dance. Still, Freder's gaze opens up for Maria the possibility of circumventing the position of iconic, maternal reproductive medium that marriage would ultimately bring. Carol Diethe's contention that the real Maria "has no sexuality to speak of" (116) may hold true in the beginning of *Metropolis,* but the visual narrative of the film revises this hypothesis immediately thereafter. It is precisely through her discovery of sexuality that, despite her pleas for patience among the workers, Maria threatens to transgress the rigid boundary between the upper and the lower classes. If this combination of pleasure and motherhood makes Maria a serious threat to paternal authority and to the social divide between the rich and the poor, it then makes sense for the capitalist ruler to produce a unidimensional robot-like prototype—the incarnation of "pure" female sexuality cleansed of all maternal feelings. Beside the cyborg's emotional incompatibility with the role of a mother, it is also safe to assume, given her mechanical origins, that the false Maria could never give birth. Like the prostitutes of the Eternal Gardens, she may restore the separation between sexuality as pleasure and sexuality for procreative purposes. The fact that Joh can only bring this cyborg to life by artificial means comments ironically on the ideological function of the false Maria, since she keeps capitalism in place by discouraging a subversive model of hybrid sexuality that combines pleasure and procreation. Yet the outcome of Joh's endeavors is hardly negative. In fact, the successful separation of sexuality and the maternal becomes apparent already at the end of Rotwang's experiment. Two Marias instead of one virtually undoes the real Maria's earlier attempt to unite pleasure and the maternal within herself. Furthermore, the original Maria and her double subsequently emerge as two distinct and irreconcilable characters, as if to demonstrate that sexuality and motherhood have indeed been distilled and can be kept apart successfully for the benefit of political and economic ideology: "By the end of the film, Maria is no longer an object of sexual desire for Freder" (Huyssen, "Vamp and Machine" 215).

But in order for the ruling ideology to be restored completely, divorcing sexuality from motherhood and reassigning each of them to the thinkers and the workers respectively would have to be replicated exactly and be successful on the much broader scale of social action. The first step toward implementing this strategy involves a detour from its intended goals. Through provocative vocabulary and body language during her inflammatory speech to the proletariat, the cyborg Maria introduces the crowd of workers to a sexual drive that had previously been denied to them: [Cyborg Maria to the workers:] "Who lubricates the machine joints with their own blood?" In theory the transgression of social boundaries presupposed by this sexual awakening increases the potential for genuine revolutionary action. The actual odds of bringing about a revolution are, however, very small if we bear in mind the political apathy that the good Maria advocates in the catacombs. Despite her virginal appearance, Maria espouses a dangerous regime of repressive tolerance that acknowledges the workers' latent revolutionary energies but also finds, quite literally, a Christian way to keep them bottled up.[8] Since, in Josaphat's words, "only their hope for a mediator is keeping the workers in check," Joh should be content that Maria preaches passivity to the lower class. Joh's decision to send the robot-woman to the workers appears at best superfluous from a political point of view, but it makes sense in light of my earlier suggestion that what Joh fears is primarily Maria's attempt to erase the distinction between hedonism and procreation.

In this context the unexpected appearance of women workers finds a surprising justification. With sexuality as the driving force behind the crowd's rampant actions, the presence of women workers casts motherhood as a temporarily repressed force that returns all the more vigorously to perform its initial, ideologically prescribed function: to keep sexuality in check among the workers. Realizing that they have left their children in the flooded abodes underground, the workers surprisingly do not return to save them but instead turn against the cyborg. They chase the false Maria through the city until they have destroyed her. The proletarians' thirst for revenge trumps their concern for their own children until Grot, the chief foreman of the Heart Machine, announces that the workers' children had been rescued and led to safety in the Club of the Sons. This turn of events presents an unsavory view of the workers, one that points to the film's ideological bias. More telling is how the workers blame their absent-mindedness solely on the women. As a consequence, women once again disappear from the screen just when the outcome of the rebellion is negotiated.

This return to a repressed femininity had been announced from the very beginning of the rebellion by a musical reference to the French Revolution, in which thousands of women fought but were similarly excluded from politics by the end of the insurgency. In the sequence where the false Maria rallies all the adult inhabitants of the workers' city on the central plaza, a shot of the female cyborg moving her head convulsively accompanies an acoustic reworking of the Marseillaise. The same musical score continues in the next shot, in which two women run out of the tenements toward the camera. By the end of the film, however, no women remain in the crowd. The renewed invisibility of workers' wives in the final shot of *Metropolis* suggests that motherhood has first been demonized, then put in its proper place along with hedonistic female sexuality, as male workers' patriarchal interests are reactivated.[9] If the upper and the lower classes cannot unite to pursue a common political goal, they can still co-exist peacefully in the face of a common threat, namely woman, with all her excesses. What makes the final reconciliation in *Metropolis* possible is precisely the "healthy and strong" partnership of patriarchy and capital that Socialist Feminists like Heidi Hartmann have long decried (360). Paradoxically, this partnership renders Harbou and Lang's male workers blind to the immediacy of their own defeat. The artificiality and unexpectedness of workers' docility at the end of the film can only suggest the price male workers pay for excluding women from the final shot. Like prostitutes, and with an equally indirect involvement in the capitalist mode of production, proletarian women keep the revolutionary energies of male laborers in check, thereby policing the boundaries between the higher and the lower classes: "The family [...] has been [...] the best guarantee that the unemployed do not immediately become a horde of disruptive outsiders. [...] On this family depends the support of the class, the survival of the class—but at the woman's expense *against the class itself*" (Dalla Costa 48, 50; my emphasis).

Metropolis curbs revolutionary impulses and puts them in the service of a highly adaptable system of large-scale repression designed to keep capitalist ideology in place. To cite Heidi Hartmann again, "in the absence of patriarchy a unified working class might have confronted capitalism, but patriarchal social relations divided the working class, allowing one part (men) to be bought off at the expense of the other (women)" (361). In a way, one could hypothesize that most critics' skepticism vis-à-vis the artificial, regressive ending of *Metropolis* is fueled by their nostalgia for the imagined benefits of class unity. The question that lingers is whether we recognize that imagining class unity remains utopian if we fail to address and acknowledge the importance of gender issues for political struggle.

What then emerges at the end of this investigation is the need to re-evaluate the differing effects of the industrial revolution on each member of society, given categories such as age, class, and gender. As I suggested earlier, despite the marginal position that women occupy in Harbou and Lang's filmic narrative, *Metropolis* aptly demonstrates that even the lives of those not directly involved in the process of production are affected by it, more often than not negatively. One of the most painful lessons of the French Revolution is forgotten in Harbou and Lang's film: instead of boosting the subversive potential of women's autonomous participation in revolutionary struggle, their exclusion from direct production relegates them to the private sphere of the household, where women better serve capitalists' goal of curbing male workers' illicit energies. Whether demonized or idolized, female sexuality emerges as perpetually subject to ideological manipulation. *Metropolis* does not promote the naïve alternative of re-introducing women into the labor force, but it also does not suggest a better alternative for women's emancipation. Faced with the problematic resolution of Lang's film, we can only hope that, if everyone realized that the primary social and political distinctions are not based on wealth or rank but rather on sex (Millett 65), things might change. We have no way of knowing whether this hope will ultimately prove realistic. But at least it is a start.

Notes

I would like to thank Professors Karin Crawford, Laurie Johnson, Brigitte Peucker, and Henry Sussman for their useful comments on earlier versions of this article.

[1] "Les débauchés rentraient, brisés par leurs travaux" (Baudelaire 84).

[2] "Le crépuscule du matin."

[3] All quotations and analytic references to individual scenes contained in this film are taken from the authorized restored version put together in 2002 by Enno Patalas and his Munich team of film restorers.

[4] The large ten-hour clock has multiple functions within and beyond the opening sequence of *Metropolis*. First of all, it fits in quite nicely with the other mechanical devices that dominate the opening sequence. Like them, it does not produce anything, but instead measures things, although the arrangement of shots does ascribe to it generative powers since it sets off the shift whistle. Marx himself suggests yet another connection between clocks and the industrial revolution: "The two material bases on which the preparations for machine-operated industry proceeded within manufacture during the period from the sixteenth the eighteenth century [...] were the clock and the mill. [...] Both were inherited from the ancients.... The clock as the first automatic device applied to practical purposes; the whole theory of production of regular motion was developed through it. [...] There is no doubt that in the eighteenth century the idea of applying automatic devices (moved by springs) to production was first suggested by the clock" (qtd. in Benjamin 695). Secondly, the clock's ten-hour dial may be a historical reference to a reform campaign that took place in England throughout the 1830s and was designed to secure legislative protection for child workers by limiting the working hours of all children below the age of eighteen to ten hours per day. Critics and historians, such as Marc Harbor and Heidi Hartmann, argue that the real purpose of the so-called Ten Hour Movement in England and elsewhere was to increase adult male employment by reducing the number of hours women and children could work: "Protective labor laws, while they may have ameliorated some of the worst abuses of female and child labor, also limited the participation of adult women [and children] into many 'male' jobs" (Hartmann 361). In this context, the ten-hour clock can be directly related to some of Marx's writings in volume 1 of *Das Kapital* on the length and extension of the working day under capitalism, as well as on the struggle for the limitation of working hours.

[5] It is estimated that by 1910 women and children made up almost one third of the workforce in early European factories. Factory owners needed cheap labor and docile workers, and they found both of these in the underage and female segments of the population. With few alternatives for work, women took whatever pay and conditions were offered in order to feed themselves and their families. They became even more attractive as laborers once World War I broke out and many men had to leave. As soon as the war was over, however, women were expected to return to their traditional

domestic roles. Marc Harbor and Heidi Hartmann suggest that efforts to reduce the presence of women and children in factories to an absolute minimum had begun as early as the 1830s under the guise of protective labor laws.

[6] Earlier in this article I identified at least one previous sequence with visual cues implying the presence of women. Therefore, the sequence that captures the outbreak of the proletarian revolution does not mark the first time women's presence is felt but rather the first time that the camera captures a visual impression of them.

[7] Having a narrative revolve almost exclusively around the figure of a prostitute was common practice among modernist writers and artists, most notably Walter Benjamin in his monumental monograph on the Paris arcades.

[8] This brings to mind the antidemocratic potential of the very principle of freedom of thought, detected a hundred years ago by Gilbert Keith Chesterton: "Managed in a modern style, the emancipation of the slave's mind is the best way of preventing the emancipation of the slave. Teach him to worry about whether he wants to be free, and he will not free himself" (qtd. in Žižek 2).

[9] Incidentally, the incrimination of women on grounds of neglectful parenthood is something that was actually practiced in the nineteenth century as part of the housewifization campaign. Marx takes a so-called medical inquiry from the year 1861 as conclusive proof that the high death rates in young children were "principally due to the employment of the mothers away from their homes, and to the neglect and maltreatment consequent on their absence [...]; besides this, there arises an unnatural estrangement between mother and child, and as a consequence, intentional starving and poisoning of the children" ("Machinery and Modern Industry").

Works Cited

Baudelaire, Charles. *Selected Poems*. Trans. Geoffrey Wagner. New York: Grove P, 1974.

Benjamin, Walter. *The Arcades Project*. Trans. Howard Eiland and Kevin McLaughlin. Cambridge, MA: Harvard UP, 2002.

Dalla Costa, Mariarosa and Selma James. "Women and the Subversion of the Community." *Materialist Feminism: A Reader in Class, Difference, and Women's Lives*. Eds. Rosemary Hennessy and Chrys Ingraham. New York: Routledge, 1997. 40–53.

Diethe, Carol. "Beauty and the Beast: An Investigation into the Role and Function of Women in German Expressionist Film." *Visions of the*

'Neue Frau': Women and the Visual Arts in Weimar Germany. Eds. Marsha Meskimmon and Shearer West. Aldershot, England: Scolar P, 1995. 108-23.

Goldman, Emma. "The Traffic in Women." *Feminist Theory: A Reader.* 2nd ed. Eds. Wendy Kolmar and Frances Bartkowski. Boston: McGraw-Hill Higher Education, 2005. 120-24.

Harbor, Marc. "Why was legislation to improve factory conditions enacted between 1833 and 1850, and how much change did it bring about?" *A Web of English History.* Ed. Marjie Bloy. 11 Dec. 2005. Mimanet. 3 Nov. 2005 <http://www.historyhome.co.uk/peel/factmine/factories.htm>.

Hartmann, Heidi. "The Unhappy Marriage of Marxism and Feminism: Towards a More Progressive Union." *Feminist Theory: A Reader.* 2nd ed. Eds. Wendy Kolmar and Frances Bartkowski. Boston: McGraw-Hill Higher Education, 2005. 356-65.

Huyssen, Andreas. *After the Great Divide: Modernism, Mass Culture, Postmodernism.* Bloomington: Indiana UP, 1986.

──────. "The Vamp and the Machine: Technology and Sexuality in Fritz Lang's *Metropolis.*" *New German Critique: An Interdisciplinary Journal of German Studies* 24-25 (1981-82): 221-37.

Marx, Karl. "Co-operation." *Capital, Vol. 1.* Pt. 4, Ch. 13. Chicago: Charles H. Kerr and Co., 1906. Trans. Samuel, and Edward Aveling Moore. Ed. Frederick Engels. Library of Economics and Liberty. 5 June 2006. <http://www.econlib.org/library/YPDBooks/Marx/mrxCpA13.html>.

──────. "Machinery and Modern Industry." *Capital, Vol. 1.* Pt. 4, Ch. 15. Chicago: Charles H. Kerr and Co., 1906. Trans. Samuel, and Edward Aveling Moore. Ed. Frederick Engels. Library of Economics and Liberty. 5 June 2006. <http://www.econlib.org/library/YPDBooks/Marx/mrxCpA15.html>.

──────. "Simple Reproduction." *Capital, Vol. 1.* Pt. 7, Ch. 13. Chicago: Charles H. Kerr and Co., 1906. Trans. Samuel, and Edward Aveling Moore. Ed. Frederick Engels. Library of Economics and Liberty. 5 June 2006. <http://www.econlib.org/library/YPDBooks/Marx/mrxCpA23.html>.

Metropolis. Screenplay by Thea von Harbou. Dir. Fritz Lang. Perf. Brigitte Helm, Alfred Abel Gustav Fröhlich, and Rudolph Klein-Rogge. Kino International, 2002.

Mies, Maria. "Colonization and Housewifization." *Materialist Feminism: A Reader in Class, Difference, and Women's Lives.* Eds. Rosemary Hennessy and Chrys Ingraham. New York: Routledge, 1997. 175-85.

Millett, Kate. *Sexual Politics.* London: Virago, 1997.

Poldervaart, Saskia. "Theories about Sex and Sexuality in Utopian Socialism." *Journal of Homosexuality* 29.2/3 (1995): 41–68.

Ruppert, Peter. "Technology and the Construction of Gender in Fritz Lang's Metropolis." *Genders Online Journal* 32 (2000).

Spencer, Lloyd. "Allegory in the World of the Commodity: the Importance of *Central Park*." *New German Critique: An Interdisciplinary Journal of German Studies* 34 (1985): 59–77.

Žižek, Slavoj. *Welcome to the Desert of the Real!—Five Essays on September 11 and Related Dates*. London: Verso, 2002.

"She's Got Her Own Way of Asserting Herself": Interview with Seyhan Derin

Angelica Fenner

Introduction

Seyhan Derin was born in Caycuma, Turkey in 1969. In 1972, she moved with her parents and three sisters to the Federal Republic of Germany, where her brother was born. Derin experimented with Super-8 film as a teenager and received her formal training at the Hochschule für Film und Fernsehen in Munich. Her first feature-length film, *I Am My Mother's Daughter* (1996; *Ben Annemin Kızıyım*), was a thesis project sponsored by her film school in cooperation with the Middle Eastern Technical University in Ankara. Tasked to produce a project on three generations of women, Derin documented the different circumstances faced by her two sisters raised in Germany, her mother as a Turkish migrant, and her grandmother who remained in Turkey. *I Am My Mother's Daughter* garnered four international prizes in 1996. The following interview, which has been translated from German, was conducted in July of 2005 during my research on women's diasporic documentaries, with a follow-up interview in April 2006. It also explores Derin's views on production conditions in contemporary Germany since the completion of her second film, *Between the Stars* (2002; *Zwischen den Sternen*), and touches upon her work for the German television series *Good Times / Bad Times* (*Gute Zeiten / Schlechte Zeiten*). A filmography and further scholarly references have been appended.

Interview

Angelica Fenner: *Looking back now, since the release of* I Am My Mother's Daughter *in 1996, it would appear that your first film set something in motion among other filmmakers of the second generation, as for example with Fatih Akin's autobiographical documentary* Denke ich an Deutschland—Wir haben vergessen zurückzukehren.

Figure 1: Seyhan Derin

Seyhan Derin: I know Akin personally. Before he made his documentary, he attended a screening of my film. Afterward we talked about my biography and why I made the film. At the time, I had the sense that it made a strong impression on him.

Yes, that influence seems palpable. But I think your film is more effective due to its dialogical quality. Akin used voice-over, instead of subtitles, to translate his relatives' comments in the film. By translating their speech and foregrounding his voice over theirs, I think he created a hierarchy within the film discourse.

There are actually two versions of my film. The German one does not have subtitles because there was no funding left, so we used the voice-over technique. I spoke my own lines, while others dubbed the other people. One person spoke my mother's lines and someone else spoke my father's, since my German is too good to be convincing for that. But I don't find voice-over very effective. That's why we chose to use subtitles for the English version. Had there been enough money, we would have redone the German version. But we never got the funds together for it and at some point it had been shown so many times that I thought, okay, let's leave that for now and move on to new projects.

While we are on the topic of sound, music is also quite important for your film. How did you decide which Turkish songs to use?

When I work on a script I usually listen to music, and then it may occur to me, "Oh, that would fit well here!" I'm already very influenced at that stage. We knew that we would not be able to include many musical excerpts, maybe one or two pieces, and it was more about finding a certain rhythm for the editing or a melody that would match well. Then I played these songs for our composer, Georg Schaller, explaining, "Here, while we were writing, shooting, or editing this scene we listened to this music and it conveyed this particular feeling to me." This provided the basis for his own score, and we used that along with a few songs by Sezen Aksu. Those fit in beautifully. It was clear to me from the start that I would use those. The music in the scene where an old woman sings about the bride on her wedding day is from a CD of folk songs from the Black Sea Region released by Sezen Aksu. There's another song, "Ben annemin isterim" (But I Want My Mother), that I would have liked one of the women in the village to sing. Unfortunately, we never got around to that. I would have liked to do more of that sort of thing.

There are these scenes in the film that offer a glimpse of women's daily work life in the village. For example, when they are working with the dried corn, it seems almost ethnographic. It is striking to see that these women are still engaged in the same forms of labor as an earlier generation.

I found it really interesting that the local women were claiming that nowadays there's no work to be done in the village. I could see that they were working very hard, even by today's standards! There may be a few more machines than there used to be, but they don't have that big of an impact. It was a hard life back then, and it still is now.

I found it intriguing how you managed to produce this subtle observation about women's hard work via the editing process. There's the scene where women are carrying pails of water from the pump and walk past a café where men are sitting around and smoking.

I struggled with whether or not to evoke that impression, because it's not entirely accurate. After we shot that scene, I sat down among these men and asked, "How are you?" "What are you doing?" and so forth. And then I found out that several of them, including the one who yawns in that one scene, had just finished the night shift at the local mine. So they were just relaxing after their own work. So it's not about lazy men sitting around while women do all the work. It's a scene in which men happen to be resting and women happen to be working. But I also noticed that women were *always* working. They never had a break where they could just lean back and relax. They would do housework or schlepping for days on end. Some of them apparently also work in town. The men have a night shift of eight to ten hours and then they rest. There's also the image of the old man who is sitting there while his wife continues to work beside him. So I knew that for the women there was no resting, just days of ongoing work. For me, that justified using that scene to show that.

So a completely different statement is conveyed, depending on how one assembles the sequence of images. How much were you involved in the editing of I Am My Mother's Daughter?

From start to finish. I sat down with my editor [Thomas Balkenhol] and we looked at all the footage, deliberated, and discussed. At some point, we showed rough cuts to our friends and discussed their impact, what they mean and why, and then we resumed editing. So I was very much involved.

It's fascinating to sit at the editing table and get an overview of the footage one has accumulated. Then new decisions come into play, depending on how the footage came out.

First, I let the editor just create a sequence. So he cut, looked, and thought about it because he could see new connections in the footage that I hadn't previously recognized. I found that fascinating—how another person can bring a whole new perspective. What I had seen in my material was still there, but it was the editor who discovered what goes where and why. That was really nice.

I find an editor can really play a very significant role in a film. In North America, editors often are not given enough recognition for their work; it always seems about the director.

Well, in documentary films the editor has a really big influence on the production, more than even the cameraman, in my opinion. For example, there are decisions such as the one in the scene "Men Relax while Women Work." How do you edit that? There are so many different ways to write that! You can take away one part and put it somewhere completely different, and then all we see are women working and nothing else, or only men lazing about. And whether it comes across as earnest or comical, engaging or boring—the editor determines all of that. As a director you may sit next to him and think, is that what I'm aiming for or not? Or you suddenly get a new idea and then you have to go out and do more shooting. But in this case, I just had this feeling: I'll make a few small adjustments and let myself in for a surprise regarding the end results.

The staged scenes with the little girl on the train, which were shot in black and white, really made an impression on me. Although you have made a documentary film, there is also something lyrical about it that links it with imagination. It's not a straight talking-heads documentary. Memory work is central to the film, but it is also clear that it can't always be captured on camera in the most concrete of terms.

That's true. When I first started out, we had planned to go out and follow these three generations of women—my grandmother, my mother, and me—through their various daily routines. But we figured out early on that accompanying me in my routines didn't work at all. I couldn't direct the film and be a subject in front of the camera at the same time. I just felt really funny in that situation, and you could see that in the footage. So the cameraman suggested, "Let's just try something completely different." So we decided to just forget about making a film about me. If we are covering issues having to do with me, then it should always be in context with others, like when I worked with the little girl, or met up with my cousins or friends, or had a conversation with my grandmother or my mother. The idea was to not stage these encounters as interviews. And that was a good decision because it really helped me to relax. Instead I went out and got to know these other women and heard their stories. My own story was running parallel to theirs, of course, but I wasn't the main protagonist. This was good for the others too, because I could really focus on them. I noticed that sitting or standing next to them rather than across from them also helped them to relax more. Then they responded to me as their cousin, sister, or daughter, rather than as this filmmaker who wanted to ask this or know about that.

It can also be difficult to broach a topic directly. The film surely is about you—it's made by you and it's you who speaks in the voice-over—but you approach your own story indirectly. That can be far more effective than approaching things in a premeditated way and head on. Then the timing may be wrong and everything feels forced.

Exactly. Of course, I did discuss the general schema with my professor, with his assistant, and with the editor before we started shooting. It was clear that the cameraman would be involved from the beginning, but also the editor because he is a very good and very experienced documentary film editor. Even when he was back in film school he was already pretty much making his own films. He gave me specific pointers of what to bear in mind as the work proceeded. His most important advice to me was, "Don't let yourself be distracted, just be there and see what you find. Try to record what you are finding. And don't go into the project with too rigid a plan!" So even though I had a structure during the actual shooting, I was supposed to just forget it and go forward. The first question he asked me in the cutting room was, "Did you discover anything? And what is it that you've discovered?" And I realized that I could summarize in one sentence what I had discovered: my mother is not who I had previously perceived her to be. And we built the whole film around that.

That's fascinating. So, in effect, one can't really know until later in the whole production process what it's really all about, because it's a process of revelation and discovery. One can start with an outline, but one can't necessarily fully foresee what the outcome will be.

Absolutely. But sometimes completely banal things did go entirely as I had planned them in my script. For example, I predicted that when we visited my aunt, she would slaughter a chicken to celebrate the occasion. And that's the way it was, but we didn't incorporate that into the film. Certain situations and dynamics that I remembered from earlier years played themselves out just as I had anticipated. So we had a laugh, took a look at the footage, and thought about what we could use and what could be set aside.

Are there any scenes that went completely differently than planned, but were nevertheless very effective?

Yes, there are several. One was the scene at the market in Caycuma: Mother goes to the market and shops. I thought that would be really easy to shoot. But from the very start it was a challenge because Father didn't want us to shoot at the market. He was embarrassed to have his wife and daughter making a scene, as it were, in a place where people also know him. That just drove me crazy because I knew that Mother used to go to this market and sell things to earn some money for us. So of course I had to go there with her, because I was trying to portray what her life was like before and evoke those earlier settings. So we came to the agreement that the team and I would maintain a distance of ten meters from Mother, so nobody would see a connection between her and us. And that's what we did, and then that evening we looked at the rushes. The cameraman said, "This is all totally unusable; it's so superficial. We can't even tell what your mother is doing." All the takes were set in long shot and as soon as we tried to use the zoom, the images became so shaky we really couldn't use them. Then I went to Mother and described the problem to her and explained that we needed to convince Father to let us try that again. And she argued very forcefully on our behalf. She had a real argument with him about letting us shoot this scene and show up with her at the market as a film team rather than as separate parties. And she succeeded! That's what I also try to convey in the film: she has her own way of somehow asserting herself and the proof is in the footage. She would observe a situation, and if needed, she'd get in an argument about it, and that's what she did for us, too. Without these scenes, I feel the film would be considerably impoverished.

Do you feel that this way of asserting oneself has also been a formative influence upon you?

I think so, especially since I am currently working for television to earn extra income. When I first started that job, there were only men at the job because it happens to be physically strenuous to direct in this setting. Now there are several women there. But the first thing I heard was, "Oh, you can manage, quiet and gentle as you are!" And I thought to myself, "But I don't feel that way!" But apparently that's how I come across to others when I say, "No, we're going to do it like this!"

What also turned out differently in my documentary film was the encounter with my grandmother. I tried to convey that in the letter I read aloud to her, because I hadn't anticipated that she would be that infirm and unable to communicate much. I basically had to set aside the questions I had prepared for her.

What that scene conveyed for me and what stuck in my memory was this phrase she repeated several times, "You know best" or something like that. That is also another way in which women have responded in situations where they didn't necessarily have the option of asserting themselves. Of course they have their own opinion and desires, but for the sake of appearances they might give in to the other person. Even after your grandmother lost her mental capacities, this phrase was evidently so ingrained in her speech that she invoked it like a reflex, a rote way of dealing with the world.

What also interests me is the issue of how to use the camera. I find that a camera has the potential to turn into a weapon or to be experienced that way by those being filmed, causing them to become inhibited and to act unnaturally. How did you cope with this very typical challenge?

Well, it depends first of all on who is behind the camera. The cameraman, Martin Farkas, was and is a good friend of mine. I knew that he had already made several documentaries besides mine and that he started out in documentary film. Martin is essentially a very reserved person and uses the camera accordingly. He has the ability to win the confidence of his subjects very quickly, but also to pull back again and become almost invisible. I was still worried, though, because he is German and male. And here I am going to the village of Caycuma and meeting Turkish women! I agreed to my parents' request to wear a headscarf in the village in order to be accepted by the locals. But what was I to do about this German man? So then we had Ayschin, who was the camera assistant and also doing Second Camera, and who is Turkish. In the event that there were any issues, the back-up plan was that she would then do the camera and Martin would advise her on the technical aspects and check everything beforehand and, if needed, keep a distance of ten meters. But it never came to that. It was really to my advantage that people knew me. Even if they were in the process of getting to know me again, they knew that I was the daughter of this couple and were therefore willing to interact with me while the camera was running. I wasn't standing next to the camera, but rather next to these women, so their attention was oriented toward me, not the camera, and they quickly forgot about it. My aunt, though, was totally interested in the cameraman; I literally had to lure her attention away because she was always flirting with him! I had to laugh about it, because the fact of the matter is that Martin looks very much like my uncle who died awhile back.

Did you discuss when to use a medium close-up or a close-up, or did you just leave it up to the cameraman?

In the documentary portion of the film, the cameraman normally made his own decisions. But when I wanted a particular type of shot and framing, I just made special requests. We generally reviewed the footage every evening and then made decisions about how to proceed with subsequent camera work. The staged scenes naturally had to be prepared in great detail before.

We had three different shooting sessions: a few days in Germany with my parents, a few days at my place in Munich, and two or three weeks in Turkey at my parents' place. After the first shoot with my parents in Germany we started discussing all these issues. That's when we decided that I would not be doing a self-portrait, but always appear together with other individuals. It's funny; my approach toward the first section was as if I were making a fiction film. One assistant, who had made many documentary films, was really mad at me one evening and said, "Seyhan, you can't do that. You can't just tell your mother, 'Okay, now you should go shopping.'" But I knew that she wanted to go shopping anyway, so I asked her about it and discussed what she would say and do, and then we shot it that way. It was really done like an actress working on command. That looked obvious in the footage, but that didn't bother me because I had the feeling it would be a way to guide Mother into being comfortable with the camera there, and even to have fun playing a role. But it isn't a typical thing to do in documentary filmmaking. The cameraman defended my point of view. That was really interesting, having two documentary filmmakers who had such different opinions on the project. But I still had to find my own path and try things out. Today I would do things differently, but this point of entry was necessary for Mother, and it helped the rest of the family to approach the whole project in a more playful way.

That is really clever. After all, even with documentaries, or perhaps particularly with documentaries, there are people who become completely inhibited and think, "What should I say? What do they want? I don't know how I should act." But as soon as you turn it around and say, "Okay, we're all just playing roles anyway," it gives people permission to just perform, effectively, who they are!

But it really came about as a coincidence, because I'm not trained as a documentarist; I studied fiction filmmaking, so it made sense to me to approach it that way.

Did you study the documentary genre at all during school? Was it part of the curriculum?

It was part of it, but only a small part. The primary focus was fiction film, and I think I may have taken one seminar to earn credits. But I've always loved to watch documentary films. I enjoy the focus on real people and their stories.

Are there certain documentarists who have influenced you?

Chris Marker, for sure. I've seen *Sans Soleil* (1983) so many times because I find it so fascinating. That film is also very autobiographical, with letters and journals that he reads aloud and just tons of images that he combines in different ways. And I'm intrigued by the human observations and the conclusions that he draws.

He also uses voice-over. I liked the way you evoked the dialogical via the epistolary form so that your father also gains a voice through reading aloud his letters.

Those two letters were real. They weren't written for the film. They had already been incorporated in the original plan for the film. While editing we realized that two letters might not be enough. Since the film is ultimately structured as a journey, it seemed natural to write a sort of travelogue that would contain my reflections. It was the editor's suggestion that I then continue with this form of address.

Did your relationship to your father change because of this film?

Not really. Instead, he changed. I don't feel that things between us are different now, but at some point he started to get jealous of my mother because I was making a film that is mostly about her, not him. I didn't expect that. Of course, he told us a lot about himself, but it wasn't clear to me how important it was to him that we address his story. I always felt that we already knew his story because he always shared it. If his relationship to me changed, then perhaps in the sense that he became more relaxed afterward. Previously, he wanted me to study something different and choose one of these classic careers as a doctor or a lawyer. After completing my *Abitur* (high school diploma) I said, "No, I'm going to film school," and it took another three years before I could get a position. So he was worried that I wouldn't find my way. But when he saw how hard we had to work during the shoot, he started to gain respect for that line of work. I noticed that if he happened to phone me, it was easier to get issues resolved when they came up, or he would even say, "I'll have to discuss that with your mother," instead of just making the decision on the spot. So something in their relationship definitely changed! But I would say less so between us.

It's amazing that he agreed to be in the film, because I can well imagine that the experience confronted him with his own situation and his past.

I think while we were making the film he didn't really think about what it all meant. He just went through with it. But I can remember having some confrontations with him after the film was finished. I had to finish the film really quickly for the Berlinale, so there wasn't much time for postproduction. There wasn't even time to show it to my parents before it officially premiered. Following the Berlinale, there were interviews that appeared, some in Turkish newspapers, and Father read a few things he really wasn't too happy about. He started to really worry that he might dislike the film and was ready to disavow the whole thing as if to say, "You are no longer my daughter." So I drove out to my parents and showed them the film, and that calmed him down. What bothered him in the interviews he had read was that I addressed in the film tensions between us regarding my older sister's marriage to a German man, and Father couldn't accept this new relationship. That's essentially what he says in the letter he read aloud. But apparently he hadn't really grasped that he himself had brought up that topic. So there he was reading about it in the paper and then he saw it in the film too. I had to say to him, "Papa, I can't understand why you have a problem with this issue. You wrote the letter yourself and you read it aloud! I asked you, 'Can we use this letter?' and you said yes. You actually say, 'My biggest fear is that the rest of you will also marry German men.' That statement establishes the issue in the film!" And then he was really shocked to realize he had totally overlooked this.

Later, in 2002, you used the same cameraman and composer to make a fiction film for television, Between the Stars *(Zwischen den Sternen). Following the success of* I Am My Mother's Daughter, *was it easier to recruit a producer to finance that next project?*

After that film I did receive support to write another script, but I couldn't find the right producer for that particular project, which was titled *Hidden Life*. In fact, I'm still looking for funding for it. In 1999 I approached various producers and found someone who was interested in the script but thought it would be too ambitious for my first fiction film. He suggested that we first make a short film. So I suggested this other more modest narrative material and that became the film *Between the Stars*. When I first talked to him, I hadn't written a single line. The producer just took the first exposé to an editor at ZDF/Kleines Fernsehspiel who was interested. But in the next meeting with the editorial board, he wasn't able to convince them to accept my project. So this producer went to WDR, which has a series for debut films called "Avanti Debütanti" (and also "Debüt im Ersten" and the "Six-Pack Series") funded by film grants from the NRW, and they decided to take it on. That's why that film was also shot in Cologne. After that, I was scheduled to tackle *Hidden Life,* but that's when the crisis in the German film industry hit, and my producer had his hands full just trying to keep his company from going under and couldn't come up with the funds. So we went our separate ways. Up until recently I actually had a new producer for *Hidden Life,* but he wasn't able to get the funds together either, so now I'm searching again. I feel so strongly about this project that I simply refuse to just file it away. Over the years I've continued to work on the screenplay, even though I'm also working on new projects. I'm sure I could continue for another ten years with the ideas I've been gathering.

To what extent does the script of Between the Stars *resonate with your own biography, and to what extent are there broader issues at stake for an entire generation?*

In a certain abstract sense it parallels my life, but many things are also different. The main protagonist Deniz grew up in a modern and intellectual family, whereas I come from a more traditional working-class family. Deniz's parents provide financial support for her to live an independent life and are completely shocked that their daughter would want to explore Turkey as the country of their origins. They have all but lost contact with Turkey. In fact, they have turned their back on Turkey because of the political persecution the mother had experienced earlier. I think the issues that preoccupy Deniz are normal for her generation: where do I come from, who am I, who do I want to be? And when parents repress that, as Deniz's parents do, you can be sure that a child will want to explore the issue. The issue of "Who am I?" is quite important for young people of that age anyway, but it is an even more acute question for German-Turks. Perhaps living between two cultures intensifies the problem.

When her mother says, "You have to decide where it is that you belong," Deniz retorts, "I don't have to belong anywhere." I can imagine that this is a pressing issue for the second generation.

That's true, but I don't think that applies to just the second generation. I think the issue of where we want to live is one that will be relevant for many people in the future. With today's technology there's so much contact with other countries that people are not going to stay in their native country all the time. And they will have less fear of trying new things, because returning home is easier now; it doesn't have to be a one-way ticket.

Does making a film for television influence the style or content of the production? Would you have done anything in the film differently if it had been privately financed?

In this particular case the editor working with me was a positive influence. Unfortunately, the production head noticed that we had cut certain cliché scenes. Fortunately, he noticed it too late, when we were in the final phase of editing. But as a result, he chose not to continue working with me on future projects, even though the editor and I would have liked to collaborate further. I think the shooting team was an even bigger influence, though. It was my first big fiction film production and we didn't have much money, and because of the funding from NRW I had to work mostly with people I didn't know. The production company was in Berlin and just barely fulfilled their obligations. All the responsibilities fell to me, and I was working with young and inexperienced actors who didn't get along with each other. It was very stressful, and there were certain scenes where I simply wasn't able to achieve what I had planned and would have liked to do.

And you've continued to work in television?

To earn income, I sometimes work in television and have been doing something I never dreamt I would do, namely work on a series, *Good Times / Bad Times*. But it's good, because I don't have the financial worries and can create a little space to pursue other things.

Of course, that series is very different ideologically and aesthetically from your own films. As an artist and a socially engaged person, do you experience that as a contradiction in terms or do you sort of keep these spheres distinct?

What's nice at *Good Times / Bad Times* is that people are very comfortable with one another. Most people have been working together for quite awhile, and that makes a difference. The directors come and go. From an organizational point of view, I can determine when and how much I want to work. In terms of artistic considerations, I was actually surprised how many new things I learned and am still learning. Ultimately, it's about producing stories—granted, within a specific format—but I'm the one controlling that. We have to tell the story effectively and in an engaging way given time constraints down to the very minute. I often have only a few seconds to figure out how to fix a particular shot, the acting, or the props. Sometimes there's nothing I can do because we don't have enough time, the actor isn't able to apply what I've suggested, or because the props aren't ready. Those are painful moments. But then there are other moments when I have discussions with the writers and try to take away some of this superficiality. Even though people are generally all ears, it's not always possible to bring depth to the material, so I try to do something on a different level. In any case, I've definitely shed my earlier disdainful attitude toward soap operas and television series.

What projects are you working on now?

I've got several projects at the moment. For a while, I had a producer for *Hidden Life,* but we've broken that off and now other producers are reviewing the project. It's about this law student who is half German and who travels to Turkey for the funeral of her father, with whom she hasn't had any contact since childhood. She suspects that he was murdered and begins to do some research, which gets her into trouble with her Turkish relatives and the police. My second project is a film musical, which is still in progress. I want to use music and dance to tell the story of my youth, when I ran away from home at age fifteen together with my twelve-year-old sister and took my parents to court. It's material that would normally be made into a classic social drama, but it wouldn't have been much of an artistic challenge. And amidst all of this, I'm writing and doing research for three documentary film projects. One is ready for production, but ZDF rejected it. This summer I'm going to make the film anyway, using my own funds.

What is it about?

It's about death. That is to say, about an experience I had. When I left home, I spent the years from age 15 to age 18 at boarding school. During that time period my friends and I made several Super 8 films and took lots of photos, all of which had to do with death. We were fascinated with the topic. A lot of the films used these interesting landscapes and cemeteries. Then we made a death list: seven girls who die one after another. Eva would be the first to die, then Nicki, and I was to be the seventh or last one. It was just supposed to be fun and games. And then, three months later during the summer vacation, the first one on the list actually did die in a plane crash. At the time, none of us thought much of the coincidence. But then, two and a half years later, my best friend Nicki died in a car accident. She had been the second one on the list. I was actually supposed to be with her in the car, because we had planned to meet and then somehow missed each other, so I wasn't with the other passengers after all. That's how it was, and I didn't think much further about it. But a few years ago I realized that the early deaths of my two friends were still haunting me. So I'm making a film about those left behind—mothers, fathers, siblings, friends—and how they coped with these early deaths. I'm interested in how differently people cope with death. For example, Nicki's parents traveled around the world and studied the role of death in many different cultures. That was their way of dealing with the loss of their daughter, through seeking some sort of broader meaning in other cultures. So I plan to incorporate stories like this.

Into a documentary film?

A documentary film also integrating the Super 8 footage and photos we made back then. There is this one photo of Eva, who had become a doctor, in which she stands mourning at someone's grave. As it happens, Nicki, who died a year and a half later, is now buried at that same cemetery. So it appears as if the one who died first is mourning at the grave of the one who died next. The whole thing really left its mark on me. After Nicki's death I found myself wondering whether we had somehow created this, whether it was somehow a sin to have created this list. There were such guilty feelings, and many parents, the survivors, knew nothing about this list. When I contacted Nicki's mother about my film project, she was so astonished because she had been a teacher in our school and knew nothing about our obsession with death. It was our own little world, separated from teachers and other adults.

What an unusual story, one that has landed you right back in the documentary genre!

Through this project I've rediscovered my love for documentary, and I'm sure I'll come back to this genre again and again.

It's absolutely fascinating the different ways through which one can explore reality with documentary.

It also involves more responsibility, because viewers assume that what they see is reality and some sort of truth or guidelines about how one should live or think, for example. In fiction filmmaking people just assume you've made it all up. At least that's my experience as a viewer. I don't take fictional stories as seriously. They don't impact me the way documentary does. I feel one really has to think through carefully how to make a documentary film and what kind of statement one wants to broadcast to the world.

Do you have the feeling you have to cultivate a different ethos?

Yes, I don't feel like I can just separate myself from the film material and say, "Oh, it's just a story I made up to entertain everyone." Rather, I'm making a statement about how I view the world. I think it is really interesting that an audience member once said to me that he used to think of women in headscarves as non-persons, basically invisible and indistinguishable. But through my film he learned about how a woman wearing a headscarf has a personality, and so he felt that now he would see such women in a completely different light. It's like he discovered human beings where previously there were none for him and he could just ignore them. This personal story made a difference for him and I think that is a good thing.

From a technical point of view, is it more difficult to make documentary films than to make feature films?

I wouldn't say so. It requires less money, and production can move more quickly. The team is smaller, and you can just go out with your own DV camera and shoot, whereas in feature filmmaking you have to think through every last detail in advance. The whole infrastructure involved in documentary is much less complicated, so I wouldn't say it's more difficult. But it is and always has been harder to get funding, despite the current documentary film boom in Germany.

What about funding through television?

They are just starting to get involved in that again after many departments that used to support documentary had shut down. Südwest television has a new department for young documentary filmmakers, for example.

*Last week there was the film festival in Munich where funding prizes for new German filmmakers (*Förderpreis für den deutschen Filmnachwuchs*)* *were also awarded. What would you say is the current state of German cinema? Have filmmaking conditions improved in recent years?*

I wouldn't say so. Things just seem to go up and down. There are always a few films that get a lot of attention because of some new breakthrough. Then you get the sense that things are going to change, but that hope always seems to get dashed. It's really peculiar what's going on in Germany. I don't know why that is. I witnessed this with my first fiction film; I just assumed that after making it, things would start moving and there wouldn't be any problems. But that was not the case. In fact, I found it harder to get funding for the second film than for the first because of the simultaneous decline of the German film industry and general economy. So many producers had to close shop, especially in Berlin. Film funding agencies now want lots of security. Previously, I could apply for funds as a film student. Today, even if you are a known director, you can't apply for funds without already having a producer lined up. Instead of things getting easier for independent films, it's gotten much harder! You always have to have a combination of producers lined up or a well-known name because of this huge need for a safe bet. In Germany, experimental film is basically over.

I wonder to what extent this has to do with globalization. Funding agencies may be looking for potential films with an international appeal rather than a national or regional orientation.

I never thought about that. German films have a certain, how shall I say, inferiority complex, a fear that they won't be appealing abroad. Wasn't there an article about that in *Spiegel* last week, discussing which German films have been successful outside the country?[1] It's an issue that keeps resurfacing, which would seem to indicate that there is some strange complex involved.

I wonder if this is a different phenomenon from the era of New German Cinema, during which a film had to be successful abroad before the domestic audience would embrace it.

Well, in any case, if someone is successful, then suddenly everyone accepts their work. Funding agencies that previously said no suddenly come up with funding. Directors whose films are a success abroad definitely have it easier.

New German directors of Turkish heritage seem to be a more visible presence on the film scene today.

One of the most recent rejection letters I received annoyed me because the reason given was "I already have so many projects from directors of Turkish heritage." I would have liked to know what kind of projects these are. I can't imagine they are as similar as he thinks. It was really strange to read something like that in a rejection letter! I don't want to get my hopes up. Whether I like it or not, I always have to put up with this kind of compartmentalization. I try to resist it, but it's not easy. I am a director of Turkish heritage. I don't have any problems with that. But I don't want that to be the criterion for deciding whether or not I get funded.

Notes

I would like to acknowledge Barbara Mennel for first placing me in contact with Seyhan Derin, and also thank Seyhan for her collaboration, the peer reviewers and editors of the *Women in German Yearbook* for their feedback, and the Joint Initiative in German & European Studies at the University of Toronto for research funding.

[1] "Der überraschender Exportserfolg des deutschen Kinos." *Der Spiegel* 28 (2005): 82–83.

Filmography

Between the Stars (*Zwischen den Sternen,* 2002) 89 min.
    Screenwriter and Director. WDR and Mediopolis Berlin.
    A love story about two second-generation Turkish-Germans. Deniz meets Umut while on school vacation in Turkey. They try to find a way to stay together as a couple despite many challenges. Deniz wants to finish her schooling in Germany, but Umut doesn't have a German passport and now lives in Turkey.

Good Times / Bad Times (*Gute Zeiten / Schlechte Zeiten,* 2002–present)
    Camera direction for the German television series (RTL), which was launched in 1992 as an adaptation of the longstanding Australian soap opera, *The Restless Years*. The daily series received a "Bambi" in 1999 and the German Television Prize in 2003 and often features cameo appearances by prominent guests such as Brigitte Mira, Tic Tac Toe, Gerhard Schröder, Thomas Gottschalk, and Manfred Stolpe.

I Am My Mother's Daughter (*Ben Annemin Kızıyım, Ich bin die Tochter meiner Mutter,* 1996), 89 min.

Screenwriter and Director. Hochschule für Fernsehen und Film (HFF) München.

An autobiographical essay in which the author pieces together aspects of her Turkish heritage through conversations and meetings with family members and relatives. The film is structured as a journey from Germany back to the author's place of birth in Caycumet, where she investigates the life her parents lived prior to emigration. It premiered in 1996 at the Berlinale and garnered prizes at the Munich Documentary Film Festival, Portugal's Figuiera da Foz (1997), and Saarbrücken's Saar-Lor-Lux Festival (1997).

Contact Information

Seyhan Derin
Schliemannstr. 48
10437 Berlin, Germany
seyhan-derin@T-Online.de
Tel. +49-30-44327934
Fax +49-30-44327935

Further Reading

Eren, Mine. "Die Migration neu gedacht: Arabeske Textpraktiken als Reaktion auf dreißig Jahre Immigrationsgeschichte von Türkinnen." *DAI* 61-09A (2000): 193 leaves.

———. "Traveling Pictures from a Turkish Daughter." *Moving Pictures, Traveling Identities*. Ed. Eva Rueschmann. Jackson: U of Mississippi P, 2003. 39–54.

Löwisch, Henriette."Interview with Seyhan Derin: *Ben annemin Kızıyım.*" *Triangulated Visions: Women in Recent German Cinema*. Eds. Ingeborg Majer O'Sickey and Ingeborg von Zadow. Albany: SUNY UP, 1998. 129–35.

Mennel, Barbara. "Local Funding and Global Movement: Minority Women's Filmmaking and the German Film Landscape of the late 1990s." *Women in German Yearbook 18* (2002): 45–66.

Ruth Angress Kluger:
To the Writer and Scholar on Her 75th Birthday

Helga Kraft and Dagmar C.G. Lorenz

The following reminiscences trace the career of Ruth Kluger in commemoration of her 75th birthday and celebrate her contributions to German Studies in the United States and the international scholarly and literary scene. Both authors offer an account of personal contacts with the scholar and writer in appreciation of the mentorship she has so generously granted, especially to future women scholars and members of the Coalition of Women in German. The last section features two of Ruth Kluger's poems, both in the original and in translation. (HK)

Ruth Kluger's Career as an Academic and Intellectual

Throughout her career as a professor of German literature and culture and as an autobiographer and critic in the United States and Germany, Ruth Angress Kluger has been a pioneer. She lectured and wrote about women's issues and female literary characters when doing so was considered daring, iconoclastic, and detrimental to a young scholar's career. She focused on Austrian authors and taught Raimund, Nestroy, and Grillparzer at a time when scholars of German Studies and literature subsumed Austrian texts under the rubric of German literature if the works and their authors were famous, or dismissed them as regional oddities if they were not. Ruth Kluger also discussed Jewish literary characters and their significance in major works and in the 1970s began teaching about the Holocaust at a time when German Exile literature had barely been established as part of the scholarly discourse and was still considered trendy by many traditionalists.

After the Shoah, in 1947, Ruth Kluger immigrated to New York. She enrolled as a student at Hunter College, where she graduated in 1950. She continued her studies as a graduate student at the University of California at Berkeley, where she received a PhD in German in 1967.

She began her academic career at Case Western University as assistant professor (1966–70). In the following decades she taught at the University of Kansas (1970–72), the University of Cincinnati (1972–73), and was chair of the Department of German at the University of Virginia (1974–76). Her determined anti-racist stance at the University of Virginia, where she protested against faculty membership in a country club that excluded African Americans, culminated in her resignation from that institution. Immediately thereafter she accepted a professorship at the University of California at Irvine (1976–80), and moved from there to Princeton, where she served as the first female chair of the Department of German (1980–1986). In 1987 she returned to the University of California at Irvine for personal reasons (1988–present). From 1978 to 1986 she was editor of *The German Quarterly* (volumes 51–56). In 1988 she went as program director for education abroad to Göttingen. Here, after a near-fatal accident and a long stay in the hospital, she began her autobiographical project *weiter leben,* which appeared as a book with the Göttingen Wallstein publishing company in 1992. In 2001 a revised English version of her memoirs appeared, *Still Alive*, in which Kluger specifically addresses an English-speaking public. Her appointments as guest professor took her to Smith College, the University of Göttingen, and the University of Wien.

Ruth Kluger began her career as an expert in eighteenth- to twentieth-century literature. Over the years she has published on a wide range of topics, including Kleist, Stifter, and Holocaust literature. Her autobiography about her childhood in a Viennese middle-class household, her ordeal in the concentration camps Theresienstadt and Auschwitz, and her life in the United States and Germany, made her a celebrity in German-speaking and other European countries, and eventually—after the book was translated into French, Italian, Spanish, Dutch, Swedish, Czech, Japanese, and Swedish—in the United States, where a revised version of the book appeared under the title *Still Alive: A Holocaust Girlhood Remembered* (2001).[1]

Ruth Kluger received numerous literary prizes, including the Renchen Literaturpreis of Austria in 1992, the Grimmelshausen Preis (for a book of contemporary significance) in 1993, the Niedersachsen Preis in 1994, the Marie-Luise-Kaschnitz-Preis in 1994, the Andreas-Gryphius Preis (one of three) in 1995, the Heinrich-Heine Preis der Stadt Düsseldorf in 1997, the Österreichischer Staatspreis für Literaturkritik in 1998, the Prix de la Shoah of Paris in 1998, the Preis der Frankfurter Anthologie (for a series of poetry interpretations) in 1999, the Thomas-Mann Preis der Stadt Lübeck in 1999, the Bruno-Kreisky Preis of Vienna in 2002, and the Panunzio Award for achievement by a professor emeritus, a system-wide award of the University of California in 2002. She was also awarded an Honorary Doctorate at the University of Göttingen in October 2003, the Preis der Stadt Wien für Publizistik in February 2004, and the Goethe Medaille des Goethe Instituts in March 2005. She is also a member of the Deutsche Akademie für Sprache und Dichtung Darmstadt (Academy for Language and Literature of Darmstadt).

Figure 1: Ruth Kluger, 2006. Photographer: Isolde Ohlbaum

In addition to *weiter leben* (1992), Ruth Kluger published *The Early German Epigram: A Study in Baroque Poetry* (1971), *Katastrophen: Über deutsche Literatur* (1994; Catastrophes: About German Literature), *Von hoher und niedriger Literatur: Bonner Poetik-Vorlesung* (1996; Of High and Low Literature: Bonn Lectures on Literature), *Frauen lesen anders* (1996; Women Read Differently), *Dichter und Historiker: Fakten und Fiktionen, Wiener Vorlesungen* (2000; Writers and Historians: Facts and Fiction, Vienna Lectures), *Schnitzlers Damen, Weiber, Mädeln, Frauen: Wiener Vorlesungen* (2001; Schnitzler's Ladies, Dames, Girls, Women: Vienna Lectures), *Alte Menschen in der Literatur* (2003; Old People in Literature), and *Gelesene Wirklichkeit: Fakten und Fiktionen in der Literatur* (2006; Reading Reality: Facts and Fictions in Literature). Kluger has been a guest on Marcel Reich-Ranicky's *Literarisches Quartett* (Literary Quartet) and participated in a TV production entitled *Reisen ins Leben: Weiterleben nach einer Kindheit in Auschwitz* (1996; Travel into Life: Living on after a Childhood in Auschwitz) with Gerhard Durlacher and Yehuda Bacon. Together with Hermann S. Mosenthal she edited *Erzählungen aus dem jüdischen Familienleben* (2001; Stories from the Life of Jewish Families). Ruth Kluger lives both in California and in Göttingen.

Thinking of Ruth Kluger and Her Accomplishments

I have known Ruth Kluger since my student days at the University of California at Berkeley. Occasionally we took the time to go swimming in the campus indoor pool. Being a single mother of two small sons, Ruth had little free time. I sat next to her in Middle High German class, and met her again in some of Heinz Politzer's seminars on Kafka, Kleist, and Grillparzer. Her impact on me was immediate, and I started informing myself about the Holocaust intensely after I noticed a number tatooed on her right arm. I caught up on what my German parents and schooling had neglected to tell me. Most of all, I remember Ruth's love of literature and learning. It amazed me that she went out of her way to add a non-required course in ancient Greek simply because she wanted to read certain texts in the original. She left Berkeley and entered the profession long before I did, but when I was ready, I received significant advice and encouragement from her. We knew the difficulties we faced as women entering the profession. Although in the sixties and early seventies most college students in foreign language and culture were women, with a few exceptions women were not professors. It was not easy for a woman to be taken seriously as a scholar and to find an outlet for publications, even after landing an academic position.

Through her participation in the MLA Women's Caucus (founded in 1969) Ruth was instrumental in introducing blind-blind reviews of refereed articles in the major professional journals for Germanists. She adopted the blind-blind review for the *German Quarterly* in 1978. Up until that point women used initials so that their first names would not reveal their gender. Thanks to Ruth and her active colleagues, the advent of anonymous submission meant that manuscripts by young women academics were accepted, while at times articles by established male scholars were rejected. Ruth Kluger was among the first to join the Coalition of Women in German, which was established in the mid-1970s, and she has remained a faithful member. She has even participated in the infamous satirical Cabaret, which has become a tradition and part of every WIG Annual Conference. The photo below shows her in the role of "Dr. Ruth Wienheimer" during the conference at Great Barrington, Massachusetts in 1993. In Women in German Ruth continued mentoring younger women in the profession. I still remember her answer when a beginner in the field complained about the difficulties of getting her book published by a major university press. Good reviews of a book, she reassured the young colleague, are more important than the place of publication. Remarks such as these instilled confidence in many, including myself. Ruth served on the Editorial Board of the *WIG Yearbook: Feminist Studies in German Literature and Culture,* and her high academic standards contributed to establishing the quality of our publication.

Figure 2: Dr. Ruth (Kluger) Wienheimer, Dr. Otto Speculum (Miriam Frank), and Westwindgrass (Julie Klassen)

Aside from her own publications and research, the significance of Ruth Kluger's contribution to the profession goes beyond her being an advocate for women in the profession. In 1980 I participated in an interdisciplinary NEH Faculty Summer Seminar in Irvine, which she had organized and taught. With a focus on the year 1779 the seminar initiated research on that period. The participants consisted of professors in German Studies, Philosophy, and History. I fondly remember this productive, intellectually vibrant, and inspiring seminar. The research I did during that summer found its way into several of my publications. To this day I am in close contact with some of the participants. As a teacher Ruth was an excellent facilitator, an enthusiastic analyst of history, and a champion of cutting-edge methods of interpretation. In subsequent years I would meet Ruth Kluger from time to time at national and international conferences and lectures. For instance, I encountered her in Germany in 1996 as the keynote speaker at the annual award of the Kleist Prize for Literature. In May 1998, I was overwhelmed to see around 250 paying spectators pouring into the audience of the Gasteig Black Box Theater in Munich, where she presented a lecture on Jewish women writers to spirited applause. This event left no doubt in my mind about her celebrity status in Germany, which grew steadily after the publication of her autobiography *weiter leben: Eine Jugend*. The book was presented and applauded on German television, notably by Marcel Reich-Ranitzky and his *Literarisches Quartett* in 1992. Ruth's memoir recounts her life in Auschwitz, her escape from a death march, and the incredible feat of the young survivor who had never graduated from elementary school obtaining her *Abitur* in Straubing, Germany. In 1946 she enrolled at Regensburg University and later, as a new immigrant in the United States, at Hunter College in New York. Ruth's book was not only a popular success with German readers in general, it was also critically acclaimed by experts in literary and cultural studies and continues to be studied at universities in German-speaking countries and beyond. Jonathan Yardley of the *Washington Post Book Review* named the English adaptation of the book, *Still Alive,* one of the ten best books of 2001. In the ongoing argument concerning the factuality of memoirs, Ruth Kluger's work on memory takes an important place. In her *Vienna Lecturers* she tackled the problem of authenticity long before it entered popular debates in the United States. The lectures were published in 2000 as *Dichter und Historiker: Fakten und Fiktionen.*[2] Her continued concern with this topic is apparent in the 2006 publication of *Gelesene Wirklichkeiten: Fakten und Fiktionen in der Literatur.*

As an accomplished Germanist and expert in Gender Studies, Ruth Kluger has inspired many scholars with her innovative autobiography and through her books and articles, as for instance those collected in *Frauen lesen anders,* which she dedicated to WIG.[3] This volume examines representations of women and men in texts by male authors, and she demonstrates that reading such books has a different impact on girls and women than on boys and men, because women cannot identify with the traditional hero and male accomplishment, and also because the portrayal of women lacks inspiration.

After her semi-retirement from Irvine, Ruth Kluger is more productive than ever. Since the year 2000 she has published four books on a variety of topics in German, Austrian, and Jewish Studies.

Helga Kraft

Ruth Kluger, a Teacher, Mentor, and Friend

I first met Ruth Angress Kluger in 1973 when I was a doctoral student in the Department of German Language and Literature at the University of Cincinnati. I had recently come from Göttingen, the German university town that was to play such a momentous role in Ruth's later life as the site of a near-fatal accident and the place that inspired her to write her autobiography, *weiter leben* (1992).[4] I was enrolled in her Austrian literature seminar, which had an extraordinary impact on my own professional development. My studies in Göttingen had taken place under the auspices of the radical New Critical, "werkimmanent" approach to literature represented by Emil Staiger and Wolfgang Kayser, which prioritized close textual analysis and the established literary canon. Ruth's seminar went far beyond this aesthetics- and text-oriented framework and introduced issues involving historical and social dimensions as well as gender, ethnicity, and cultural identity. Her insights as a professor of German literature and a humanist were informed not only by an awe-inspiring wealth of literary and theoretical knowledge, but also by multicultural experience, which she had acquired under harrowing conditions and which she later revealed in *weiter leben*. Like all of Ruth's students I was impressed by the intensity of her teaching and her multifaceted approach, which combined textual, cultural, and historical analysis. We marveled at the wealth of dramatic and poetic texts she had at her fingertips and that she was able to recite from memory, since she had memorized a lot of literature in Vienna when she was kept out of school for being Jewish, and at the clarity and firmness with which she set forth her point of view. I owe Ruth Kluger more insights and encouragement to become active in our profession than I can possibly repay. She made it possible for me to give my first academic lecture on Frank Wedekind before the Cincinnati Germanistik Society in a time-honored university venue called Annie Law's Drawing Room, and she suggested that I undertake editing a Reklam edition of Martin Luther's texts on marriage. In 1978 I conducted research on a book on Ilse Aichinger in California, where Ruth was teaching at the University of California at Irvine. I benefited immensely from our conversations on postwar literature, and I helped Ruth train, probably idiosyncratically and badly, her new puppy, Bella. Later that summer we secured plane tickets through a travel agency evocatively named "The Friend of China" and went on an adventurous trip to Thailand via Korea and Hong Kong in search of the "Stones of Many Colors" ("Bunte Steine") famous in that corner of the world. Rather than becoming successful ruby and diamond traders, we took home unforgettable impressions of Buddhist temples, the jungle bordering the canals of Bangkok, and a shady but elegant hotel with a German beer garden.

Later, when Ruth had begun to teach about literature of the Holocaust in Princeton, I attended one of her large lectures and subsequently decided to develop a course on Holocaust literature and film at Ohio State, which, with her encouragement, I succeeded in doing. Finally, when I was passing through Irvine in 1992, Ruth asked me to read a manuscript of hers, not an academic book, but something of a more personal nature. It was the manuscript of *weiter leben,* which I had the privilege of reading before its publication. Ruth's and my paths have continued to cross on many occasions in Göttingen, when *weiter leben* started to take on a life of its own and become famous. I visited Ruth just when she received her first invitation to Reich-Ranitzky's *Literarisches Quartett.* She was excited, surprised, and, as usual, extremely down-to-earth. Soon after, she was celebrated as a prominent writer. She was invited for readings and lectures all over Europe, including in her native city of Vienna and other cities in Austria. Yet, she continued attending and presenting at academic conferences, where she drew large audiences. Just recently, at the 2005 IVG (International Association for German Studies) conference in Paris, I heard her speak in an overcrowded lecture hall to a spellbound international academic audience.

Ruth Angress Kluger has been a constant intellectual presence throughout my career and my life, as well as a mentor, a critic, and a friend. I owe her, as do many women scholars of my generation, a debt of gratitude impossible to repay.

Dagmar C.G. Lorenz

Ruth Kluger as Poet

It is not so well known that Ruth Kluger has also written poetry since she was a child. Below are two samples of her work. The first poem was written during her incarceration in Auschwitz when she was thirteen years old. The second poem was created in 1996 when she returned to Vienna to revisit the street and the house where she grew up.

Der Kamin

Ruth Kluger

Meiner Freundin Hannah Ungar

Täglich hinter den Baracken
Seh' ich Rauch und Feuer stehn,
Jude, beuge deinen Nacken,
Keiner hier kann dem entgehn.
Siehst du in dem Rauche nicht
Ein verzerrtes Angesicht?
Ruft es nicht voll Spott und Hohn;
Fünf Millionen berg' ich schon.
Auschwitz liegt in seiner Hand–
Alles, alles wird verbrannt.

Täglich hinterm Stacheldraht
Steigt die Sonne purpurn auf.
Doch ihr Licht wirkt öd und fad,
Bricht die andre Flamme auf.
Denn das warme Lebenslicht
Gilt in Auschwitz längst schon nicht.
Blick zur roten Flamme hin,
Einzig wahr ist der Kamin.
Auschwitz liegt in seiner Hand–
Alles, alles wird verbrannt.

Written in Auschwitz (1944)

[The Chimney

To my friend Hannah Ungar

Every day behind the barracks
I see smoke and fire linger.
Jew, give in, bend down your head,
There's no escape for you in here.
Don't you see within the smoke
A distorted, sneering face?
It shouts in scorn and ridicule:

I've claimed five million up to now.
Auschwitz rests within its hands—
Burning all and everything.

Every day behind barbed wire
A purple-colored sun appears.
Yet, its light looks bleak and bland,
When the other flame bursts forth.
For Auschwitz lost long, long ago
The sense of warm, life-giving light.
Just look into the flaming red,
the chimney here alone holds truth.
Auschwitz rests within its hands—
Burning all and everything.][5]

Wiener Neurosen

Ruth Kluger

I

Es heißt
Im Hause des Henkers
sprich nicht
vom Strick.
Ich weiß –
und sprech auf Schritten und Tritten
vom Henken.
Gegen die guten Sitten
verstößt das Gedenken.

Ich bin im Hause des Henkers geboren.
Naturgemäß kehr ich wieder.
In krummen Verstecken
such ich den Strick.
Mir blieb eine Faser davon im Genick.
Meine Hartnäckigkeit war mein Glück.

Doch der Strick ging verloren
und der Henker ist gestorben.
Auf dem Galgenplatz blüht
der Flieder.

II

Ein brückenheiliger Nepomuk
steht im Hof am Bauernmarkt eins,
wo ich wohn.
Wie kommt denn der her?

Gibt's nicht Brücken genug
wo was Heiliges nötig wär,
und kriegen keins?
Hier wirkt er wie Hohn.

[Vienna Neuroses

    I
They say:
In the executioner's house
do not mention
the noose.
I know—
and with every step I take I mention
executions.
Remembrance offends
against good manners.

I was born in the executioner's house.
Naturally I return.
In crooked hiding places
I search for the noose.
A thread remained stuck in the back of my neck.
My perseverance was my luck.

But the noose was lost
and the executioner died.
Lilacs bloom at the site of the gallows.

    II
A bridge-saintly Nepomuk
stands in the courtyard at Bauernmarkt One,
where I live.
How on earth did he get here?
Aren't there enough bridges
that require something saintly
and don't get it?
Here, he appears like a mockery.

Here, he is wasted.
Many people perish
in torrential rivers,
and he greets you.
between the elevator and the garbage bin
Here he appears like a mockery.
Who needs that?

Or is here a bridge, after all
one just as invisible as the river?
No tourist on Jasomirgottstrasse
has an idea of his travail,
for he is the one who guards against evil,
he (his wood) fills the gap
and subdues the danger.
We see him next to the waste paper,
but he knows to what end
he was hauled to this place.

Saint Nepomuk, pray for us, especially
for me, so that I do not fall into the waters
that I can't see and therefore
can't watch out.
Dear sanctimonious one, do a good turn:
Look after the Jewish customers,
so that I won't drown at
Bauernmarkt One.][6]

Notes

[1] *Still Alive: A Holocaust Girlhood Remembered.* New York: Feminist P at CUNY, 2001. In Britain with the title *Landscapes of Memory.* London: Bloomsbury Publishing, 2003.

[2] *Dichter und Historiker: Fakten und Fiktionen.* Wien: Wiener Vorlesungen, 2000.

[3] *Frauen lesen anders: Essays.* München: Deutscher Taschenbuchverlag, 1996.

[4] *weiter leben: Eine Jugend.* Göttingen: Wallstein, 1992.

[5] Trans. Helga Kraft and Dagmar C.G. Lorenz.

[6] Trans. Dagmar C.G. Lorenz.

"Language Is Not an Instrument for Me but Existence":
Interview with Marlene Streeruwitz

Helga Kraft

Introduction

This interview with dramatist and novelist Marlene Streeruwitz was conducted in Vienna on 27 March 2006. She made her mark on the theater scene with critically acclaimed plays in the early 1990s. As a politically outspoken feminist, Streeruwitz belongs to a group of prominent Austrian writers who have been praised for their literary achievements but also criticized by conservative political factions. In the mid-90s she shifted to writing novels, prose texts, and theoretical essays. She holds a PhD in Germanic Studies and has lectured widely, including at the University of Tübingen, the Free University of Berlin, and the University of Illinois at Chicago. In the following interview she talks about her relationship to language, feminism, globalization, and her new novel *Entfernung*. Marlene Streeruwitz was the invited guest at the 2005 WIG annual convention in Kentucky.

Interview

Helga Kraft: *First I'd like to know your point of view as a contemporary writer. Writers work with written language, which was believed to be dependable. How have you come to terms with the instrument of language and the ease with which it can be manipulated? How have you interpreted women's linguistic boundaries or the disintegration of languages that Hofmannsthal describes in his "Letter from Lord Chandos to Francis Bacon?" And do you feel affinities with the Wiener Gruppe (Viennese Group) that startled readers with language experiments but also recognized language's influence on our thought processes and our ability to make independent decisions? We are manipulated by the media, and many profit politically or commercially from our impaired vision. Has anything changed in this respect? More specifically, has your use of language changed since you've been a writer? Do you use this medium today as you did at the beginning of your career, or has your use of language, and thus your literary output, changed?*

Figure 1: Marlene Streeruwitz; Photo by Peter Rigaud

Marlene Streeruwitz: I believe that language is for me in principle not an instrument, but existence, equal to physical or emotional being. It's a matter of life or death. Language is like skin, which both expresses and simply is life. Language, like life, develops and then exists and can then only be described and not judged in advance. Just like I only know about life after having lived it, I only know something about the sentence after it has been uttered. It's very important for me that it's not something planned within the framework of a canon. Although I know the language of the canon, as a woman I live outside of it. And these two levels cross each and make quite different demands on language than if I were Hofmannsthal representing a decadent class of society with decadent language. In this case my words would probably disintegrate, in fact would logically disintegrate, since I, as a woman, would be starting with ruins. These days everyone deals with these broken pieces, because power, most visibly in the last ten years, has brought all of language within its grasp. We know this from the media and the power structures that surround us daily, from advertising to bank statements, which present entire narratives that we have to fragment ourselves to understand. I do feel an affinity with the Wiener Gruppe, which describes precisely this process. They set out to lay bare the broken and existential aspects of language. Only the Wiener Gruppe is able to base its judgment on the familiar, on an agreement in a canon. They can depend on their destruction being generally understood. If I have to assume that many areas of importance have remained unarticulated and have not been put into language (including many of those areas with which the Wiener Gruppe dealt) because they are supposed to stay in the non-verbal region to avoid challenges to existing power structures, then I must use certain strategies to be understood. These strategies, too, need certain political preconditions. Not being understood would mean forcing oneself into silence. Therefore, there is an eternal back and forth between the breaks in the texts and the narrative line that, despite all interruptions, is nonetheless a line that still communicates and remains intelligible on a level that includes the incomplete.

Has your own written style of language changed over time?

It has to change, of course, because in time and existence nothing stays the same. Language, as my existence, functions the same way. What has been said forms a past. Thus, there is a different version of style and language for each project, but they all remain connected.

But are there stylistic similarities? When one reads a few lines of your texts, one knows that it is Marlene Streeruwitz.

That's what I mean—it's like a living person who one recognizes again and again, but who changes over time.

Yes, that's true for a writer, but for other people it's perhaps not so clear.

Yes, but that is my profession, after all. I believe part of this profession is to accept language as a form of being, not as communication.

Are you asked sometimes whether you are or think like a feminist? How do you answer? In Europe one talks about "gender mainstreaming," which would end special support. Many reports state that women are returning to "children, church, and cooking." Are these women going back to self-chosen subservience? To what extent are you conscious of gender problems while writing? And lastly, what is the situation in literature by men? Is the macho being deconstructed there?

A macho can, of course, write as well. I have never considered confessions of a certain belief a precondition for writing. Hemingway was an excellent author and is one of my favorites. I can read such literature on my own. I don't need directions in order to protect myself. This is, however, a self-acquired meta-theory that basically gives me access to all literature, because I no longer have to protect myself as a person of questionable gender. I believe that gender has been transposed, actually reduced, to the question of how to apply it as a mode of power. It is no longer possible—it got lost or given up in the 80s—to develop an active view of gender in society. The many backlashes—were there seven? eight? nine? ten?—have prevented the radicalization of Enlightenment ideas about gender identity. All of us can now be only described from the outside. That is, we are completely at the mercy of society, and our sexuality is now only a kind of marker of how society treats us, and no longer a possibility for expression. All active possibilities have been lost or given up because many women refused or considered it wrong to call themselves feminists. Backlash becomes our own fault, and it's important to say so. We all could have insisted on our emancipation, and it doesn't matter that I did insist on it, because one can't do it alone. Of course I'm a feminist; I have always been one. For me it is a bias in favor of women, girls, and life and constitutes a basic attitude toward the world. Nurtured by common experiences, it becomes a basic form of solidarity. For literature this means that we have to look at texts differently (including Hemingway, who can be read unproblematically because he has become historicized and provides an example of how time, society, and texts are related). We have to concentrate when we read texts by both men and women on what voices we hear, what "postcolonial" means, who speaks, from where they speak, the position of the author, etc., and we need to watch for multiglossality/multiculturalism. Does the author take on the task of speaking for all represented groups or is that given back to these figures? The most important matter is the author's attitude toward the subjects described, however fragmented they may be, and this is more important for me than it was perhaps 15 years ago. In other words, the power of speech, the empowerment of the characters, their care or exposure, and the dramaturgy have become more important than the linguistic version. And of course, any man can be a feminist.

Austria and the United States play a role in your texts. You live in Vienna most of the time, but also partly in New York City. For example, your play New York. New York. *takes place in a Viennese public toilet during the imperial period. California and Chicago are in* Nachwelt. *(Posterity) and* Partygirl. *And a character from the American comics, Spider-Man, appears in* Tolmezzo. *Today, nations generally show off their poets and thinkers. How do you feel as an Austrian writer, and what is your relationship to your homeland, to Europe, to the USA, and the world?*

Austria is simply the place I come from, the society that I can "read" and that taught me to read societies in general. It is in a certain way my ABCs of world interpretation, which helps me relate to the whole world, and through that I have a certain grounding, a placement of sorts, even if it consists of critical questioning. I have the good fortune to come from a place drowning in complete decadence, yet that also constitutes an avant-garde of the whole panopticum of globalization. Seen from that point of view, I live in a particularly foolish society and can therefore interpret everything foolish happening in the world. I consider this an absolute privilege because this is a small place with a surveyable history that had been at the mercy of great powers. The question of how politics operates in this world and how it throws itself obediently into the arms of power shapes my view of developments in the world.

You have written a new play again. The latest version is called "Imbiss zur Säge." (Sawmill Diner). There are cannibalistic elements in this piece inspired by a case in Germany, which was covered by the media. A man found a victim on the Internet who voluntarily allowed himself to be butchered. What sort of message can the audience take home from this production? In today's theater, where text and performance are shaped by the directors, not much is left to the author's text. Should authors have more control over productions, or should they perhaps not allow their texts to be performed?

The question, which in my opinion contemporary theater has answered in the negative, is whether the "stage play" can be a work of art in the first place. I write texts that reside within the category "stage play," texts that claim a certain autonomy because my conceptual background includes the autonomous work of art, and I cannot give up all of those concepts at once, even though I think that there ought to be a development toward a gradual obliteration of such elements. In the meantime—in the process of the autonomous text's self-obliteration into a participative text—it is extremely important that the written text be staged with the most painstaking precision, as I no longer can nor wish to avail myself of the means of auratization in order to expose the text. If I would offer up my texts for dismemberment and fragmentation, I would consider this a disastrous move from a political perspective. Because then a text could be utilized for any means whatsoever, and would be open to any misunderstanding, in an authoritarian way for example, because everything would just be a shapeless floating. To my view, that would entail a total depolitization, a descent into an arbitrarily authoritarian use of language. It is a mistake to think the fixated text is authoritarian. On the contrary, freedom is located in the tension between that which is finished and its transformation during the staging process and its performance, whereas the "project text," assembled some way or another, is to me an absolute political disaster of arbitrariness into which any Nazi text might be inserted at will. That, to me, is beyond question. This coincides with everyday language use, which I wouldn't listen to otherwise since it would simply be like the chit-chat of a talk show. In this respect we have many possibilities today, and I have no problem if the theater dissolves itself. It has given up its task as a critical institution anyway. If there's no guarantee that this very fragile text can be faithfully transformed, then I would always turn down a performance. The play can be performed according to the spirit of the text, which always still leaves open quite a bit of flexibility for interpretation. In my new play there are no stage directions, just dialogue. A spoken text provides all the instructions needed for a performance. And what does a person or the audience get out of such a performance? Well, obviously they get the message that we live in a cannibalistic culture, chiefly via our cultural myths and symbols, but also increasingly in the biological-medical cannibalism of implantation and explantation. We ourselves are only museums of our own organs, tied to a dreadful technological circulation of our bodies. It is something suggesting the final departure from religion and its rites and a newly radicalized Enlightenment way of thinking that could and should regulate things differently, especially the present compliant gray zones that are kept from the public knowledge just as religion was.

You have just written a new novel, Entfernung. *(Displacement). Previously your texts departed from traditional narrative structures and pursued different strategies. For example, you parodied the melodramatic dime novel in* Lisa's Liebe. *(Lisa's Love), you showed the impossibility of biographical writing in* Nachwelt.*, and you opened out a life story backward from the end to the beginning in* Partygirl. *Each time you invented a protagonist who lives out, and here you might want to contradict me, the longings of a female life based on rarely fulfillable social promises. Once you said that you don't invent stories since they actually serve fascist practices. What about your main characters, the protagonists in your novels? To what extent are they artificial figures who reflect social practices? After all, they are never caricatures as, for example, in Jelinek's work. They are rooted in normative structures as a point of departure, but the protagonists take action and face the world in which they live. They assert themselves, which makes them victims and perpetrators at the same time. Am I perceiving them correctly? How does this play out in your new novel? What is the narrative pattern here, and what role does the protagonist play in it?*

The characters are linguistic beings who only exist in language. Based on an anti-auratic, but joyful manner of narration, they are experimental constructs who conduct their life linguistically. Thus they reveal what the long discussions on cyborg figures have shown: life in the media is possible. And in literature it's been that way for a long time, which I consider most productive. I would think that this linguistic existence in language is the only one in which we find all aspects of existence describable, because we bounce off the outer representation but find our way into the figures themselves. That is only possible through language. And that is an enormous event, providing incredible pleasure and the greatest pain. My project is pain. How does pain enter life? Here's the whole plan: a figure caught in language, and the question, how pain enters this picture, leading to an examination, an attempt of an order—constituting the sequence of the novel—that follows its own logic to the last page, which of course is never the end. These are of course only excerpts like fabric samples, just a slice of time and not—something that I blame the male canon for—creativity that views itself as a life-giving deity: inventing figures, allocating them their own time, which becomes the narrative time. And here I would challenge every Lukács and every theory of the novel and assert that these are religious texts, and each person who still writes like this today remains caught in these criteria, and they will always remain authoritarian and metaphysical texts if it's an author, a theater, or film director who invents a figure and gives it life. That would be an act that imitates divine creation and remains in these areas of meaning, something that I do not consider art. But to describe a period of time in the medium in which someone works, then leave everything and not concede that I could now put an end to this invented life, that for me is the beginning of a type of democracy and participation. But only the beginning, of course.

Here's a question about location: we have just spoken about protagonists made out of language living in cities that you name and which in fact exist. In your new novel Entfernung. *the city is London. The city becomes incredibly lively. I read the text like a film and could see everything before me: what the main character Selma sees, what impresses and disgusts her. Is this city of London an inner landscape or an external power that Selma must confront?*

Well, film is my competition. A film script would be a better comparison. What justifies such a story is exactly the possibility of a linguistic existence, a complete inner existence within language, where the inner world would be narrated, and we can assure each other that we are human beings, something I consider the most important foundation of the human community right now. We are again at the point at which Rousseau began to write, and we must find out what connects us, makes us similar or equal. I believe that this report from the inner world describes and activates exactly what lies between us and makes understanding possible. There is, after all, something that lies between us, which is named differently again and again, something I call a secret in the sense that we do not know exactly how we communicate. But when we report on our inner life, we know this is a human being, that I am a human being. It's also important for me that this being human is conditioned by gender, and that gender is a locality in which social possibilities are played out. The city is simply the inner stage where this life takes place in the time that is narrated. London is important for me as an extreme example of globalization, where globalization is fully played out and where the conditions under which we will live in the future are described. London was interesting for me because of this mix of the complete dissolution in diversity combined with an incredible threat to the bare facts of life. Globalization teaches us a fear of life, a survival fear, which London represents in its incredibly sharp, hard struggles around life.

In your novel you treat diversity and the problems you recognize in London due to globalization. Do you see transnational powers that abet the situation?

I see no solution here. On the contrary I see only increased problems. A fight for survival is being created that pits everyone against each other.

That is now very clear on the streets of London, also in the countries where London's inhabitants come from. Belonging to some kind of community can protect one in such a struggle and in threatening, everyday scenarios. But this struggle is transferred to our inner life; it is conveyed to us as a threat so that we, as obedient modern subjects, are actually forced into racism in order to win this fight for survival, because the threat is always dealt with in terms of nationalities. And that is exactly the reality underlying this novel. Through neo-liberal globalization we are forced into a steady upward movement to get ahead in order to safeguard our position. First we have to name things and describe facts, then understand and integrate them, to draw conclusions and not accept a situation per se and merely react to it, which is only possible via aggression, exclusion, and fascist social methods. I believe that we are seduced into taking care of things ourselves, that we are supposed to be encouraged to produce fascism ourselves, so that we no longer recognize large fascist systems but make the daily small fascisms of the world possible for the neo-liberal globalization, thereby maintaining tension and disharmony. This war of survival keeps us all busy so that we no longer think of ourselves, of the salvation of our souls as critical persons who want to develop. We no longer have the time or capacity to evolve, because we have made ourselves fascist and can no longer act critically against the powers that be. This concerns us all. Gender determines reactions to this problem. I believe that men are called to participate in power differently than women, who give up right away and return to old patterns, because they offer the best possibility of survival. But death's proximity is constantly simulated, which is not so far-fetched when one talks to the so-called "people of the street." The protagonist encounters all of this in London. Everything is taking place in another language; our worlds are taking place in other languages, and we can't keep up learning all these languages. But we are familiar with that from our places of work. When I consider how evaluative language evolved around academic achievement, it seems that we are always occupied with learning another language so that we might know what the world looks like and how we are supposed to act. That happens on all levels, and in the new novel it applies just to one person who is really threatened.

You do show in your novels from the last ten years these eruptions, as for instance the explosions in the London subway in Entfernung. *that are a sign or an element that fills you with fear, a fear that you can't escape.*

No, but in that case it was the question of whether the protagonist can escape or not, and if language dissolves here, which could have happened. I can only make that part of a process, but I can't control it. And it turns out that language can overcome and remain, that it does not disintegrate. The danger is great, but it has always been great. But it's nothing different, just one more overcoming of something.

There is a certain level of optimism in this novel. You are against fatalism.

It is "of course" quite difficult. One of the problems that arises is the question of how to treat reality. Do I bring in fundamentalism, for example? That does not work and is not possible. There need not be a guilty party, and the perpetrators don't have to appear. This existence through language first circles around itself in order to gain strength, to understand this survival. And what the real problem is develops at a new, but not yet existing level of language, for instance a cautious level of description of transnationality. I have found no language to describe the various places of origin simply and matter-of-factly. There is no level of language on which classifications of a cultural sort can be described. This parallels the different levels of the female experience that have no language, for example birth and pregnancy. The existence of a person not born in our society has no language. And it is very difficult to describe a world in which Afro-Britain women stand at the register as cashiers and are possibly also very fat; it is hard not to use a description that is automatically a put-down and places this person in a certain corner, but only just to say who is standing there. Describing skin color is quite important because it is there, and these people have a right to be described without prejudice, but at the same time it is almost impossible. This was a very big problem when writing the book. We see that all areas in the shadow of power are without language, and we work here matter-of-factly to find language not tied to power, possibly a description appropriate for the person that is democratic, participatory, and positive, not just witty put-downs and ironic quasi-funny forms of description, which are actually the only ways we have. For me, one of the most important results of this work is that I cannot describe a walk through London without having to use a totally intolerant, dreadfully devaluating language from the realm of available possibilities. It's a little easier in English because communication functions differently due to historical necessities. But we know that "Afro-American" is not really an adequate description, that the social problem is mirrored in the impossibility of finding a description. There is no matter-of-fact description of multiculturalism. There are only fraught levels of language, and that reminds me very much of the way women of various ages are described. There are older women for whom there are no descriptive expressions, just put-downs, such as "the mother-in-law," a family constellation that can't be uttered without all kinds of jokes illuminating it. That's how it is with people from other parts of the world. This describes what cannot be said. "From other countries" is not correct; one has to take these strange verbal detours. I believe we know it, but it is always good to show how our language is an instrument of hegemony, and that we have to work on expanding the language so that non-qualifying expressions can be developed, even friendliness expressed.

In your earlier texts you have dealt with the mother-daughter constellation. In Tolmezzo. *you show a Jewish-Viennese woman who, after many years in the US, returns to her birthplace in Vienna with her daughter. In* Sloane Square. *you chart a relationship between a mother-in-law and a daughter-in-law. In* Nachwelt. *the famous daughter of Alma Mahler is a main character and in* Verführungen. *being a mother is of course the main theme. You have two daughters yourself and you obviously consider the relationship between different generations of women very significant. Could you say something about that? Which problems do you think are important to describe?*

First off it's a matter of describing what the relationship is. From literature we know father-son relationships in unending constellations. We have few daughters described as part of these complex problems. I am not a missionary, and I am not concerned with creating positive frames into which people can insert themselves. Instead, it is a matter of describing how these relationships are at least as complex as those between fathers and sons, in all their possible forms. There are good ones, bad ones, antagonistic ones, beautiful ones, well-turned-out ones, boring ones. Only within this diversity can the feminine evolve and not be throttled by stereotype. I often hear, "Yes, we know of course that this exists." It is simply necessary to archive the possibility of this relationship, with all its rich possibilities. You can't do it any other way. I show positive or painful relationships, but also the complexity, the beautiful, and the dreadfulness at the same time and that this always applies to female relationships. I came to believe that they are more complex and richer than those of men, because the maids have to arrange themselves in a more multi-faceted way than their masters. But it is exactly this rich variety from the worst to the best that should lead femininity out of its valley of humorous definitions, which I see even in the condescending shape of Hollywood beauties, which remains unopposed. Therefore it is important to simply fill up the archives, nothing else. That is what's necessary. These are the relationships in which most people live, and that is why they are interesting. The old story that the link between mothers and daughters is interrupted in order to prevent the history-forming function of generational narratives is something that applies to all sexes today. The reason for this of course lies in the culture of brand-name companies—our actual nations—that are interested in seeing youth groups separated from their elders in order to sell them something different and allow the definition of clear marketing goals on a global level. I believe that this process applies to Asian youth just as it does to ours; they are separated and become the target of a very definite and globalized marketing strategy.

But something different is being sold to the sons than to the daughters, and the parents, specifically the mother, whether consciously or unconsciously, support the things that are being sold to the daughter. A certain status quo is reestablished, and the mothers or fathers support what is being sold to the children. So it becomes a certain kind of gender performativity that gets reaffirmed but can't progress.

We interrupted this trend for a short time in the 70s and 80s, but it has returned full force, I believe. Today I would see it across history. I, of course, always notice that fashion performs like gender, that is like the latest gender edict. Powerlessness hovers over the whole generation, men and women. This applies to both young people and who we now call young adults in order to describe this extended puberty without employment; it applies to both genders. Yet, how it applies to them is determined by gender. There is no entry into society in the form as we knew it. I believe the question of gender is nowadays more emphatically associated with the entry into society and power, and that applies clearly to everyone. The fact that gender roles are again emphasized in their reactionary form has probably something to do with the fact that young people have to flee into these roles. I see it less as something being passed on, but rather as something that is necessary if one wants to exist at all. If a young person is not finding a place in society—which is becoming a world-wide problem—then there will be nothing left other than an economy of movements in flight that are necessary in order to define oneself. One will have to become "a whole man" and "a whole woman" in order to create a self or a mirror image. Because on the job there is no mirror image that would define itself differently (not even through the bank account), so a man or woman would have to flee to traditional concepts. Parents are now probably satisfied, because it confirms something that they have assumed anyway, that is their reactionary feelings toward sexuality. I believe it all fits together. Therefore, I would consider it more like a renewal that takes place between the generations, rather than a transfer. It is tragic that reactionary gender constructs from the past have to be adopted, and it is wrong. I consider it a disastrous and misguided backward development, paid for at a high price, because the power involved here is so perfidious. The old gender stereotypes have to be overcome as a road to power itself. People who are presently roughly twenty-three years old and fully integrated in a peer group that defines their gender role in its old-fashioned form have to transcend this form of appearance in order to even get the idea of producing a critical thought. It is a wonderful and perfidious form to keep people busy with totally new thresholds, and that is something that we did not have to do in the 60s and 70s. The *Zeitgeist* has done this for us, and for that I express great gratitude.

I am looking forward to the appearance of Entfernung. *and "Imbiss zur Säge." Finally I would like to ask one more question: is it too early to ask about new projects, or are you just beginning to think about them?*

Yes, I intend to follow the Austrian elections this fall in some literary form. I will express my present world anger and involve myself in everyday affairs, because I believe it is necessary to do so at this time.

Thank you very much for the interview!

Selected Works by Marlene Streeruwitz

Ocean Drive. Frankfurt a.M.: Suhrkamp, 1991.
Tolmezzo. Eine symphonische Dichtung. Frankfurt a.M.: Suhrkamp, 1994.
Verführungen. 3. Folge. Frauenjahre. (1996). English Version: *Seductions.* Vancouver Island: Oolichan Books, 1998.
Sein. Und Schein. Und Erscheinen. Tübinger Poetikvorlesungen. Frankfurt a.M.: Fischer, 1997.
Können. Mögen. Dürfen. Sollen. Wollen. Müssen. Lassen. Frankfurter Poetikvorlesungen. Frankfurt a.M.: Fischer, 1998.
Nachwelt. Roman. Frankfurt a.M.: Fischer, 1999.
Lisa's Liebe. Roman in drei Folgen. Frankfurt a.M.: Fischer, 1998.

Waikiki Beach. Und andere Orte. Die Theaterstücke. Frankfurt a.M.: Fischer, 1999.
Majakowskiring. Erzählung. Frankfurt a.M.: Fischer, 2000.
Partygirl. Roman. Frankfurt a.M.: Fischer, 2002.
Jessica, 30. Frankfurt a.M.: Fischer, 2004.
Morire in Levitate. Novelle. Frankfurt a.M.: Fischer, 2004.
Gegen die tägliche Beleidigung. Vorlesungen. Frankfurt a.M.: Fischer, 2004.
Entfernung. Frankfurt a.M.: Fischer, 2006.

Excerpt from the Novel *Entfernung*.

Marlene Streeruwitz

This excerpt from Marlene Streeruwitz's new novel—followed by an English translation—features the writer's unique stylistic expression. *Entfernung*. chronicles the life of a woman on the brink of destruction, since Selma Bechthold experiences globalization as a personal attack that threatens her very identity. Fear becomes reality when a terrorist attack paralyzes London. In order to survive, she must find her own truth, a process in which language plays an integral part. (HK)

Die Sängerin stand auf einem kleinen Podest. Hinten rechts. Sie hatte ein Standmikrophon vor sich. Sie stand ganz still. Ruhig. Sang in das Mikrophon. Sie war groß. Graublonde lange Haare. Sie trug ein Chanel-Kostüm. Der Stoff war weiß und schwarz durchwebt. Die Ränder waren schwarz und silbern abgesetzt. Weiße Knöpfe mit Goldrand. An den Taschen und an den Jackenärmel die Borte und die Goldknöpfe. Die Frau trug eine hellrote Seidenbluse unter der Jacke mit einem Maschenkragen. Die Masche hing vorne über die Jacke. Wie ein Jabot. Schwarze Slingpumps. Sehr hohe Absätze. Die Gitarristin sprang zu ihr auf den Podest und sang den Refrain mit. Sie wiederholten den Refrain. Dann sprang sie wieder herunter. Lief an den Bühnenrand. Und wieder die gejagte, jagende Musik. Der drängende Rhythmus. Der Zwang sich bewegen zu müssen. Selma begann den Kopf mit der Musik. Sie fand sich im Takt nicken. Heftig mit dem Kopf zu nicken. Der Refrain war zum Kreischen geworden. Alle schrieen mit. Alle reckten die Arme. Schlugen mit den Fäusten in die Luft. Dann ein Spinett. Eine Barockphrase. Die Stimme. Vorschlagend. Bittend. Freundlich drängend.

"Little girl. Promote yourself.
Rip out your ribs.
Bust up your tits.

Cut in. Cut out. Cut up.
Promote yourself. Little girl. Promote yourself."

Alle sangen mit. "Cut in. Cut out. Cut up." Die Sängerin lachte wieder. Die Sängerin war keine junge Frau. Sie stand hinten. Sie sah von hinten ihrer Band zu. Dem Publikum. Sie stand in ihren high heels ganz ruhig da. Sie bewegte sich nicht. Nur ihre Stimme. Sie schickte ihre Stimme über die Bühne in das Publikum. Eine süße Stimme war das. Nicht jung. Es war eine wissende Süße. Tröstend. Eine wiedergefundene Süße. War das mütterlich. Selma stand in der Stimme. Sie hatte ein großes Verlangen sich dieser Stimme mitzuteilen. Mit dieser Stimme mitzugehen und ihr alles zu erzählen. Die Frau, deren Stimme. Diese Frau sah nicht mütterlich aus. Nicht ein bisschen. Sie sah kühl aus. Wirkte kühl und unbeteiligt. Abweisend. Eigentlich. Und nur die Stimme eine Verführung. Die Stimme mehr von der Frau als sich zeigte. Als die Frau sehen ließ. Selma hätte alles gestanden. Dieser Frau hätte sie alles gestanden. Selma nahm die Tasche ab. Stelle sie zwischen ihre Füße. Klemmte die Tasche zwischen ihre Schuhe. Sie pfiff. Sie pfiff auf den Fingern. Sie hatte das lange nicht gemacht. Aber es ging. Sie konnte es noch. Und mit jedem Pfiff wurde sie besser. Dann kam wieder eine leisere Stelle. Die Sängerin sagte wieder den Satz, dass die Dinge, die heute gehasst würden, die sein könnten, die morgen notwendig würden. Die morgen gemacht würden. Die das kleine Mädchen, das dann nicht mehr das kleine Mädchen sein würde. Die das kleine Mädchen machen würde. Machen müsste. Machen wollte. Machen gemacht werden würde. Machen gemacht werden wollte. Alle schrieen die Liste dieser Dinge mit. Selma pfiff im Rhythmus. Mit dem linken Arm schlug sie den Rhythmus in die Luft. Die Sängerin nahm das Mikrophon. Sie trug das Standmikrophon in der rechten Hand. In der Linken hatte sie eine brennende Zigarette. Sie ging nach vorne. Sie ging ohne jede Bühnenhaltung. Sie ging einfach. Stellte das Mikrophon vorne rechts auf. Stellte sich dahinter. Ihre Bewegungen waren linkisch selbstverständlich. Ohne jede Konzession an die Zuschauerinnen. Ohne Pose. Die Frau beugte sich über das Mikrophon. Sah zu Boden. Wartete. Tippte den Takt mit der Schuhspitze.

"Fuck your father.
Rape your mother.
Rip open their guts.
Mix entrails and hearts.
Do unspeakable acts
But take. But take. But take.

Excerpt from *Entfernung*.

Please. Little girl. Please little girl.
Whatever you get on the road to menopause."
Die Stimme hatte alle Süße aufgegeben. Die Sängerin sang tief aus der Brust. Stieß die Sätze aus. Hart. Sie stand über das Mikrophon gebeugt und stieß die Sätze von oben in das Mikrophon. Warf die Befehle aus ihrer Brust in die Lautsprecher. Bei "Fuck your father." begann das Gejohle. Der Tumult war so laut wie die band. Der Rhythmus fuhr zuckend zwischen die Sätze. Stimme und Schlagzeug. Stimme und Bassgitarre. Das Publikum. Selma sprang mit hoch. Sie hatte ihre Linke zur Faust geballt und schlug mit der Faust in die Luft. Sie pfiff im Rhythmus. Sie wurde von den Frauen rund um sie angefeuert. "Fuck your father." Sie pfiff. Dreimal lang. Einmal kurz. Die anderen Frauen klatschten. Die Sängerin stieß die Worte von sich weg. In Befehlsform. Aber mit der tiefen Stimme der Rhapsodin. Nicht im Falsett des Kasernenhofs. Selma sprang. Reckte die Faust. Pfiff. Sie keuchte. Sie war vollkommen in die Musik aufgelöst. In ihre Reaktion auf die Musik. Dieser Stimme. Und diese Stimme. Diese Stimme wollte sie selbst sein. Die Reichweite dieser Stimme. Die Selbstgewissheit dieser Gestalt. Die Akkorde sammelten sich. Fielen ineinander. Ein crescendo. Ein winziges Gitarrensolo. Eine Arabeske. "Thank you." Die Sängerin stand einen Augenblick über das Mikrophon gebeugt. Sah auf. Sie nahm das Mikrophon wieder auf. Sie trug es zurück. Nach hinten. Als räumte sie auf. Machte Ordnung. Dann ging sie nach rechts. Sie sah sich nicht um. Verbeugte sich nicht. Sie verlässt uns, dachte Selma. Sie pfiff mit den anderen. Schrie nach einer Zugabe. Die anderen Bandmitglieder verbeugten sich. Immer wieder. Dann ging das Licht auf der Bühne aus. Das Publikum. Die Frauen zerstreuten sich. Verteilten sich im Raum. Selma suchte nach ihrer Tasche. Sie war auf der Tasche herumgesprungen. Die Tasche war flachgetreten. Schmutzig. Selma überlegte, ob etwas zertreten sein könnte. Die Füllfeder. Das Parfum. Sie hob die Tasche auf. Hielt sie vor sich hin. Schaute, ob es irgendwo heraustropfte. Eine Frau sah ihr zu. Sie hatte lange rotorange Haare. Sie war nicht ganz jung. Sie sahen beide die Tasche an. Selma zuckte mit den Achseln. Die Frau nickte. "Unsalvagable," stellte sie fest und nickte wieder. Selma wollte sie fragen, wie die band hieße. Sie wollte sagen, dass sie nur zufällig in dieses Konzert gekommen wäre und nichts über die band wüsste. Dann sah sie einen Tisch links. Gleich neben der Bar. CDs lagen aufgestapelt. Selma klopfte ihre Tasche ab und ging hinüber. "Dickopraphia." Und "The Little Girl's Guide." stand auf den CDs. Der Name der band war "The Singing Tampons."

Translation of Excerpt from *Entfernung*.

The singer stood on a small podium. In the back to the right. She had a microphone standing in front of her. She stood very still. Motionless. Quiet. Sang into the microphone. She was tall. Grey-blonde long hair. She wore a Chanel suit. The material was a black and white weave. The edges were black and silver. White buttons with gold borders. On the pockets and on the jacket sleeves the border and the gold buttons. The woman wore a pale red silk blouse under the jacket with a woven collar. The loop was hanging over the jacket in front. Like a jabot. Black sling pumps. Very high heels. The woman guitarist jumped up onto the podium and sang along. They repeated the refrain. Then she jumped down again. Ran to the edge of the stage. And again the driven, driving music. The urging rhythm. The urge to move. Selma began moving her head with the music. She found herself nodding with the rhythm. Forcefully nodding with her head. The refrain turned into screams. Everyone screamed along. Everyone stretched their arms. Beat their fists into the air. Then a spinet. A baroque phrase. The voice. Suggesting. Pleading. Friendly urging.

> "Little girl. Promote yourself.
> Rip out your ribs.
> Bust up your tits.
> Cut in. Cut out. Cut up.
> Promote yourself. Little girl. Promote yourself."

Everyone sang along. "Cut in. Cut out. Cut up." The singer laughed again. The singer was not a young woman. She stood in the back. She watched her band from the back. The audience. She stood there quite still in her high heels. She did not move. Only her voice. She hurled her voice across the stage into the audience. A sweet voice it was. Not young. It was a knowing sweetness. Comforting. A found-again sweetness. Was that motherly. Selma stood in the voice. She had a great longing to communicate with this voice. To go along with this voice and tell her everything. The woman, whose voice. This woman did not look motherly. Not a bit. She looked cool. Came across cool and uninvolved. Rejecting. Actually. Only the voice was a seduction. The voice was more of the woman than what could be seen. Than the woman allowed to be seen. Selma would have confessed everything. To this woman she would have confessed everything. Selma took her handbag off. Put it between her feet. Squeezed the bag between her shoes. She whistled. She whistled with her fingers. She had not done this for a long time. But it worked. She could still do it. And with each whistle she got better.

Excerpt from *Entfernung*.

Then there was a more quiet passage. The singer spoke each sentence again. That the things that are hated today could be those that become necessary tomorrow. That would be done tomorrow. That the little girl would no longer be a little girl. That the little girl would then no longer do what a little girl would do. Had to do. Wanted to do. Do, what she was made to. To do that wanted to be done. Everyone screamed along with the list of these things. Selma whistled in rhythm. With the left arm she beat the rhythm into the air. The singer took the microphone. She carried the microphone in her right hand. In her left hand she had a lit cigarette. She went to the front. She walked without any stage posture. She just simply walked. Set up the microphone on the right side in front. Stood behind it. Her movements were of course awkward. Without any concession to the female audience. Without pose. The woman bent over the microphone. Looked to the floor. Waited. Beat the rhythm with the tip of her shoe.

"Fuck your father.
Rape your mother.
Rip open their guts.
Mix entrails and hearts.
Do unspeakable acts.
But take. But take. But take.
Please. Little girl. Please little girl.
Whatever you get on the road to menopause."

The voice had given up all its sweetness. The singer sang deep from her chest. Pushed out her sentences. Hard. She stood bent over the microphone and pushed the sentences into the microphone from above. Threw the order from her chest into the loudspeakers. At "Fuck your father" the howling started. The commotion was as loud as the band. The rhythm drove twitchingly between the sentences. Voice and drums. Voice and bass guitar. The audience. Selma jumped up, too. With her left hand clenched into a fist she hit the air. She whistled with the rhythm. She was spurred on by the women around her. "Fuck your father." She whistled. Three times long. One time short. The other women applauded. The singer pushed the words away from herself. In a special order. But with the deep voice of a rhapsodist. Not in the falsetto of the boot camp. Selma jumped. Pushed up her fist. Whistled. Panted. She was totally dissolved in the music. In her reaction to the music. This voice. And this voice. This voice she wanted to be herself. The reach of this voice. The self assurance of this figure. The chords were gathering. Fell into each other. A crescendo. A tiny solo of a guitar. And arabesque "Thank you." The singer stood bent over the microphone for a moment. Looked up. She picked up the microphone again. She carried it back. To the rear. As if she were cleaning up. Put things in order. Then she walked to the right. She did not turn around. Did not bow. She is leaving us, Selma thought. She whistled with the others. Yelled for an encore. The other members of the band bowed. Again and again. Then the lights went out on the stage. The audience. The women scattered. Dispersed in the room. Selma looked for her bag. She had jumped repeatedly on top of her bag. The bag had been flattened. Dirty. Selma wondered whether something could have been broken. The fountain pen. The perfume. She picked up the bag. Held it in front of her. Looked to see if anything was dripping out of it. A woman watched her. She had long orange-red hair. She was not quite young. They both looked at the bag. Selma shrugged her shoulders. The woman nodded. "Unsalvageable." She concluded. And nodded again. Selma wanted to ask her what the name of the band was. She wanted to say that she had come to this concert accidentally and knew nothing about the band. Then she saw a table on the left. Right next to the bar. CDs were lying there piled up. Selma pounded on her bag and went over there. "Dickopraphia." And "The Little Girl's Guide." was printed on the CDs. The name of the band was "The Singing Tampons."

Translated by Martha Kaarsberg Wallach

Feels Like Teen Spirit:
Teaching Cultural Difference through Bodies, Gender, and Affect

Richard Langston

Foreign-language pedagogy, cultural theories of affect, and feminism can join forces to help foster cross-cultural understanding among advanced language learners. This fusion is especially useful for commercial popular cultures whose surfaces evince few self-evident cultural distinctions. Theory's investment in affective difference and bodily movement broadens pedagogy's concern for optimizing affective learning factors in the classroom; affect resides in both the form of instruction *and* in its cultural content. Feminist epistemology operates as a vital moderator in this dialogue, for it alone can grapple with the functionalization of gender difference endemic to both native and foreign popular cultures. (RL)

The Problem: Contemporary Commercial Culture

The global reach of contemporary commercial culture can wreak havoc on fostering cross-cultural understanding in the foreign-language classroom. This is especially the case for advanced learners capable of exploring both their own culture's frame of reference and that of the target culture. According to Claire Kramsch, cross-cultural pedagogy aims to uncover and negotiate distinct discourses at work in "insiders' and outsiders' view of cultural phenomena" (*Context* 229). Yet what if the object of study calls into question regional, national, and international borders such that the sought-after interstices between self and other become fleeting mirages? This postmodern predicament is particularly pronounced when the object in question stems from commercial popular culture, an arena in which transnational networks have made possible the instantaneous worldwide production, distribution, and consumption of sounds, images, and words. This simultaneity, what cultural theorist David Harvey calls the postmodern compression of time and space, thwarts longstanding notions about the origins, contexts, and semiotic use value of cultural artifacts (293). As a result, contemporary commercial culture geared for young adult audiences—like popular music, film, television, and literature—can run the risk of giving students the impression that the only apparent difference between the target culture and theirs is purely linguistic.[1] Nothing could be further from the truth. As I argue in the course of the following article, behind the facade of sameness that students see, foreign popular cultures can and do conceal significant differences when measured up against a native culture. Nonetheless, arriving at an interstitial place between contemporary popular cultures—what Kramsch calls a "fault line" or "third space" where meaningful intercultural dialogue unfolds—is so complicated that ferreting out a modicum of cultural difference becomes a theoretical problem, one well suited for scholars of culture, not students in the foreign-language classroom (205, 210). I contend that a cross-cultural pedagogy must not settle for popular culture's superficial sheen of sameness, nor should it refrain from profiting from cultural theory's lofty high-wire acts. In what follows, I bring into dialogue the disparate realms of cultural theory and foreign-language methodology, a dialogue in which feminism will play a singularly important role. The stakes in this dialogue are high, for the middle ground between these three interlocutors marks the space where teaching for cross-cultural difference can succeed if it chooses to incorporate a target popular culture's bounty of attractive, authentic, and appropriate artifacts.

Cultural theory has hardly discovered the antidote for undoing the spell of global sameness endemic to postmodernity. Nevertheless, cultural difference—according to one loose faction of theorists invested in the corporeal experience of affect—is best thought of as a function of feeling, not thinking. According to one of the pioneers of affect's importance in popular culture, affect refers to structures of feeling that determine the terrain of each individual's everyday life. "Some things feel different from others," Lawrence Grossberg writes; "some matter more or in different ways than others" (80). Out of the qualitative and quantitative investments individuals make in the field of popular culture arise unique maps with which they "navigate their way into and through the various moods and passions" of quotidian experience (82). Affect not only engenders borders within and between cultures, but it also fosters identity formations and aligns people vis-à-vis various hubs of power and authority. Since Grossberg, scholars of affect have come to fashion their work as a necessary theoretical intervention in prevailing poststructuralist thought, which, on the one hand, did help in the eighties and nineties to unveil the extensive range of postmodernity's dominion but, on the other hand, never advanced ways out of the mess.[2] By turning their attention to affect, this new theoretical camp reinserts the concrete, feeling body into the cultural equation that the poststructuralist turn had omitted entirely. Like feminism before it, theories of affect insist that the body can and does demonstrate an unyieldingness and even obstinacy toward the simulacral forces of postmodern commercial culture that whitewash cultural difference.

However, as very recent feminist reflection has made clear, the proliferation of theories of affect is not without its oversights and excesses.[3] As I elucidate in the first two theoretical sections below, feminist thinking not only accounts for the blind spots in affect theories, but also serves as a crucial arbiter between theories of affect and the very different role affect plays in the foreign-language classroom. By joining forces, feminism, theories of affect, and foreign-language teaching methodologies together point toward an approach to unlocking cultural difference as a unique experience people feel with their bodies. Taking the confluence of affect and the gendered body as its twin foci, this essay—*neither the exclusive province of teaching methodology nor pure cultural theory*—seeks out a liminal space between these disciplines in order to improve upon theories of affect using foreign-language methods and to enrich these methods with the insights of these theories.[4] In other words, by elevating the material body as an immutable index of cultural difference, I maintain that overcoming the postmodern challenges that contemporary popular culture poses for teaching for cross-cultural understanding must begin by reflecting on how theories of affect can offer a powerful framework with which to generate an awareness of difference where none appears to exist. Conversely, teachers out to sharpen their approach to teaching cross-cultural understanding must also account for the blind spots in theories of affect that feminism brings to light in order to ensure that knowledge generated in the classroom is squared with lived experience. Laid out in the following pages, the reader will thus find not a set of instructions per se for mastering the challenges of commercial popular culture, but rather methodological reflections on and an accompanying suggestion for how to bring cultural theory and foreign-language pedagogy into productive dialogue. In order to set the stage, I first take a closer look at two very different notions of affect, one a longstanding concern in second-language research and the other the centerpiece of this recent wave of cultural theory.

Two Ideas of Affect

The chasm that separates pedagogy's attention to affect from cultural theory's interest in affect could not be wider. For teachers of foreign languages, and in particular those committed to task-based instruction, affect is a factor contingent on a student's disposition as well as the methods and materials used in the classroom. Since the mid-seventies, affect has been recognized as a function of each individual student's propensity for acquiring subconsciously a new linguistic system. According to Stephen Krashen, who has done much with his "Monitor Model" to advance the importance of affect in language-learning, affect is largely used to describe three attitudinal factors among students: their motivation to acquire a second language, their self-confidence to succeed, and the level of their anxiety toward the overall learning experience (30–32). In order to maximize motivation and self-confidence and reduce student anxiety as well as the "affective filter," instructors are encouraged to design, examine, and modify their classroom environment such that input is comprehensible, students refrain from producing output prematurely, and error correction does not stigmatize learners (73–76). Affect in foreign-language pedagogy is thus understood as swinging in one of two directions. With little motivation, no self-esteem, and debilitated by a glut of anxiety, students encounter a mental block that impedes the intake of comprehensible input. When students' affective filters are fully raised, language acquisition comes to a halt. Conversely, when motivation and self-confidence are fostered and anxiety is kept at bay, the affective filter is negligible and the students' "acquired system," as Krashen calls it, proceeds to develop. An ideal pedagogy would successfully manage, therefore, every operative learning factor such that students are awash only in positive affect. And lest one think Krashen's theory and its methodological application (for example, Tracy Terrell's "Natural Approach") only apply to beginning language instruction, the confluence of psychological, neurobiological, and linguistic research has shown that affect, in general, and anxiety, in particular, impact intermediate and advanced learners as well.[5] As Dolly Young has argued, attention to affect in the advanced classroom is essential; both positive and negative affect play a direct role in many an intermediate and advanced student's decision to continue studying a foreign language (4).

Unlike these humanistic language-learning theories and their concomitant teaching methods that contend instructors can manipulate the quality and quantity of affect, cultural theorists insist that affect can never be mediated or mitigated. For them, affect describes a corporeal condition neither exclusively synonymous with emotional states nor vulnerable to environmental engineering. Affect goes beyond the realm of subjective cognitive feeling to include an irreducible bodily condition that resides within each individual person, a corporeal state of being.[6] The growing scholarly interest in affect among cultural theorists thus rests on the conviction that affect encapsulates the possibility for resistance insofar as a person's affective intensities can escape social forces that shape thought and behavior. In contradistinction to forms of power from above that subjugate people according to capitalist or patriarchal imperatives, affect, writes Michael Hardt, must be conceived as biopower from below. More often than not a gendered labor, affect, he claims, possesses the potential for autonomy, networking, and liberation (98–100). All in all, the affective intensities of interest to cultural theorists are unquantifiable, non-narrativizable, and unassimilable. Because of this, affect proves more powerful than even the most complicated positionality models of identity and agency (Massumi 2–3, 27). A disparate scholarly field that encompasses psychoanalysis and the unabashedly anti-Oedipal postmodern philosophies of Gilles Deleuze and Félix Guattari, these theories all share in common a celebration of affect, the effects it has on oneself and others, and the de-territorialized possibilities it creates.

Were these theories to dialogue with foreign-language pedagogy's interest in affect, they would certainly challenge language teachers' presumption that there is such thing as an optimal affective condition and that teachers have any influence over its constitution. According to these theories, affect's importance rests on the fact that it is unruly, unpredictable, and disruptive. Affect theorists would hence invite pedagogues to consider how affect resides not just in the form of instruction, but also in its content *as an object of cross-cultural study*.[7] In other words, affect must be framed as belonging to culture insofar as it embodies, quite literally, the very means with which individuals negotiate the dominant forces within that culture. As I will suggest shortly, in the era of global capitalism, being German can and does feel different from being American. Bringing then cultural theory's idea of affect to the classroom would thus involve building upon pedagogues' attention to learner factors. In addition to the order of affect pertinent to foreign-language acquisition (A1), a more comprehensive model of affect would include how students assume affective relationships vis-à-vis their own native cultures (A2) and how their perceptions of this affect (A3) inform students' classroom experiences. Add to this Kramsch's framework of cross-cultural pedagogy attentive to the tensions between cultures and a fourth order of affect (A4) comes into view: a target culture will surely incite affective responses within language-learners because of its foreignness. Fifth, a target culture generates affect with its own culturally bound constituency (A5). And lastly, the target culture evokes affective responses in the native culture (A6) just as much as a native culture undoubtedly elicits affective responses within the target culture (A7). The relationship of these affective fields can be imagined as three overlapping circles (Figure 1):

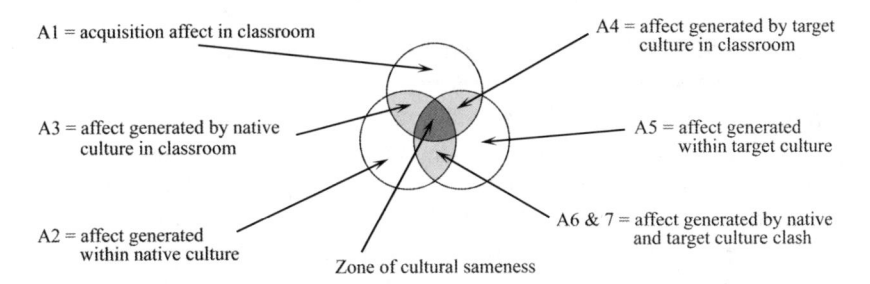

A1 = acquisition affect in classroom

A4 = affect generated by target culture in classroom

A3 = affect generated by native culture in classroom

A5 = affect generated within target culture

A2 = affect generated within native culture

A6 & 7 = affect generated by native and target culture clash

Zone of cultural sameness

Figure 1: Orders of Affect

Cultural theory's insistence on the ubiquity of affect at home, in the classroom, abroad, and in all the in-between spaces urges foreign-language pedagogues to think about how affect is culturally specific, what gains its didacticization would elicit, and to what degree this difference can be elevated as the focal point of cross-cultural understanding. How, for example, does German popular culture feel different to Germans than to Americans? Yet if cultural theory encourages instructors and students to investigate how Germans feel differently from Americans, it must nevertheless retain skepticism toward these theories of affect and question, as feminism has, whether and how affect is truly liberating. In order to throw this intervention into relief, I must first delve deeper into the intricacies of this cultural theory and establish its implications for the classroom.

Feminist Interventions: Re-Placing Gender in Theories of Affect

Largely unintelligible, the Seattle rock band Nirvana's lyrics to Generation X's anthem of disillusionment, "Smells like Teen Spirit," never really mattered as much as the sonic blasts of the song did. Although the words "Here we are now, entertain us" resonated clearly through the din of the song, not much else was left to decipher. One American chronicler of the early nineties aptly wrote that it was clear to him from the overall "feel" of the song that "the singer was pissed off [even] though I couldn't understand a word he was saying." This twenty-something Nirvana fan goes on to say, "But [Kurt Cobain] was also reaching into the melodic stratosphere and coming back with a simple tune that made you want to do something [...]."[8] In the recent history of pop culture, Nirvana's success as a global generator of feeling, movement, and agency among youths exemplifies perfectly what Lawrence Grossberg calls a site of "affective alliances." According to Grossberg, affect constitutes a central component in the relationships individuals assume with the field of popular culture, for "one cannot exist in a world where nothing matters" (84). Understanding affect proves to be a crucial avenue for accessing how individuals mold identity through a sense of belonging and difference that their investments in the popular generate. In this respect, the arrival of Nirvana and its humalong ode in the early nineties could not have been timelier, for they together afforded an entire "grunge" generation with the means to articulate feelings of disenchantment and disgust and therewith distance themselves from the dominant, conservative ideologies of the day. But the differences and concomitant empowerment that Nirvana made possible were fleeting. The postmodern culture industry reacted quickly and marketed the signs of grunge's difference to a mass audience. Soon Nirvana no longer mattered because everyone was investing affectively in the band's structures of feeling. In the words of Grossberg, the feel of Nirvana's teen spirit was no longer authentic. It no longer made a difference that Nirvana mattered.

Affect among youth, Grossberg claims, "is not only a state of the mind but a state of the body [...]" (183). "Visceral responses," he claims, "which often seem beyond our conscious control, are the first mark of the work of popular culture: it is sentimental, emotional, moody, exciting, prurient, carnivalesque." In short, "popular culture inscribes its effects directly upon the body" (79). Grossberg goes on to note that in the rock 'n' roll heyday of the fifties, the youthful body was once capable of indulging in a range of movements because of its affective alliance such that it momentarily delivered itself from the dominant structures of everyday life. In postmodern times, this is no longer possible. While youthful bodies may continue today to invest in the popular and therewith glean from it both affective intensities and mobility, the movement won from contemporary popular culture fails to deliver them to alternative places. This is because pandemic postmodern cynicism no longer sees anything existing outside of dominant culture. Grossberg's proposed solution entails jumpstarting affect and reinvigorating bodily mobility according to Deleuze and Guattari's concept of the "politics of the minor" that moves beyond the stakes of identity politics (378). Highly critical of pronouncements that decry the "postmodern condition" as a hopeless quagmire in which agency and difference vanish, Deleuze and Guattari advance an alternative to identity politics that opens avenues of transformation and differentiation. Instead of identifying individuals as inhabiting a static site within a social grid—the intersection of race and gender, for example—Deleuze and Guattari shift their attention to the body in motion and proclaim, "We know nothing about a body until we know what it can do" (257; Massumi 2–4). Taking stock of Deleuze and Guattari, Grossberg makes clear the political advantage behind this shift: their attention to the body in motion sidesteps the isolation and fragmentation brought about by the proliferation of identity claims. In other words, the intricacies of and infighting common to the politics of difference has taken a toll on the potency of progressive strategies needed to oppose the hegemony of postmodern conservatism. By extension, a move from multiple identities to the body allows for the generation of common commitments that matter to a much larger collective body (Grossberg 380–83).

In their translation of Deleuze and Guattari to the classroom, Christa Albrecht-Crane and Jennifer Daryl Slack echo Grossberg by emphasizing affect's heuristic ability to go beyond the binaries (woman/man, black/white, heterosexual/homosexual) that underpin positionality models of identity politics (192). Of greatest interest to Albrecht-Crane and Slack is the degree to which all bodies are capable of negotiating the social forces that comprise everyday life in spite of their pre-established identity affiliations. How, they ask, do bodies affect other bodies, and how, in turn, are they affected themselves? Furthermore, what degree of movement and in which direction does affect afford a body within a social space? Albrecht-Crane and Slack illustrate the effects of affect in terms of an actual interpersonal conflict among college students. Student A offends student B on the grounds of his national otherness. Affected by the provocation, student B retorts by insulting student A in terms of his gender and sex. Equally shaken by one another's attacks, each individual affects and is affected such that they, pushed to their affective thresholds, stand down and enter into meaningful dialogue (201–05). To be sure, classroom conflict is not the only terrain onto which a pedagogy of affect can transpire. As Elspeth Probyn rightly points out, students and teachers must also direct their attention to the messy ways bodies, affect, and movement operate within texts, between texts and students, as well as between students, instructors, and the institutions in which they find themselves (29). Both Albrecht-Crane and Slack and Probyn are not far from Deleuze und Guattari's original reason for wanting to know what a body's affects are and "how they can or cannot enter into composition with other affects, with the affects of another body, either to destroy that body or to be destroyed by it, either to exchange actions and passions with it or to join with it in composing a more powerful body" (247). Precisely because of affect, bodies establish points of contact and exchange that identity politics otherwise foreclose.

While focusing on bodies, affect, and mobility might initially strike foreign-language teachers as a novel and potentially effective tack to teaching artifacts from a target culture, embracing Deleuze and Guattari's model as-is comes at a considerable cost, as feminist scholarship has made clear. As Elizabeth Grosz and others have convincingly argued, Deleuze and Guattari's stress on a genderless body—what they call a "body without organs"—dissolves the particularity of embodied female experience, especially feminism's political struggles, in the name of transcending altogether the detrimental forces that arise out of sexual difference (161-64, 182). With their post-gender vision, they defuse women's sexual specificity, deactivate the political agency found in that difference, and therewith advance phallocentric thought. Paying attention to bodies while atomizing gender difference would therefore sidestep a central concern for feminist teachers of foreign popular cultures. This approach would downplay the fact that these postmodern commercial cultures are not only saturated by, but also functionalize gender difference affectively and usually do so to the detriment of women and other minorities.[9] Spelled out in the most basic of terms, the potential sacrifice in adopting Deleuze and Guattari is the celebration of the obstinate genderless body at the price of devaluing the cognition of difference. By supplanting epistemology with ontology as the privileged site of intervention, a pedagogy of bodily affect would therefore have no place for the corpus of situated feminist knowledge to which women's oppression is singularly important. A proponent of this shift away from epistemology and to ontology, Brian Massumi stresses the importance of affect's autonomous place outside of representation and identification, its primary address being the genderless body's surface. For him, to make sense of postmodern culture's smorgasbord of images, one must break free from the realm of signification and instead investigate the affective potentials that culture generates and that resist ideology (42-44). But as Clare Hemmings points out in her feminist critique of Massumi, such a move is as undialectical as it is unnecessary. Feminist attention to affect can and already has been mining the "relationship *between* the ontological, epistemological, and transformative" (557). She cites feminist standpoint theory as a prime example, a divergent field ranging from Marxist feminism to postmodernism that has wrestled with the problems of essentialism and attended to the challenges of multiple and conflicting standpoints while retaining a commitment to "political accountability [...] and the importance of positive affect for both belonging and change" (558).[10] Massumi's oversights notwithstanding, Hemmings insists that many theories of affect, and by extension Deleuze and Guattari, must not be dismissed. She motions that matters of the mind can and must be articulated with bodily responses, that judgment is vital for linking the primacy of affect with the social world, and that only through cognition can a knowledge of affect over time assume mnemo-political value.

On Discovering the Gender-Affect Dialectic: An Anecdote

It was my students' reaction to a piece of popular German fiction that spawned my initial thinking about the cultural distinctness of embodied feeling, the importance of a broadened understanding of affect for teaching contemporary popular culture across and between national boundaries, and the validity of bringing feminism to bear on cultural theories of affect and foreign-language methods. For a fifth-semester syllabus modeled around the topic of contemporary German popular culture that I intended for intermediate-high to advanced students of German, I chose Benjamin Lebert's novel *Crazy* (1999).[11] In many respects, Lebert's story seemed ideal for the course commonly called Conversation and Composition at many North American colleges and universities. According to Kramsch's selection criteria, *Crazy* is arguably of thematic interest to college students, as I will establish in the following section (*Context* 138). An example of the road-trip genre, its narrative is both predictable and full of unique twists. Linguistically, the story is manageable even for intermediate readers and is discursively rich as well. The novel invites readers to tap into both factual and poetic information. And it is chock-full of pregnant pauses that raise readers' curiosity. In short, *Crazy*, I thought, provides students with plenty about which to write and talk. Nevertheless, the cultural allusions in this popular novel are less than obvious. A huge commercial success in Germany, the story of *Crazy*—a coming-of-age tale of a disabled teenager thrown into a private boarding school—encapsulates much of the postmodern condition typical of German pop novels: it illustrates the divorce of affect and ideology, it exchanges interest in national history with detailed attention to the everyday, and it indulges in the identifications with and pleasures of consumerism. Considered by some critics to be the swan song of reunified Germany's "pop literature" boom of the nineties, *Crazy* also replicates a phallocentrism endemic to this recent literary niche that exalts the narrative consummation of male desire.[12]

When asked to write about what they thought was particularly German about the stories discussed in their conversation and composition course, my students were especially divided over the cultural difference conveyed through language and representation of bodies. As to whether Lebert's piece of pop literature evinces national differences between the United States and Germany, twenty-year-old sophomore Mark exclaimed, "We read a lot of texts in this course that were fun, others were strange, and a few were just plain weird. But the only thing that separated these texts from American culture is the German language."[13] For him, the youths portrayed in works like *Crazy* were identical to both the real people and fictional characters that purportedly populated his own lived existence. A *lingua franca* of sorts, youth required no translation in this student's eyes, for all youths apparently endure the same experiences: puberty, heartbreak, peer pressure, and even loss. In contradistinction to Mark and several others who did not sense any difference in the contemporary popular culture read and discussed in class, other students were convinced that the texts did indeed represent a culture very different from their own. For example, Susan read *Crazy* according to her personal experiences in Germany, especially when she insisted that the independence enjoyed by German youths in Lebert's novel reflects what she sees as the liberal values ingrained in German society. She continued by claiming that, unlike at home, a level of trust prevails in Germany that curbs parents from policing their kids' bodies, in general, and their consumption of tobacco, alcohol, and drugs, in particular. *Crazy* reflects this state of affairs accurately, she insisted. And in her reading of the same text, Jennifer claimed to witness a reversal of American values. The protagonist's philosophical ruminations on sex and love made it clear in her mind that "German men have all the emotions" while "women have all the hormones." My students were neither entirely right nor wrong. On the one hand, the look and feel of German popular culture, in this instance represented by Lebert's *Crazy,* seemed in their eyes much like its American counterpart. On the other hand, something was amiss. Independent of any theoretically informed inference on my part, some of my students were instantaneously drawn to the role of the teenage body with the hunch that cultural difference resided therein. According to what they wrote in their final essays and professed in class, they sensed this difference not just in terms of the divergent kinds of corporeal experiences like sex, intoxication, and pain, but also in how representations of embodied experience from abroad appear to be accompanied by emotions that are distinct from the ones familiar to them.

Of my many students drawn to the question of bodies, it was Polly who was most dismayed by what she saw as an unmistakable cultural difference. On the first of December, the eve before the last week of classes, Polly, a self-described "part-time feminist," wrote me an e-mail declaring that she was disillusioned by a majority of the texts in our class. "At first I was particularly interested in the females," she wrote, "but I eventually looked at the males as well. I even made a list of the major characters, and the majority of both sexes (although I found myself listing more females) fell into the 'questionable' or 'negative' character category." "The rest," she concluded, "were either sluts or...umm...sluts." With respect to *Crazy*, she remarked that feminism

> isn't even an issue or something to be considered. Change? Who cares? [...] I mean, the climax of the novel was going to a strip joint?! 'This is living'?!?! WTF?! [...] I just about died! (Almost) [...] And the thing is, now that I think about it, I don't understand these characters much at all. [...] I'll admit that even I have a few things in common with SOME of them, but I don't feel like I can really relate.[14]

With its excessive use of exclamation points, Polly's confession about her inability to feel like the German characters was unequivocally charged by and with affect. As such, it underscored at once the presence and impenetrability of something different at work in German pop literature. She made clear that from her vantage point the stories left her feeling confused; her built-in frame of reference—gender, in general, and a feminist sensibility, in particular—brought her to indict nearly every male and female character as being unworthy of her identification because of what she called their sluttishness. Toward the end of her e-mail she remarked that a desirable change in the narrative would have accomplished the exact opposite of what the novel's band of boys did: instead of identifying "women [as] mere objects and toys," they should have acknowledged the "power," "dignity," and "sexiness" that she believes women are capable of today.

The affective response *Crazy* elicited in Polly arose from her underlying sense that attention to undifferentiated bodies is not enough. As she established in her e-mail to me, knowledge of difference, attention to identity, and above all respect for women as subjects were, in her opinion, entirely absent from the narrative. In other words, she was not willing to dismiss lightly a story in which women's bodies were objects. Her reaction echoed the very dialectic that Hemmings seeks to reintroduce into the current theoretical discourse on affect, namely the importance of the epistemological alongside the ontological. For Polly, it is precisely because male and female bodies express sexual difference, exist within the discursive field of normative gender roles, and do what they do as a result of affect that makes Lebert's novel so shocking for her. This is not to suggest, however, that Mark's position on the indecipherability of cultural difference in *Crazy* is any less legitimate. Together, these anecdotes demonstrate how popular literature does certainly insinuate that affect from both the target and native cultures can appear to blend into one another, such that the zone of cultural sameness eclipses any and all room for cultural difference. Traced back to my model of affective orders, popular culture can indeed give the impression to some that the affect engendered by foreign and native cultures in the classroom (A3 and A4) overlap entirely. As a result, students may downgrade culture clash outside the classroom (A6 and A7) to a dismissible instance of copycat. On the other hand, responses to *Crazy* like Susan's, Jennifer's, and Polly's point to the fact that the standpoint(s) of women is/are already at work in the classroom uncovering the link between feeling and embodiment that Hemmings advocates. More importantly, these responses demonstrate that this link can indeed demystify the illusion of metastasized sameness that popular commercial cultures propagate around the globe.

Teaching the Affect-Gender Dialectic or How to Get *Crazy* in the Classroom

While my students' experiences with *Crazy* lend credence to my initial theoretical propositions about the problem of cultural sameness under postmodernity (Harvey), the centrality of affect in popular culture (Grossberg), the effects affect has on other bodies (Deleuze and Guattari), and the need to reinstate the category of gender in the genderless theories of affect (Hemmings), neither they nor these theories themselves provide pedagogues with a systematic approach for singling out affect as a vehicle for teaching cross-cultural understanding. Similarly, Albrecht-Crane and Slack's as well as Probyn's calls to didacticize students' affective reactions fall short of addressing the intricacies of teaching across and between cultures in the foreign-language classroom. Like Kramsch, I propose therefore that teaching affect effectively is only possible when instructors reflect well in advance on the function of affect in the proposed artifact of study. Of all the pre-teaching activities a teacher must perform, the art of reading formal and substantive codes of affect is most crucial (*Context* 138–39). In the case of a novel like *Crazy*, such a preliminary investigation is necessarily framed by the affective intensities captured at every level of the work's composition, from vocabulary to intertextuality, from grammar to genre, from poetic strategies to narrative construction. In other words, teachers must first ferret out the culturally specific discourses of affect at work in *Crazy* and establish how their traces can, with pedagogical assistance, jump off the page as perceived difference. These discourses will, in all likelihood, orbit around and intersect with representations of bodies in motion and interrelations between genders in the artifact. The most potent examples include those moments when Benni and his friends seek out the opposite sex: their clandestine trip to the girls' dorm, their visit to the local sex therapist, or their road trip to the strip joint in Munich. As Kramsch has rightly argued, this behind-the-scenes discourse analysis of affect in a literary text like *Crazy* ensures that instructors are well poised to focus their students' attention on those textual features most salient to the target culture. Only then are teachers well equipped to modify Kramsch's sequential model for teaching literary texts in their cultural context, which begins with pre-reading and reading, progresses toward narrative comprehension and discourse exploration, and concludes with cross-cultural dialogue (*Context* 140–56, 229–32). In the case of *Crazy*, instructors would be wise to take Polly's astonishment at the novel's climax as a starting point for cracking open the affect at work in the novel. In order to illustrate how this pre-teaching phase could go on to influence an affect-sensitive reading of *Crazy*, I devote the remainder of my remarks to the question: why do the boys go to a strip joint in the first place?

Let us first briefly establish the story of *Crazy*. Benjamin, a sixteen-year-old born with hemiparesis (the partial paralysis of one side of his body) enters a private boarding school in rural Bavaria. Told entirely from his perspective, the narrative initially establishes information about Benjamin (aka Benni), the nature of his disability, his relationship to his family, the hardships he endured in previous schools, his obligation to repeat eighth grade, as well as his misgivings for his new environs. After Benjamin gradually befriends a motley clique of boys, his story gains full momentum when they decide to run away from school and head for the big city. After eight chapters detailing their road trip, the boys arrive in Munich where they—without any prior warning—promptly head for a strip joint in Schwabing, one of the city's most bustling neighborhoods for natives and tourists alike. Dared by his roommate to slip a ten-Mark bill in a stripper's bikini, the protagonist Benni, already in a state of euphoria for inhabiting an exclusively adult male space, rises to the challenge and then, as if the exhilaration were beyond his physical limits, admits that he feels ill. After pronouncing "we're the best" and calling his friends "heroes" and "crazy," Benni passes out (165).[15] In the novel's next and final chapter, the reader learns that months later he has failed school for the fifth time on account of his poor grades and will be enrolled in a special school (*Sonderschule*) with an abridged curriculum.

Polly's reaction to the novel's narrative and libidinal climax resulted because of her objection to the female spectacle on which the boys feast and because of the language that the narrative deploys, which fulfills the boys' scopophilia and reduces woman's body to her genitals. In order to move from the affective shock an American reader like Polly may experience in this passage (A4) to the question of why the boys seek out the strip joint in the first place and, more importantly, why Benni feels euphorically ill after making contact with an erotic dancer (A5), an instructor must jump backward to the outset of the narrative. An initial exploration of the affective discourse within the represented target culture must begin by considering Benni's own body, for the novel's exposition is in large part a description of its embodied otherness. Described as a "spastic paralysis" and "partial paralysis" by his mother (12), a "handicap" by the school's principal (13), and "disabled" by Benni himself (17), Benni's body is precisely what makes him more than just "a little different" from the rest of the girls and boys at his school (9). A careful close reading must consider Benni's body physiologically (how does hemiparesis manifest itself?) and pinpoint how it determines the rhythms and, above all, movements of his everyday life (what can Benni do?). More importantly, an instructor's reading should establish how Benni's "handicapped" body, to use his principal's term, is constructed discursively by the "normal" male bodies around him. This move can weigh his doting mother's pre-Oedipal overemphasis of his differently abled body against the school administration and faculty's wholesale disregard of it. Furthermore, it can assess Benni's own melancholy that emanates from his own perceived limitations: "My disabled leg. How often I have wanted to chop it right off. [...] What do I need them [his arm and leg] for anyway? Just to see what I cannot do: run, swim, jump, be happy. But I wouldn't do that. Perhaps I need them for math. Or for fucking. Yeah, I might just need my goddamn left leg for fucking" (17). Attention to Benni's real and perceived restricted movement, his teenage desires to have sex, along with his anxiety of ever being able to engage in sex as a "cripple"—he uses the German *Krüppel*—can also assess how his desires target "normal" male bodies and their ability to procreate as seemingly unattainable signs of fulfillment (40–41). Above all, this close reading can uncover how Benni's body comes in contact with other male and female bodies, which of those bodies are affected and how, and what sort of affective "compositions" arise from these encounters. This focus would illuminate how Benni's body joins with those of his male friends and becomes, to use Deleuze and Guattari's idiom, a more powerful "assemblage" capable of a much wider range of movement that ultimately allows him to fulfill his desire: to desire like a "normal" body by assuming the male gaze among grown men. In this instance, the boys' affect results in the scopic fragmentation of the female body.

Kramsch contends that "constructing the cultural context" within an artifact from the target culture must also entail a comparative examination of other texts that intersect, collide, complicate, and enhance the meanings initially unearthed in the primary text (*Context* 139, 216). Establishing a collage of discursive intertextuality is absolutely essential for teachers committed to answering my question in its entirety: why do the boys go to a strip joint? Were instructors to consider, for example, how German law defines disability in terms of a diminished capacity to work (Hamilton 233) and then question why the German state refuses to designate Benni as disabled (Lebert 153), it would become clearer that an entire range of social forces are far more influential on his maneuverability than his own body. Seen from the vantage point of labor, Benni does not believe he can rise to the socio-economic expectations for becoming a useful working male member of society, for his corporeal difference and concomitant degree of mobility are entirely ignored. (This is perhaps most obvious when one ponders the German school system and asks why a sixteen-year-old is repeating eighth grade in his fifth different secondary school when he should be in tenth grade.) A different reading could entail situating Benni's understanding of self within a larger field of self-identifying disabled voices in Germany. Such a move would allow instructors to evaluate an entire community Benni disregards and to inquire into ways differently abled Germans actively position themselves with respect to the myth of a normal German body. Returning to the novel, instructors might also question the ways in which knowledge of and reflection on Benni's identity as a differently abled youth influences his desires and bodily movement. Instructors would also discover that in those moments when Benni and his friends experience emotional highs, they fail to imagine and desire lines of flight out of their current circumstances that would have delivered them from dominant discourses that determine not only what it means to be happy, but also how to perpetuate the oppression of women. Instead, they desire to become part of an adult phallocentric order and exactly at the point when this becomes near reality, Benni passes out.[16] While two radically different worlds, the school from which they escaped and the strip club in which they reveled are in effect only degrees apart from one another.

These are big questions to ask of a seemingly modest novel like *Crazy*, questions that certainly exceed advanced learners' linguistic proficiency. Nonetheless, they illuminate for instructors absolutely essential questions about how masculinity in contemporary German pop literature is embodied, how the social formation of gender influences embodiment and mobility, how this ideology obfuscates and even assails other forms of embodiment, and how the desire to comply with this ideology produces one body of knowledge at the price of obviating another, namely that of women. Instructors who "pre-teach" *Crazy* according to affect, bodies, and gender thus gain a firm grasp on how to proceed toward fleshing out cultural difference in the classroom. To begin with, this background information helps to determine what kinds of background knowledge (for example, normalcy and embodiment) instructors should elicit from students, how to present the overarching problem (for example, becoming a man) at work in the forthcoming reading, where and how they might focus their attention while reading the novel (for example, the strip joint scene), and what they should expect from their cross-cultural dialogue (for example, seeing different feelings at work in Germany and America). Moving onto the reading phase, instructors can entertain any number of processing-techniques to explore what Kramsch calls the "when? what? why? and how? of the story-line," in general, and the representations of affect, bodies in motion, and gender, in particular (*Context* 140–41, 143).[17] Once students are prepared to move beyond the story, instructors must ensure that activities intended to explore the novel's affective discourses tend to its epistemological voids. To this end, students could consider, for example, possible women's perspectives on the novel's climax *from within the framework of the text* by revising the narrative point of view from the vantage point of one of the story's many minor female voices (for example, the stripper, the community sex therapist, Benni's high school sweetheart, his lesbian sister, or his mother).

Identifying feelings within a text's discourse as something different from the structures of feelings that students of foreign languages bring to their reading is without question a tricky task. Success will certainly be a function of how well instructors help students differentiate, for example, their own North American perspectives on women's oppression from those both represented within the narrow purview of *Crazy* and the great range of German culture. The instructional goal must unveil those cultural discourses that shape affect. Accordingly, instructors would be wise to provide students first with opportunities to situate Lebert's novel within a wider discursive context in which gender and disability in contemporary Germany play a role. For this, students will need to question how the feelings in *Crazy* compare to the voices and affective registers of other differently abled Germans.[18] Students will also need to investigate analogous voices from their own culture. In this case, screening a recent Hollywood coming-of-age film like *American Pie* (1999) or even Katie Roiphe's controversial post-feminist reflections on college date rape, *The Morning After: Sex, Fear, and Feminism* (1993), can provide students with a rich foil with which to investigate their own culture's nightmares and fantasies apropos the teenage libido. Such texts would tackle only one half of the necessary self-introspection, for much of mainstream American popular culture refrains from featuring any teenage embodiment that veers from normative bodies. Beyond the realm of literary and cinematic narratives, students could explore the Americans with Disabilities Act of 1990 as a watershed for civil rights in the United States, work through the definitions of disability therein, research the degree to which differently abled persons are integrated into American schools, or dive into scholarship on the confluence of disability studies and gender (Orgassa 96–97). Equipped with a sensitivity for the cultural forces at work in the German novel as well as those that they might overlook in their own culture, students would begin to stack up important questions positioned at the precipice of cross-cultural analysis: Why is a teenage boy in a strip joint something entirely unacceptable or shocking to an American reader? How would Lebert's novel need to alter its representation of young women and men in order to conform to American expectations of teenage erotics, sex, and desire? How does a feminist perspective or a disabled perspective on *Crazy* and an American counterpart provide students with the means to carve out the makings of a third space for cross-cultural understanding? To what degree are disabled protagonists like Benni visible in American popular culture? Why does the German state fail to recognize Benni as disabled, and how might he have fared differently in the United States? What kinds of alternative lines of flight within American culture might Benni have considered had his story taken place here? Do these possibilities exist within Germany? From here, students would be well on their way to scrutinizing the cultural differences that emerge when each culture sees the other through its own artifacts and then discussing how and why the struggles of being a teenage boy or girl are indeed different in present-day Germany and the United States.

Conclusion: Knowing Different Feelings

Identifying the body as the primary site of learning is nothing new to foreign-language methodologies. Since the forties, empiricist methods like audiolingualism advanced the idea that learning is a matter of conditioning an organism within a carefully orchestrated environment (Omaggio Hadley 110). In reaction to this biologism, rationalists' approaches like Total Physical Response insisted a couple of decades later that learners are especially successful when language instruction is synchronized with corresponding body movements (Asher 1, 30–35). Gender has also been recognized, albeit belatedly, as a fundamental learner factor that instructors must acknowledge in order to tailor their instruction to the needs of their diverse students (Chavez 13–16, 133–97).[19] As I established at the outset of my essay, scholars have recognized affect for almost thirty years as a pivotal variable for instructors who seek to maximize student performance and pleasure. Although all three pedagogical issues—the body, gender, and affect—are certainly analogous in terms of their role in optimizing the learning experience, they have been relegated to the arena of student performance in the classroom (Arnold 5). The crux of my argument here has been the assertion that foreign-language pedagogy has much to gain if it expands upon these existing concerns by relating them to questions of culture, cultural difference, and cross-cultural awareness. By incorporating the ideas from recent theories of affect, instructors can equip themselves and their students with the heuristic tools capable of making sense of the vast array of attractive contemporary cultural documents, which under initial inspection hardly look foreign but feel, to quote my student Mark once again, inexplicably "strange" and "weird." When instructors and students attend to how bodies feel in these documents, they begin to explore not only the effects that bodies have on one another, but also the range of movement available to them as determined by the cultural context into which they are placed. The kinds of emotions that teenage bodies feel in the United States and in Germany may very well be identical, but the movement they derive from these affects, the direction that those movements assume, and the effects they have on others will certainly be different because of the distinct discursive forces at work within each culture. A foreign-language pedagogy attentive to affect is especially successful when it tempers such an approach with a commitment to feminist epistemology. Women's perspectives from within and without a target culture imbue readings of affect with a crucial sensitivity to the fields of power that differentiate bodies according to gender, sex, and disability. Moreover, fostering an awareness of feminist knowledge in cross-cultural awareness can lead students to explore how knowledge and subjecthood commingle outside of the cultural document in question to produce positive forms of affect that enable minorities to seek out forms of resistance and agency either in the cultures in question or in the fault line between them.

As my analysis of *Crazy* demonstrates, the knowledge a feminist perspective on affect can bring to a literary text in a foreign language might initially frustrate the goals of cross-cultural awareness, namely fostering empathy toward the target culture (Omaggio Hadley 355). Nevertheless, contemporary German popular culture, when combined with a sensitive pedagogy attentive to bodies, gender, and affect, can reveal substantial cultural differences that deepen and complicate students' preconceived notions of unfettered teenage liberties in a liberal German society, for example. Similarly, such texts and approaches can also succeed in providing students with a critical space from which to appraise their own culture's highly contradictory and contested discourses on youth and gender. With respect to instructional priorities, it is not farfetched to imagine how instructors can integrate this sensitivity to affect into culturally comparative approaches to foreign-language teaching. Of equal importance, with affective approaches to contemporary texts like *Crazy,* instructors confirm that, in spite of the visual thrust of much of postmodern culture, language alone can and does convey structures of feeling (Massumi 25–26). Similarly, they can verify how this relation exists simultaneously on numerous levels in the teaching and learning context: in the classroom, between readers and texts, and within the text itself. And finally, they can prove that the affect conveyed through language brings people to do things that are culturally very distinct. While foreign-language teachers have rightly tagged affect as a learner factor that can impede learning, a wider and carefully framed understanding of affect in contemporary postmodern culture can facilitate the discovery of that sought-after third space between home and abroad.

Notes

[1] The original predicament that inspired this essay grew out of a discord between what Kramsch calls the "pre-teaching" phase in teaching literary texts and what I saw as a pervasive inclusion of contemporary German popular culture in commercial textbooks and advanced language syllabi for the college level. According to Kramsch's criteria, contemporary popular culture might not merit inclusion in foreign-language curricula

because the cultural allusions therein are unclear (*Contexts* 138). However, there exist ample examples from popular culture that do meet Kramsch's other criteria for selection: thematic interest, linguistic simplicity, aesthetic character, narrative complexity, and the intelligibility of semantic gaps.

[2] See Hemming for an overview of this poststructuralist conundrum and the response from two more recent contributors to the theorization of affect (Massumi and Sedgwick). I am most grateful to Clare Hemmings for sharing with me her unpublished essay.

[3] One such intervention into affect studies is Hemming's article. I shall address Hemming's critique in greater detail in the following section. For a more affirmative feminist account on the value of affect for "feminist theorizing of queer bodily matters," see Clough 362.

[4] I take Kramsch's *ADFL Bulletin* essay on social, semiotic models of language instruction as a model for the bridge I seek to build between the disparate discourses of cultural theory and foreign-language pedagogy.

[5] In addition to anxiety, Arnold lists socio-psychological factors (student inhibitions, personality, self-esteem, motivation, and learner styles) and relational factors (empathy, student-teacher interactions, and culture shock) as belonging to the field of affect (8–23). For a brief overview of the massive body of research on academic, cognitive, social, and personal effects on anxiety development, see Peter D. MacIntyre, "Language Anxiety: A Review of the Research for Language Teachers," in Young 24–45.

[6] Brian Massumi's engagement with affect does much to interrogate and problematize the conflation of affect with emotion (à la Grossberg) and thus petitions that affect be understood as having as much, if not more, to do with the body (27–28). To be sure, Massumi's Deleuzean emphasis on the body is not symptomatic of all theoretical work on affect. Others, like Sedgwick and Hardt, articulate it with drives and emotions. My interest in cultural theory and affect engages in particular that tendency among theoreticians to fold the body back into the emotional realm of affect, a moment where the latest in cultural theory could be said to have finally caught up with one of feminism's most central yet vexed categories, the body. For more on the position of the body in feminist thought, see Grosz 3–5, 13–19.

[7] Research in foreign-language teaching has indeed addressed the problem of affect in the study of a target culture, primarily in terms of culture shock. Unlike these approaches that stress a clash between a native learner's cultural frame of reference and a target culture, I am interested here in culturally distinct forms of feeling common within a target culture. While the anxiety generated by culture clash has certainly not vanished entirely, I argue that with contemporary popular culture in Germany this culture shock has become negligible. For an overview of research on culture shock within the larger context of affect, see Arnold 21–23.

[8] Jamie Allen, "Smells like Teen Spirit," *Salon* 15 Apr. 2002, 16 Nov. 2003 <http://www.salon.com/ent/masterpiece/2002/04/15/teen_spirit/>.

[9] Coming to the problem from the arena of critical pedagogy, Henry Giroux contests in a similar vein that the sexual body has been and continues to be the primary site of a volatile representational politics of youth in the United States (53). In the postmodern context, he argues, any pedagogy involving popular culture must first acknowledge the dominant forces that relentlessly commodify, demonize, and discipline the teenage, gendered body and provide young students opportunities to engage these forces critically (68).

[10] For an overview of the history of feminist standpoint theory, the postmodern and poststructuralist challenges leveled at it, the rationale for its preservation, and attempts to update its claims to truth in postmodern times, see Hekman.

[11] Barbara Kerce of the International Import Book Service in Lynchburg, TN, a German book distributor that supplies North American colleges and universities with course textbooks, confirmed for me in an e-mail from 11 January 2005 that *Crazy* has remained a high-selling text for language instruction. Bookseller Schoenhof's of Boston, MA reported in a telephone interview on 12 January 2005 that, compared to canonical texts by Frisch and Dürrenmatt, *Crazy* is not a title frequently ordered as a course textbook. An Internet search for syllabi that incorporate *Crazy* in North American colleges and universities produced approximately twenty examples in early 2005. A similar search for use of the novel in German schools produces innumerable instances. As of the writing of this article, pedagogical interest in *Crazy* in North America has manifested itself in the form of a few unpublished conference papers, for example, Cornelia Becher, "Literature and Culture in the Language Classroom: What's up with German Texts?" UC Language Consortium Conference on Theoretical & Pedagogical Perspectives, University of California, Santa Cruz, 27 March 2004.

[12] What exactly the rubric "pop literature" designates is not yet clear. Literary historian Thomas Ernst suggests, for example, that the emergent pop writers from the mid-nineties rejected the reflective, anti-fascist stance of the elite, literary intelligentsia published by the Suhrkamp Verlag and who dominated the West German cultural landscape up until the fall of the Wall. In its place, younger writers embraced the pleasures of entertaining narratives and the promise of commercial success. Other than Lebert, Christian Kracht, Benjamin von Stuckrad-Barre, Thomas Brussig, and Alexa Hennig von Lange are considered part of this phenomenon (67).

[13] This and all other quotes are actual student responses culled from work originally written in German. I have translated their work along with subsequent quotations from Lebert's novel into English. Student names have

been changed in order to ensure anonymity. This and all following responses were submitted on a final written exam in which students were asked to describe what, from their perspective, was so German about the materials read and discussed in class.

[14] For the sake of space, I have condensed Polly's e-mail (written in English) from 1 December 2002 considerably. I nevertheless have preserved the many punctuation marks in order to preserve her affective intensities to the novel. WTF is an acronym for "what the fuck," a vulgar expression of disbelief commonly used in online chats and blogs.

[15] Because of my emphasis on teaching the German original in the foreign-language classroom, I am citing Lebert's novel instead of Carol Brown Janeway's 2000 English translation. All translations from the German are my own.

[16] I am grateful to one of my anonymous readers for suggesting the juncture of Benni's collapse and his entrance into the desired realm of male adulthood. It is arguable that by falling unconscious, Benni's body actually opposes the very thing that his mind desires. Such a reading would echo recent cultural theory's insistence on the affected body as a site of resistance.

[17] With respect to the question of affect, students could attend to each character's ability to affect and be affected by others, the beneficial or harmful effects of affect on male and female bodies, the varying degrees of mobility that affect affords them, the kinds of desire different bodies articulate, the proportionality of desire and a body's range of movement, and the direction of a body's movement away from or back into the clutches of patriarchal norms.

[18] Several intermediate German language textbooks do incorporate disability. David Crowner and Klaus Lill's *Impulse: Kommunikatives Deutsch für die Mittelstufe* features an entire chapter on basketball players in wheelchairs (314-40). Jack Moeller and co-authors' *Kaleidoskop: Kultur, Literatur, Grammatik* includes a short biography about the professional life of a disabled woman named Carolin (137-38). Both these texts could be used as intertextual complements to a discussion of Benni and disability in Germany.

[19] For research specifically on negative affect (anxiety) and gender, see Christine M. Campbell, "Language Anxiety in Men and Women: Dealing with Gender Difference in the Language Classroom," in Young 191-215.

Works Cited

Albrecht-Crane, Christa, and Jennifer Daryl Slack. "Toward a Pedagogy of Affect." *Animations (of Delueze and Guattari)*. Ed. Jennifer Daryl Slack. New York: Peter Lang, 2003. 191–216.

Arnold, Jane, and H. Douglas Brown. "A Map of the Terrain." *Affect in Language Learning*. Ed. Jane Arnold. Cambridge: Cambridge UP, 1999. 1–24.

Asher, James F. *Learning Another Language through Actions: The Complete Teacher's Guidebook*. Los Gatos, CA: Sky Oaks Productions, Inc., 1986.

Chavez, Monika. *Gender in the Language Classroom*. Boston: McGraw-Hill, 2001.

Clough, Patricia Ticineto. "Affect and Control: Rethinking the Body 'Beyond Sex and Gender.'" *Feminist Theory* 4.3 (2003): 359–64.

Crowner, David, and Klaus Lill. *Impulse: Kommunikatives Deutsch für die Mittelstufe*. 2nd ed. Boston: Houghton Mifflin, 1999.

Deleuze, Gilles, and Félix Guattari. *A Thousand Plateaus: Capitalism and Schizophrenia*. Minneapolis: U of Minnesota P, 1987.

Ernst, Thomas. *Popliteratur*. Hamburg: Europäische Verlagsanstal/Rotbuch 3000, 2001.

Giroux, Henry. "Body Politics and the Pedagogy of Display: Youth under Siege." *Body Movements: Pedagogy, Politics and Social Change*. Eds. Sherry Shapiro and Svi Shapiro. Cresshill, NJ: Hampton P, 2002. 45–73.

Grossberg, Lawrence. *We Gotta Get out of This Place: Popular Conservativism and Postmodern Culture*. New York: Routledge, 1992.

Grosz, Elizabeth. *Volatile Bodies: Toward a Corporeal Feminism*. Bloomington: Indiana UP, 1994.

Hamilton, Elizabeth C. "From Social Welfare to Civil Rights: Representation of Disability in Twentieth-Century German Literature." *The Body and Physical Difference: Discourses of Disability*. Eds. David T. Mitchell and Sharon L. Snyder. Ann Arbor: U of Michigan P, 1997. 223–39.

Hardt, Michael. "Affective Labor." *Boundary 2* 26.2 (Summer 1999): 89–100.

Harvey, David. *The Condition of Postmodernity: An Enquiry into the Origins of Cultural Change*. Cambridge, MA: Blackwell, 1989.

Hekman, Susan. "Truth and Method: Feminist Standpoint Theory Revisited." *Signs: Journal of Women in Culture in Society* 22.2 (1997): 341–65.

Hemmings, Clare. "Invoking Affect: Cultural Theory and the Ontological Turn." *Cultural Studies* 19.5 (Sept. 2005): 548–67.
Kramsch, Claire. *Context and Culture in Language Teaching*. Oxford: Oxford UP, 1993.
———. "Language and Culture: A Social Semiotic Perspective." *ADFL Bulletin* 33.2 (Winter 2002): 8–15.
Krashen, Stephen D. *Principles and Practice in Second Language Acquisition*. Oxford: Pergamon P, 1982.
Lebert, Benjamin. *Crazy*. Köln: Kiepenheuer und Witsch, 1999.
Massumi, Brian. *Parables for the Virtual: Movement, Affect, Sensation*. Durham: Duke UP, 2002.
Moeller, Jack, et al. *Kaleidoskop: Kultur, Literatur, Grammatik*. 6th ed. Boston: Houghton Mifflin, 2002.
Omaggio Hadley, Alice. *Teaching Language in Context*. 3rd. ed. Boston: Heinle & Heinle, 2000.
Orgassa, Ute C. "Max versus Max: Disability-Related Services in the U.S. and Germany." *International Perspectives on Disability Services: The Same But Different*. Ed. Francis K.O. Yuen. New York: Haworth P, 2003. 87–100.
Probyn, Elspeth. "Teaching Bodies: Affect in the Classroom." *Body & Society* 10.4 (Dec. 2004): 21–43.
Sedgwick, Eve Kosofsky. *Touching Feeling: Affect, Pedagogy, Performativity*. Durham: Duke UP, 2003.
Young, Dolly Jesusita, ed. *Affect in Foreign Language and Second Language Learning: A Practical Guide to Creating a Low-Anxiety Classroom Atmosphere*. Boston: McGraw-Hill College, 1999.

The Making of Transnational Textual Communities: German Women Translators, 1800–1850

Andrew Piper

By portraying the work of female translators from the first half of the nineteenth century, this essay explores how women created new textual communities that capitalized on the increasing diffusion of print networks. In doing so, women used translation to negotiate new relationships to print and publishing that facilitated their emergence as a professional writing class. Translations by women also promoted the creation of new, increasingly international cultural geographies in which translation functioned not as a force for homogenization, but as a means of identifying cultural differences. (AP)

> *"How shall our voices, on a foreign shore*
> *(We answer'd those whose chains the exile wore,)*
> *The songs of God, our sacred songs, renew?"*
> —Felicia Hemans's translation of Camões, "Sonnet 239"

In chapter 5 of book 1 of Goethe's *Wilhelm Meister's Journeyman Years,* Hersilie hands Wilhelm a translation one evening that he is to read before going to bed. The translation is entitled, "Die pilgernde Thörin" ("The Foolish Woman on a Pilgrimage"), and Hersilie is said to be its translator. The translation was based on an eighteenth-century French novella, *La folle en pélerinage* (1786), which Goethe himself had translated. Not only did "Die pilgernde Thörin" serve as the opening novella published in Goethe's two-decade-long publication of *Wilhelm Meister's Journeyman Years* (functioning like a *Tor* [gate] to the larger project), but Hersilie herself would go on to play one of the most important authorial roles within the entire novel (Piper 133–36). In his late literary work Goethe had seen the woman translator as a key figure for thinking about authorship and writing, and yet we scholars have taken little notice of her as either a fictional construct or real-world practitioner.

Much work has been done on the importance of translation to the field of German literature around the turn of the nineteenth century (Huyssen; Apel; Tgahrt). As Clemens Brentano famously exclaimed, "The Romantic itself is a translation" (*Godwi* 294).[1] Studies abound on the role of translation in the work of A.W. Schlegel, Friedrich Hölderlin, or Goethe, and yet translation played an integral role in the work of women writers too, such as Dorothea Tieck, Sophie Mereau, and Fanny Tarnow. At the turn of the nineteenth century, numerous women writers were actively translating and contributing to the rising circulation of literary works across Europe. While recent studies by scholars such as Daniel Purdy, Britta Hannemann, Sabine Messner, and Michaela Wolf have begun to address the intersections of women and translation around 1800, we are only just beginning to understand the extent to which women were translating, the questions that most urgently occupied them, and the impact they exerted on the larger literary landscape.

In her work on gender and translation, Sherry Simon has asked whether discussing women as translators is a way for women writers to lose their voice, whether it reproduces a gender hierarchy of men as producers and women as reproducers. This is an important question to bear in mind, and yet in leaving translation out of women's literary history we recreate a generic hierarchy that denigrates women's writing. The more we uncover about women's writing and the important position that translation has played as both a practice and an idea within it, the more translation becomes a space to recover, not lose, women's voices. As a growing body of theoretical work on the relationship of women's writing to translation has argued (Godard; Flotow 1991, 1997; Levin; Lotbinière-Harwood; Simon; Chamberlain; Brisset), translation captures the mediations, displacements, and contradictions that surrounded, and continue to surround, women's place in the literary market. It brings to the foreground precisely those aspects of women's writing that have been emphasized in recent feminist literary histories, like Catherine Gallagher's emphasis on the poetics of dispossession in women's writing, Susanne Kord's argument about the problem of the proper name for emerging professional women writers, Barbara Hahn's notion of the "broken lines" of women's literary history, or Margaret Ezell's emphasis on shifting the site and definition of "publication" and "public" in order to recover women's innovative contributions to the world of writing.[2] Translation can be seen as a key component of such paradigmatic scholarly models that try to capture the fundamental and enduring mediations surrounding women's writing.

At the same time, leaving translation out of literary history in general, whether by men or women, does a disservice to the important and very often innovative role that translation has played within the evolution of literary form. Including translations in our histories—and our classrooms—is a way of emphasizing the increasingly crucial role that translation plays today in creating new cultural, political, and media geographies.[3] It allows us to rethink notions of authorship and creativity as far less sovereign undertakings and far more collaboratively organized. It emphasizes the process of adaptation over origination. At the same time, it identifies the encounter with a foreign language, with language as something foreign, indeed, with language itself, as an impetus to creativity.

This essay thus contributes to a larger history of the relationship between women writers and the field of translation, as well as translation's relationship to the field of literary study. In offering a portrait of different women translators' works, it aims to do away with the older, more simplistic notion of women as *les belles infidèles* and asks instead why, what, and how women were translating. What were the strategies women used to get into print, to circulate foreign literary texts, whether by men or women, and, in the process, to create new textual communities? How did such communities establish alternative and increasingly international publics? With the emergence of various nationalisms at the turn of the nineteenth century, how did translation, and particularly translations by women, potentially allow for new cultural geographies to emerge that capitalized on the increasing spread and diffusion of print networks? How was translation understood by women not as a force for homogenization, but instead as a way of identifying cultural differences?

While an enormous amount of research has been done in the past two decades on the nationalism of writing and literature at the turn of the nineteenth century, we have overlooked the growing internationalism of writing and authorial identity during this same period and the important role that women played in this process. My work thus takes as its point of departure such important new books as David Damrosch's *What Is World Literature?* and new series such as Princeton's "Translation/Transnation" series edited by Emily Apter. These works emphasize precisely the international identity of literary communities and the crucial role that translation assumed within their construction. I want to explore how the emergence of the professional woman writer around 1800 transpired in an always intimate relationship to the foreign and the practice of translation. How might this fact force us to rethink not only our understanding of this particular period in literary history, but also the larger issue of writers' relationships to their own language and works that have subtly shaped the profession of literary criticism?

* * *

While Goethe's Hersilie offers us a particular ideal of a woman translator, there was in fact no one model at the turn of the nineteenth century. Nineteenth-century women translated a variety of source texts from different languages, genres, and periods in numerous ways with varying degrees of recognition and compensation. Some female translators, such as Henriette Schubart (Sophie Mereau's sister), who translated, among other things, Walter Scott's ballad collection into German (orig. 1802/3, trans. 1817),[4] suffered their entire lives from not making enough money through translation. Others, however, were well compensated for their work, like Mereau herself, who commanded as much as any man for a translation (Schwarz), or Fanny Tarnow, who in 1846 stopped translating altogether because she had simply earned enough (Wägenbauer). Indeed, Tarnow enjoyed a reputation as one of the nineteenth-century's great translators, evidenced by repeated accolades in reviews of her translations. As the editors of the *Blätter für literarische Unterhaltung* (Journal for Literary Entertainment) flatly stated, "Fanny Tarnow translates better" (12 Mar. 1842).[5] Or as they recommended in an earlier review, "The German public does not need to long for the original; the best of it has been given to us by the translatress [*Nachbilderin*], who is certainly also superior in style to its British author; for how many writers either here or abroad can compare themselves in matters of style with Fanny Tarnow?" (17 July 1826).[6]

If women's fortunes from translating varied greatly, so too did their relationship to their source texts. One needs only to compare the relative "fidelity" of Dorothea Tieck's translations to her English and Spanish originals with the interventions that Elise von Hohenhausen sometimes offered in translating Byron (see below) or Therese Huber's invented ending for Jean-Baptiste Louvet's *Emilie de Varmont, ou Le Divorce nécessaire* (*Emily of Varmont, or The Necessary Divorce*; orig. 1791, trans. 1794), where Emilie remarries in the German translation but not in the French original. As Wilhelmine von Gersdorf argued in the preface to her translation of *Redwood: A Tale* (orig. 1824, trans. 1825), which was mistakenly attributed to James Fenimoore Cooper but was actually written by Catherine Maria Sedgwick:

> Such reasons moved me to translate this work into German. I did not anxiously bind myself to its style and language, but rather concerned myself with abridging this all too verbose narrative, like

a gardener who cuts the ivy's overly exuberant protuberances with his sheers. I hope that friends of my work will not consider this current one a superfluous endeavor for their entertainment.[7]

Gersdorf's image of the translator as a gardener pruning the unruly ivy of her original should certainly be added to the archive of translation anecdotes, like Cervantes' quip that reading a translation was like looking at the back of a Flemish tapestry.

Some women concentrated almost exclusively on translating canonical texts by men, such as Hohenhausen, who contributed translations to the German editions of Byron's and Walter Scott's collected works. Others, such as Sophie Mereau, concentrated largely, but not exclusively, on creating a female literary canon (Madame de Lafayette, Ninon de Lenclos, María de Zayas, but also Boccaccio). Finally, translation played differing roles in the lives of women. For some, like Mereau, it stood alongside a rich body of original works, while for others, such as Sophie Mayer (pen name: Sophie May), who translated numerous volumes by Walter Scott and other early nineteenth-century novelists, it was their sole activity as writers. Women remained both very present on the page in their translations, as in Hedwig Hülle's translation of Homer's *Odyssey* (trans. 1826), but also concealed and anonymous, as in the case of Dorothea Tieck, whose name never appeared on any of her translations and who was referred to by her father in print as "mein junger Freund (my young male friend)." Finally, the idea of translation also played an important role in women's original writing as well, whether it was Mary Shelley's Frankenstein monster, who overhears a young woman learning foreign languages while wandering far from home; Jane Austen's Elizabeth Inchbald, who adapts Kotzebue's *Lover's Vows* in *Mansfield Park* as Inchbald did in real life; or Madame de Staël's multilingual heroine, who translates Shakespeare in *Corinne, ou L'Italie* (*Corinne, or Italy,* 1807), which was then translated into German by Dorothea Schlegel (1807). Translation was thus not only a key element to fictional women's imaginative universes, but as in the case of *Corinne,* it also seemed capable of motivating its practice and continuing this international network of translating women.

Due to the particular nature of women's education around the turn of the century, the acquisition of foreign languages was an integral part of a woman's upbringing (Hooke-Demarle). It is simply astonishing for a modern reader to encounter someone like Dorothea Tieck, who was able to read English, Italian, Portugese, Spanish, Latin, ancient Greek, and of course her mother tongue German.[8] And it is important to emphasize that women not only learned and contributed to the circulation of modern language texts, but were also deeply familiar with classical languages as well, and in certain instances contributed to their translations. By far the boldest literary experiment in this direction was Hedwig Hülle's translation of Homer's *Odyssey,* a text that had become in Johann Heinrich Voß's translation (1781) and Werther's imagination one of the key works that motivated the formal revolutions of German poetics around the turn of the nineteenth century. Hülle's experiment almost half a century after the rebirth of Homer in German literary circles implied a series of reversals from the Voßian revival, first and foremost in her choice of rhyme and meter. While Voß had draped Homer in dactyllic hexameter, a form made popular through Klopstock's argument that it was precisely the dactyl and not the iamb that was the rhythm more closely related to the nature of the German language (Klopstock), Hülle, on the other hand, used the much shorter and swifter form of rhyming iambic tetrameter. One need only compare Hülle and Voß to feel the full force of her compression of the original, as in the passage from Odysseus's encounter with the Cyclops:

Hülle: Da, mit listigem Bemühn,
Sprach ich: du willst meinen Namen
Wissen; gerne sag' ich's dir:
Niemand heiß' ich; doch nun reiche
Die versprochne Gabe mir. (224)

[Then, with cunning attention,
I spoke: you want to know my
Name; gladly I tell it you:
Nobody am I called; now give
Me the promised gift.]

Voß: Meinen berühmten Namen, Kyklop? Du sollst
  ihn erfahren.
Aber vergiß mir auch nicht die Bewirtung, die du ver-
  hießest!
Niemand ist mein Name; denn Niemand nennen mich
  alle,
Meine Mutter, mein Vater, und alle meine Gesellen.
  (163)

[My famous name, Cyclops? You shall learn it.
But do not forget the hospitality that you promised!
Nobody is my name; for everybody calls me Nobody,
My mother, my father, and all of my friends.]

If Hülle's translation could be read in one sense as an answer to Voß, as the enactment of what Hersilie said about the role of women in a patriarchal society—namely, that they reversed the maxims of men and thus challenged their universality[9]—it was also in conversation with its poetic environment. Faust's opening monologue in the rhyming couplets of *Knittelvers*—also iambic tetrameter—was naturally one important source for Hülle, as was the echo of Faust's "mit heißem Bemühen" in Odysseus's "mit listigem Bemühen." But the larger nineteenth-century revival of Shakespeare, too, was a constant pull on German poetry to be more English. In the same year as Hülle's translation of Homer, Dorothea Tieck's translation of Shakespeare's sonnets appeared in the journal *Penelope,* twenty-six examples of iambs arranged according to a very rigid rhyme scheme.

Hülle thus inserted herself into one of the most influential poetic debates at the turn of the nineteenth century, which revolved around the difficult question of incorporating and domesticating a foreign text into the German cultural landscape. In place of Werther's fantasy of Homer offering the reader a reassuring image of the patriarchal home (*Werther* 59), Hülle saw in Odysseus the playful trickster capable of reversing fortune at numerous turns. Her own "playful translation" (*freie Nachbildung*) importantly does not begin with an appeal to the muse, like Homer's source text, thus effacing in the process one of the more prevalent and restrictive notions of femininity as the male poet's silent inspiration. Instead she begins with the word "Hellas" and, unlike many of her peers, places her proper name front and center on the title page of her translation, turning woman as muse into woman as author. Translation, like the fortune-reversing hero of the work Hülle chose to translate, became a means of reversing not only the text's particular *fortuna,* but also a woman's relationship to writing in general.

If Homer represented one of the central points of attraction for nineteenth-century translators, then it was of course Shakespeare who occupied another key position (Arac; Habicht). While a good deal of work has been done on the impact of the so-called "Schlegel-Tieck" edition of Shakespeare's works, which still remains a standard edition used today, very little work has been done on Dorothea Tieck's role in its production, and even less has on her work on the sonnets (Jansohn). In another problematic case of the relationship between gender and naming, the Schlegel-Tieck edition was named after Dorothea's father, Ludwig Tieck, who helped edit the translations but contributed none of his own, unlike Dorothea, who contributed six to the overall project (*Coriolanus, Timon of Athens, Macbeth, Cymbeline, The Two Gentleman of Verona,* and *A Winter's Tale*).

In addition to her work on the plays, Tieck also became the first author to translate the entirety of Shakespeare's sonnets into German. While the sonnet, particularly the translation of sonnets, played an important role in romantic poetic production in both England and the German states (Curran; Mönch; Kemp), Shakespeare's sonnets always maintained an uncomfortable relationship to such sonnet revivals. The romantics' circumvention of Shakespeare's sonnets was part of a persistent uncertainty about their position within both the Shakespearean "corpus" as well as the literary canon itself.[10] To take up the sonnets in their entirety was thus to address precisely those problems of supplementarity that were at the heart of both translation and women's position in the literary market. How was a work, a corpus, or even a canon to be constituted, closed, and completed?

Such questions about the place of the sonnets were of course not only limited to textual concerns surrounding the sonnets, but were also integral to the content of Shakespeare's sonnets as well. The dialogical structure of this epideictic genre, the emphasis on begetting and reproduction in Shakespeare's opening subset, and the gender reversals enacted through addressing a young man all posed problems to early-nineteenth-century poetic theory. Such problems challenged the translator, and in particular the woman translator, to reflect on her art. The intricate nexus of exchange and loss that coursed through Shakespeare's sonnets offered uniquely interesting material for Dorothea Tieck to explore her relationship to writing, literature, and the rising public sphere of printed material.

Tieck not only spent much of her writing life engaged with Shakespeare, but also translated Cervantes' last novel, *The Trials of Persiles and Sigismunda* (1837; *Los trabajos de Persiles y Sigismunda,* 1617). In translating *Persiles and Sigismunda,* Tieck was doing for Cervantes—and German nineteenth-century literature—precisely what she had done for Shakespeare in attending to the "supplementary" genre of the sonnets. Cervantes's final novel was extraordinarily different from *Don Quixote,* which Tieck's father had translated in 1799–1801 and which had become one of the key landmarks for a romantic aesthetics of the novel. In place of the wit and humor of the earlier work, *Persiles and Sigismunda* was a more somber novel, one produced by an old man, who, like Goethe in his late work, had become historical to himself.

Persiles and Sigismunda is interesting, however, not just for this turn from the comic to the serious, from the revelatory to the reflective, but also because it enacted its own fantasies about the possibility of world literature. On the one hand, the text repeatedly called attention to the difficulties of interlingual communication, with numerous scenes deploying the figure of the interpreter and the problem of misunderstanding. At the same time, in its depiction of a multinational, multilingual band of pilgrims on a spiritual quest from the farthest reaches of the North (Thule) to the Catholic center of Rome, it also argued for a particular trajectory, a move away from the difficulties of communication and toward its possibility. The novel opens in the following way:

> Voces daba el bárbaro Corsicurvo a la estrecha boca de una profunda mazmorra, antes sepultura que prisión de muchos cuerpos vivos que en ella estaban sepultados, y, aunque su terrible y espantoso estruendo cerca y lejos se escuchaba, de nadie eran entendidas articuladamente las razones que pronunciaba sino de la miserable Cloelia, a quien sus desventures en aquella profundidad tenían encerrada. (117–18)

> [At the top of his voice Corsicurbo the barbarian was shouting into the narrow mouth of a deep dungeon which seemed more a tomb than a prison for the many living bodies buried there. And although the terrible and frightening din could be heard both near and far, no one clearly understood his words except miserable Cloelia, whose misfortunes held her locked in those depths.] (Weller 17)

Dorothea Tieck translates:

> Laut rief der Barbar Corsicurbo vor der engen Öffnung einer tiefen Grube, welche eher einem Grabe, als einem Kerker für eine Anzahl lebendiger Leichen glich; und obgleich seine furchtbar tönende Stimme nahe und fern gehört wurde, so vernahm doch die ausgesprochenen Worte nur die unglückliche Clelia deutlich, welche ihr Mißgeschick in jener Kluft gefangen hielt. (3)

> [Loudly the barbarian Corsicurbo called in front of the narrow opening of a deep cave, which seemed more like a grave than a prison for a number of living corpses; and although his horrible sounding voice was heard near and far, his spoken words were only clearly understood by unhappy Clelia, whose misfortune held her captive in that abyss.]

The novel begins with a scream by the "barbarian" (from Greek *barbaros* for 'foreigner,' although linked to the Latin *balbus* for 'stammer') and continues with an opening that only one person could understand ("his spoken words were only understood by unhappy Clelia"). It begins, in other words, with the narrowing of communication. The novel ends, however, in the "South" at the Catholic kingdom of Rome with Persiles and Sigismunda shedding their pseudonyms and their fictional sibling relationship, since they have posed as brother and sister throughout their journey. As Cervantes's final work and Dorothea Tieck's final translation, we end with a text that proposes—in anticipation of Benjamin's landmark translation essay almost a century later—the possibility of a universal language in place of national vernaculars. It ends not so much with the notion of *translatio imperii* as with the idea of the *translatio spiriti* and a universal mode of communication and understanding.

Dorothea Tieck and Hedwig Hülle thus engaged through their translations of Homer, Shakespeare, and Cervantes three of the most important points that defined the horizon of "classics" for nineteenth-century German literature. And in each case their work offered a counterpoint to these authors' reception by male poets and writers. They provided a significantly different perspective on what their texts meant, not as a form of rejection or protest, but instead as an alternative or a supplement. Their work identified ways of redefining the classical itself as something open and in motion.

Where Tieck's career was largely determined by translating the work of canonical texts by men, thus having her identity simultaneously obscured by them, Sophie Mereau, on the other hand, established a corpus of translations largely of seventeenth-century women authors (Purdy; Hannemann). In translating the letters of and writing a biography of Ninon de Lenclos, as well as translating the novellas of María de Zayas, *Novelas Amorosas y Ejemplares* (*Exemplary and Amorous Novellas*; orig. 1637, trans. 1804), Mereau not only recovered, promoted, and shaped a literary tradition by and about women, she also actively promoted the sexual freedoms of women that posed a direct challenge to the common turn-of-the-century image of decorous, proper women. As one reviewer said of Mereau's translation, which listed her as editor, not translator: "What? The Mad. Mereau, who was once so celebrated by us, is now writing Spanish novellas, is writing sonnets, burlesques? She too inclines to that invidious school? Down with her immediately!" (*Der Freimüthige* 118).[11]

What was equally, if not more interesting about the works Mereau chose to translate were the communicative transgressions they enacted. Taken together, one can see how the works she chose to translate consistently addressed the central problem of "overhearing": the risks, but also possibilities, inherent in the increasing appropriatability of narrative material. From the characters of Zayas' novellas to the Princess in Madame de Lafayette's *La Princesse de Clèves* (*The Princess of Clèves*; orig. 1678, trans. 1799), which was one of the earliest works Mereau translated, we repeatedly encounter situations in which characters are not in complete control of their own narratives. On the one hand, such a poetics of communication framed translation as an act of empowerment, a means of appropriating material that was not addressed to oneself. Precisely that which Socrates had criticized about writing in the *Phaedrus*—that it could be taken out of its context of address and thus lose or change its meaning[12]—was here valorized by Mereau as a source of power and a means of entry into the written world. Both the growing circulation of printed texts and the practice of translation that capitalized upon and promoted such circulation were understood by Mereau to be the very preconditions for new voices to be heard.

Such a point was amplified in how Mereau chose to translate her source texts at certain moments. In moving the princess's confession from direct to indirect speech in her translation of Lafayette, for example, Mereau narratologically highlighted the mediation and overhearing already at the heart of the confessional moment overheard by the object of the princess's confession, M. de Nemours, and then later anonymously circulated at court. As the narrator speaks for the princess—precisely during the otherwise deeply individualized speech act of the "confession"—she underscores the appropriatability of the princess's narrative material that the narrative itself will then enact. Mereau inserts a formal device, in this case indirect speech, into her translation that motivates the very poetics of overhearing encoded in her source text, thus emphasizing for women writers a way of facilitating their entry into the world of writing. Whether formal or thematic, such overhearing authorized women writers to construct their own literary tradition from the existing canon of world literature, which had excluded them as either addressor or addressee.

At the same time, such narratives of overhearing also offered Mereau the opportunity to explore the limits that such taking implied. How was one to make someone else's material, whether a single work or an entire literary heritage, one's own? The complex lines of communication developed in the stories Mereau translated were mirrored in the vertically "broken lines," to use Barbara Hahn's expression, of the same narratives' genealogical structures, whether it was the death of the mother in Lafayette, the fatherless daughters and motherless sons in Zayas, or the breaking of the incest taboo in the biography of Lenclos, who unknowingly sleeps with her own son. There were very palpable limits to the ownership depicted in such texts of overhearing that Mereau chose to translate. In her translation, for example, of a novella from the tenth day of Boccaccio's *Decameron* entitled "Nathan," which concerned the impossibility of ever assuming another person's identity, Mereau explored through translation the essential limits of translation. Her corpus of translations thus aimed to explore the increasingly complex circuitry of transmission and partial ownership made possible by the expanding landscape of print communication around 1800 and in which translation had an increasingly important role to play. In addressing this crisis of address, Mereau highlighted the contradictions that continued to surround women's roles as writers.

Women writers at the turn of the nineteenth century were not only engaged with the preservation and discovery of older texts, they were also active participants in the growing market for new material. Nowhere is this more obvious than in the translation of contemporary novels. And no one seemed to rival the productivity and popularity of Fanny Tarnow, who, between 1830 and 1846 and after publishing an edition of her own collected works, produced fifty translations from French and English sources (Wägenbauer). While it is hard to discern a definitive pattern from Tarnow's translation choices, which included many novels that have been lost or forgotten like *Pfarrer Moritz* (*Pastor Moritz,* 1837), certainly her choice of novels, such as Honoré de Balzac's *Eugenie Grandet* (orig. 1833, trans. 1835) and George Sand's *Indiana* (orig. 1831, trans. 1836), indicates a programmatic move to circulate works that commented upon and redefined women's role in nineteenth-century society. Both Balzac's and Sand's works belonged to that genre of the female utopia, providing the construction of alternative, feminine universes whose power of social critique, as in all utopian fictions, is divided between the unity of its vision and the impotence of its explicit fictionality. At the same time, few works of fiction addressed more directly the particular social plights of women in the nineteenth century. The success of each depended, one suspects, on their capacity to hold both of these registers in well-orchestrated tension.

Among its various allures, including the intersecting positions of the colonial and the feminine, George Sand's *Indiana* was most famous for its depiction of the wife who rejected her procreative duties. With its version of the female Bartleby who proclaims "I prefer not" in the bedroom and not the office, Sand's novel explored a way to articulate woman's sexuality that was not implicated in the traditionally patriarchal structures of sexual exchange. Such exchanges included the marriage contract and the harsh servitude it entailed for women (at one point Colonel Delmare, Indiana's husband, almost crushes her head with his boot in anger). They also included the extra-marital affair whose benefits, as portrayed by Sand, largely accrued to the man and whose risks were borne by the woman (Indiana's servant Noun is ultimately driven to her death when she becomes pregnant through her affair with Raymon). The novel was thus a larger exploration of cultural resistance in general, of how to say no in a greater sense. In place of open opposition, heroics that were explicitly compared in the novel to Don Quixote breaking his lance against a windmill, Sand developed a much more nuanced theory of resistance, one very suggestive of the indirect role that translation itself might play as a form of cultural resistance. In the powerful words of defiance uttered by Indiana to her husband:

> Vous avez usé de violence en m'enfermant dans ma chambre: j'en suis sortie par la fenêtre pour vous prouver que ne pas régner sur la volonté d'une femme, c'est exercer un empire dérisoire. J'ai passé quelques heures hors de votre domination; j'ai été respirer l'air de la liberté pour vous montrer que vous n'êtes pas moralement mon maître et que je ne dépends que de moi sur la terre. (226)

> [You used violence in locking me in my room. I left by the window to prove to you that if you don't control a woman's will, your power over her is a mockery. I spent several hours beyond your power. I went to breathe the air of liberty, to show you that morally you're not my master and that I depend only on myself on the earth.] (Raphael 177)

Rendered by Tarnow as:

> Sie haben eine Gewaltthat gegen mich verübt, als Sie mich in mein Zimmer einsperrten und ich bin aus dem Fenster gestiegen um Ihnen zu beweisen, daß es eine lächerliche Anmaßung ist, den Willen einer Frau beherrschen zu wollen. Ich habe mich auf einige Stunden Ihrer Herrschaft entzogen, ich habe die Luft der Freiheit geathmet, um Ihnen zu beweisen, daß Sie nicht moralisch mein Herr sind und daß ich auf Erden nur von mir selbst abhänge. (97)

> [You exercised violence against me when you locked me in my room, and I climbed out through the window to show you that it is a laughable assumption to want to rule over the will of a woman. I removed myself from your rule for a few hours, breathed the air of freedom, in order to show you that morally you are not my master and that on earth I depend only on myself.]

While Tarnow lost some of Sand's vocabulary that emphasized the husband's monarchical status (*régner, empire,* nonetheless captured in *Herrschaft*), she made Indiana's rejection of his reign far more emphatic. In place of Sand's conditional, "que ne pas régner sur la volonté d'une femme, c'est exercer un empire dérisoire" ("if you don't control a woman's will, your power over her is a mockery"), Tarnow asserted the absolute position, "daß es eine lächerliche Anmaßung ist, den Willen einer Frau beherrschen zu wollen" ("it is a laughable assumption to want to rule over the will of a woman"). According to Tarnow, one could *never* control the will of a woman and thus could not rule over her.

Fanny Tarnow was of course not the only woman who translated numerous novels in the course of her career. One should also mention the work of Elise von Hohenhausen, Sophie Mayer, or Wilhelmine von Gersdorf, who all participated in the vigorous industry of translating Walter Scott's poetry and novels in the nineteenth century. Indeed, it is interesting to note that so many of Scott's translators were women. What was it about this corpus that made it attractive to nineteenth-century women writers and how did they treat his works in translation?[13]

However much women partook in the rise of novels around the turn of the century, they were also intimately involved in poetic translation as well. I have already mentioned Hülle's *Odyssey* translation, but I would like to focus for a moment on the work of Elise von Hohenhausen, whose translations of Byron are some of the most interesting poetic translations of the nineteenth century. In addition, they contributed to the growing celebrity of Byron as a writer capable of appealing to both male and female readers. Hohenhausen's engagement with Byron could thus be seen as the contemporary equivalent of Tieck's engagement with Shakespeare or Hülle's with Homer.

Beginning in April of 1820 in a series for the *Morgenblatt für gebildete Stände* (Morning Newspaper for the Educated Classes), Hohenhausen published translations of excerpts from Byron's *Childe Harold's Pilgrimage* (1812–18), signing each one. The very act of selection suggested an important stance toward her original, i.e., that it was something that could be disassembled. Her translations thus seemed to empower readers to interact with the texts that they read, not to treat them as sacred objects, but as malleable, multifaceted materials for further creativity.

At the same time, the parts that Hohenhausen chose to translate, the way she translated, and, at times, the way she invented new lines in her translation, suggested important points about a woman's relationship to Byron's poetry. In her second selection for the *Morgenblatt,* Hohenhausen chose Childe Harold's own farewell song, "Good Night," performed after the thirteenth stanza of the first canto. On the one hand, the choice of translating a lyric interlude from within a narrative poem, indicated for readers by the quotation marks that were reproduced in the translation, intensified the poetic voice's individuality so crucial to Byron's international celebrity (Mole). This choice also reversed or covered over precisely the pluralization of voices that a translation necessarily performed.

On the other hand, in choosing a selection that began with the words, "'Adieu, adieu! My native shore'" (26), rendered into German as, "'Leb wohl, mein Heimathstrand, Ade!'" (*Morgenblatt* 24 Apr. 1820), Hohenhausen constructed a feminine poetics that transgressed confines and expanded identities, whether those of the national tongue or the walls of the domestic home. The foreign word that remained untranslated, although respelled ("Adieu/Ade") in Hohenhausen's selection disclosed—at both the linguistic and semantic level—the fundamental condition of departure or exile that defined a woman writer's position and that was echoed in Felicia Hemans's translation of Camões's sonnet cited as my epigraph above. "Adieu/Ade" signified "departure" both in its literal meaning and non-meaning as a foreign word. And yet at the same time, in not being translated it also emphasized that a common thread connected such internationalism, that something stayed the same even when it crossed borders. In this we can see how Hohenhausen functioned as an exemplary participant in a larger project by women writers to establish their own international republic of letters.

In its typographical appeal to direct speech alongside its linguistic appeal to the foreign, the first line of Hohenhausen's selection thus condensed the essential competing tensions of any translation. It simultaneously appealed to the reader to overlook the multiple personages behind the reconstruction of this singular voice at the same time that it drew immediate attention to the limits of what could be "brought over" (*übersetzen*). One of the sources of Byron's international fame was arguably his work's concern with internationalism itself (Cardwell), and in this regard he offered ideal material for the translator to address the role of translation in giving shape to such transnational literary networks.

A year later Hohenhausen published another excerpt, this time from stanzas 98–109 of the third canto, which she entitled, "Der Morgen am Genfersee" ("Morning on Lake Geneva"), and in it we can witness not only some of Hohenhausen's most exquisite work in moving from English to German, but also her capacity to work with gender as she did so. From Byron's lines:

> The morn is up again, the dewy morn,
> With breath all incense, and with cheek all bloom,
> Laughing the clouds away with playful scorn,
> And living as if earth contain'd no tomb,— (133)

Hohenhausen writes:

> Der Morgen kommt zurück mit Perlenthau,
> Mit Balsamathem und mit Blumenwangen,
> Mit leichtem Spiel theilt er der Wolken Grau,

Als wär kein Grab mehr in der Erdenau'—. (*Morgenblatt* 10 July 1821)

[Morning returns with pearls of dew,
With balsam breath and floral cheeks,
With ginger playfulness he divides the clouds' grey,
As if the earthy meadow contained graves no more.]

If the opening lines attested to her sheer poetic facility (turning "dewy morn" into "Perlenthau" and the repetitive "all incense" and "all bloom" to the alliterative "Balsamathem" and "Blumenwangen" with its subtle phonic shift from "Bal" to "Blu"), we can also see in the seventh stanza (stanza 104 of the original) the way she highlights the feminine in Byron's otherwise ungendered original:

Byron: 'Twas not for fiction chose Rousseau this spot,
                Peopling it with affections; but he found
                It was the scene which passion must allot
                To the mind's purified beings; 'twas the ground
                Where early Love his Psyche's zone unbound,
                And hallowed it with loveliness; 'tis lone,
                And wonderful, and deep, and hath a sound,
                And sense, and sight of sweetness.

Hohenhausen: Der Dichtkunst wegen, wählte wohl allein
                Einst Rousseau diese himmlischen Gefilde,
                Er fand: hier sey der Ort, wo Liebe rein
                Den Gürtel Psyche's löst im Glutverein,
                Wo lieblich blühen geistige Gebilde, –
                Wohl weht auch hier ein wonnesüßes Seyn,
                So wunderbar erhaben, doch voll Milde.

                [It was for poetry alone Rousseau once
                Likely chose these heavenly fields,
                He found: here is the spot, where pure Love
                Psyche's girdle unbinds in fervid union,
                Where lovely bloom such spiritual shapes, –
                Well wafts here too a blissfully sweet self,
                So wonderfully sublime, yet full of mildness.]

Psyche's "zone unbound" in Byron became in Hohenhausen "wo Liebe rein / den Gürtel Psyche's löst im Glutverein" ("where pure love / Psyche's girdle unbinds in fervid union"), a substitution of important and vivid proportions. Imagination as the object of literature was given a distinctly female body, and the horizontal and vertical expansions implied in "zone unbound" are transformed instead into an erotic undressing, into an act of focalization, concentration, and penetration. In echoing Faust's imaginary encounter with Gretchen and the elaborate drama of unwrapping it enacted (lines 2678–2804), Hohenhausen's translation participated on one level in a larger turn-of-the-century hermeneutical discourse in which translation was understood as a crucial mode of interpretation and "uncovering" (Antonetti; Kittler 9). At the same time, Hohenhausen identified in her translation an altogether different "self" who occupied this space of sustained attention, not one marked by its sensuality and femininity (the undressed woman's body), but instead as *wonnesüß* ("blissfully sweet"), *erhaben* ("sublime"), and *voll Milde* ("full of mildness," but also "full of clemency"). It was both a site of contradiction (sweetness, sublimity, and charitable tenderness all at once), but more importantly a site of exchange captured in the final word, *Milde* ("mildness," but also "clemency"). In addition to the element of erotic discourse, Hohenhausen's translation highlighted the giving and reciprocity that seemed to motivate a particular way of thinking about the translator's relationship to her source text. In her attention to the notion of exchange, one could see Hohenhausen doing something similar with her translation of Byron as Dorothea Tieck had done with Shakespeare's sonnets, where translation itself was figured not as an act of falling away or secondariness, but importantly as a return, a giving back, a reply, and perhaps most interestingly, as a form of clemency or pardon for the original.

Hohenhausen's trials in the *Morgenblatt* were a key testing ground for her work as a translator and ultimately made possible her participation in the translated collected edition of Byron's works. Hohenhausen translated the entirety of volume eighteen, containing *Cain* and *Prophecy of Dante,* and volume nineteen, which contained a collection of shorter poems, including such important Byronic poems as "Prometheus" and "To Thyrza." It is to the eighteenth volume that I would like to turn as my final example, offering us a case where we can observe a woman's relationship not just to a single "work," but also to the media object of the "book" as well.

The eighteenth volume opens with an excerpt taken from Goethe's periodical, *Ueber Kunst und Alterthum* (*On Art and Antiquity*) in which he wrote a review of Byron's *Cain*. On one level, such a gesture worked to domesticate and contain Byron's challenging and, in terms of the larger literary market of its day, scandalous play. It placed the controlling voice of the canonical German poet as the frame through which readers could approach this increasingly canonical English poet. On the other hand, such a gesture only increased the polyphony surrounding this work. Not only did Goethe's judgment follow Byron's own dedication to another writer, Walter Scott, but Goethe's review was only written in response to his having read a review of a French translation of Byron's play in *Le Moniteur universel* ("[T]hus he once again spiritedly awakens our own reflection").[14] Furthermore, when the narrator who inserted Goethe's piece emphatically concluded, "So sagt Göthe" ("so says Goethe"), which I suspect might have been written by Hohenhausen, we are meant to see a certain amount of irony in this proclamation. Significantly, what Goethe has just said at the end of his piece, which belongs to one of the most cited judgments about Byron's play,[15] is in fact said to have been by someone else, named by Goethe as "an ingenious woman who is related to us in her high estimation of Byron,"[16] believed by scholars to be Goethe's daughter-in-law, Ottilie von Goethe, later editor of the multilingual journal *Chaos*.[17] In other words, the prefatory material that seemed to perform a stabilizing function contributed in fact to the increasing proliferation of "I's" that populated this volume and the growing distance between the reader and the source. Additionally, the words, "So sagt Göthe," refers instead to a *woman's* indirect mode of speech, and this was precisely how Hohenhausen assumed her own speaking position in the volume, although in reverse: instead of Ottilie being spoken for by Goethe, Hohenhausen was speaking for Byron. Whether speaking for or being spoken for, however, women in Hohenhausen's "book" only ever achieved an indirect presence in print.

I want to emphasize that the very three words that Goethe's daughter-in-law identified as so crucial to the history of world literature—Cain's last words, "But with me!"[18]—are rendered by Hohenhausen instead as two words (to remain metrically consistent) followed not by an exclamation point but a question mark: "Aber ich?" In place of the certainty of the final judgment we have a question, and it is importantly a question about the status of the "I." The emphasis shifted in Hohenhausen's translation from the damnation, and thus definition, of this "me" to its disintegration. Her organization of the codex, and the material it contained, was thus arranged to emphasize the multiplying and unraveling positions of speaking subjects that made translation conceptually possible. The book itself was thus arranged according to a poetics of translation.

* * *

In a letter to her friend Friedrich von Uechtritz on being a translator, Dorothea Tieck wrote, "I think translation is actually more of an activity for women than men, precisely because it wasn't bestowed upon us to produce something of our own [*etwas Eigenes hervor zubringen*]" (Sybel 157).[19] On the one hand, Tieck articulated a familiar and deeply engrained cliché about women writers' lack of inventiveness, which could be found in the correspondence of numerous other contemporaneous women. As Fanny Tarnow wrote to a friend, "I have no creative genius [*kein schaffendes Genie*], no new ideas, everything is just appropriated" (Wägenbauer 179).[20] But on the other hand, Tieck was also making a powerful argument about the nature of women's writing and its relationship to textual property. What women writers lacked, according to Tieck, was something of their own ("etwas Eigenes"), and by association, something they could own (*Eigentum* 'property'). In place of a poetics of genius (Tarnow's notion of the "schaffendes Genie") that depended on the exclusive ownership of one's language and work, what we find in the work of women translators and in the work of women writers is a far more dialogical poetics of interaction and exchange. And yet such "dialogue" had much more in common with Sophie Mereau's notion of "overhearing" than any Habermasian idea of equal exchange. There was always an incompleteness, a partiality to these exchanges, whether it was the deficiencies of what one could take in Mereau or the empowering, deforming appropriations of Hülle, who effaced the self-effacing Muse. Translations by women did not simply highlight what was lost or found, however, but were also seen as a form of amplification, whether it was the multiplication of the "I's" in Hohenhausen's volume of Byron or Tarnow's project of reproducing, and thus extending, feminist narratives like Sand's of the woman who says no.

These are just a few of the examples of the way translation intersected with the life and work of women at the turn of the nineteenth century. There is of course still much that we do not know. How many more women were active as translators, whether alongside their other writerly activities or as their sole means of production? We need much more reliable bibliographic details to begin to recover and record such activity. At the same time, there is also a tremendous amount of work to be done to recover the correspondence of women translators with publishers to gain a better understanding of their own agency in the translating process. How much were these selections the choices of women writers versus the choices of their publishers or other, very often male, intermediaries? Finally, we need more information on how women thought about translation, whether gleaned from the prefaces that often accompanied their translations, their diaries, or their correspondence with one another.

The value of such an undertaking, however, is that the work of women translators opens up for us a literary space that transcends the narrow confines of a single national and linguistic entity. Their work illustrates for us how texts themselves articulated the protocols to motivate their own continued circulation, how literature was and continues to be used and adapted to promote more international cultural configurations. Like Dorothea Tieck's choice of Cervantes's *Persiles and Sigismunda,* we can find numerous examples of translations by women that dealt with the very issues of translation and transnational identity. At the same time, studying translations is a way of internationalizing the study of national languages and literatures. It illustrates for us the limits and the constructedness of working in one single language. It forces us to be more attentive to the mobility of texts, a mobility that is only increasing today with the accelerating expansion of communications technologies. Finally, studying translations also allows us as literary historians to construct more interesting histories with far more complex synchronic and diachronic grids. Through a synchronic account of German women writers around 1800, one also encounters a group of writers who pass through the temporal and spatial points of Homer, Boccaccio, Shakespeare, Cervantes, Lafayette, Balzac, and George Sand—a far more accurate representation, in my view, of how individuals were reading and thinking about writing at the turn of the nineteenth century.

Notes

I would like to thank Anna Sigg and Olivia Landry for their assistance in researching this article.

[1] All translations from the German are my own unless otherwise noted. Brentano's text reads in the German: "Das Romantische selbst ist eine Übersetzung."

[2] Ezell writes: "We still need histories of authors and readers, often women, who resided away from the centers of publishing and technology of 'modern' authors. In short, we still need studies that are not focused on the 'advanced' or modern concept of authorship during this period of transition but instead on all the varied aspects of the material culture of literature" (11–12).

[3] See Apter for a discussion of translation as the foundation for a "new comparative literature."

[4] For the sake of clarity, all works of translation cited in this essay are listed separately below and not in the body of the article.

[5] "Fanny Tarnow übersetzt besser."

[6] "Das deutsche Publikum braucht sich nicht nach dem Original zu sehnen; das Beste davon reicht ihm die Nachbilderin, die gewißlich auch an Styl dem Briten überlegen ist; denn wie viele Schriftsteller des In- und Auslands dürfen sich an Gediegenheit der Schreibart wohl mit Fanny Tarnow vergleichen?"

[7] "Diese Gründe haben mich bewogen, das Werk in's Deutsche zu übersetzen. Ich habe mich nicht ängstlich an den Styl und die Sprache gebunden, vielmehr mich bemühet, die allzu wortreichen Erzählungen abzukürzen, wie der Gärtner mit seiner Schere die allzu üppigen Auswüchse der Rankengewächse verschneidet, und hoffe, daß die Freunde meiner Arbeiten auch die gegenwärtige für eine zu ihrer Unterhaltung nicht überflüssige Bemühung halten werden."

[8] For a self-description of Tieck's reading list, see her correspondence with the writer Friedrich von Uechtritz (Sybel).

[9] "Wir Frauen sind in einem besonderen Zustande. Die Maximen der Männer hören wir immerfort wiederholen, ja wir müssen sie in goldnen Buchstaben über unsern Häupten sehen, und doch wüßten wir Mädchen im stillen das Umgekehrte zu sagen das auch gölte, wie es gerade hier der Fall ist" ("We women are in a unique position. We persistently hear the maxims of men repeated, indeed we have to see them above our heads in golden letters, and yet we young women knew to say them to ourselves in reverse, which also proved to be true, as is the case here"; Goethe, *Wanderjahre* 326).

[10] As Margreta de Grazia has demonstrated in her work on the history of editing Shakespeare, the sonnets persistently occupied a troubled position within Shakespearean editions and criticism well into the twentieth century.

[11] "Wie? die von uns so gefeierte Mad. Mereau—schreibt jetzt Spanische Novellen, schreibt Sonetts, Burlesken? auch sie neigt sich zu der gehässigen Schule?—Sie muß gleich herunter!"

[12] In Plato's *Phaedrus* we read: "When it has once been written down, every discourse rolls about everywhere, reaching indiscriminately those with understanding no less than those who have no business with it, and it doesn't know to whom it should speak and to whom it should not" (81).

[13] For a discussion of Scott's translations from the 1820s, see Ebert.

[14] "[S]o weckt er unsere eigene Betrachtung wieder lebhaft auf" (*Kunst* 53).

[15] Goethe's review reads, "Alles was religios [sic] und sittlich in der Welt gesagt werden könne, sey in den drey letzten Worten des Stücks

enthalten" ("Everything religious and ethical in the world that can be spoken is contained in those last three words of the play"; 56).

[16] "eine geistreiche, in Hochschätzung Byrons mit uns verwandte Freundin" (*Kunst* 56).

[17] Discussed in Goethe, *Ueber Kunst und Alterthum* 991.

[18] The entire metrical unit reads: "*Cain*: O Abel! *Adah*: Peace be with him! *Cain*: But with me!—" (Byron 938).

[19] "Ich glaube, das Uebersetzen ist eigentlich mehr ein Geschäft für Frauen als für Männer, gerade weil es uns nicht gegeben ist, etwas Eigenes hervor zubringen."

[20] "Ich habe kein schaffendes Genie, keine neue Ideen, es ist alles nur angeeignet."

Works Cited

Translations

[Gersdorf, Wilhelmine von]. *Redwood: Ein amerikanischer Roman von Cooper*. Wien: Kaulfuß und Krammer, 1825.

Hohenhausen, Elise von. "Lord Byron's Abschied vom Vaterlande." *Morgenblatt für gebildete Stände* 98 (24. Apr. 1820).

Hohenhausen, Elise von. "Der Morgen am Genfersee." *Morgenblatt für gebildete Stände* 164 (10. July 1821).

Hohenhausen, Elise von. *Cain: Ein Mysterium. Lord Byron's Poesien aus dem Englischen. Uebersetzt von Elise von Hohenhausen. Achtzehntes Bändchen*. Zwickau: Schumann, 1825.

[Huber, Therese]. *Emilie von Varmont: Eine Geschichte in Briefen von Herrn Louvet. Nebst einem Anhang aus dem Französischen übersetzt und mit einer Vorrede begleitet vom Verfasser des heimlichen Gerichts*. n.l., 1794.

Hülle, Hedwig. *Irrfahrten des Odysseus in vier und zwanzig Gesängen: Freie Nachbildung in gereimten Strophen nach Homer von Hedwig Hülle, geborne Hoffmeier*. Bremen: n.p., 1826.

Mereau, Sophie, ed. *Spanische und italienische Novellen*. Vol. 1. Leipzig: Dreililien Verlag, n.d.

[Mereau, Sophie]. *Die Prinzessin von Clèves: Frei nach dem Französischen bearbeitet. Romanen=Kalender für das Jahr 1799*. Göttingen: Dieterich, 1799.

Mereau, Sophie. *Fiametta: Aus dem Italienischen des Boccaccio übersetzt von Sophie Brentano*. Berlin: Realschulbuchhandlung, 1806.

[Mereau, Sophie]. "Nathan." *Die Horen* 7.9 (1796). Ed. Rolf Michaelis. Weimar: Böhlaus, 2000. 85–94.
[Schlegel, Dorothea]. *Corinna, oder Italien: Aus dem Französischen der Frau von Staël, übers. und hrsg. von Friedrich Schlegel*. Berlin: Unger, 1807.
Schubart, Henriette. *Schottische Lieder und Balladen von Walter Scott: Uebersetzt von Henriette Schubart*. Leipzig: Brockhaus, 1817.
Tarnow, Fanny. *Eugenie: Ein Genre=Bild. Nach Balzac von Fanny Tarnow*. Leipzig: Kollmann, 1835.
Tarnow, Fanny. *Indiana von George Sand: Uebersetzt von Fanny Tarnow*. Leipzig: Kollmann, 1836.
[Tieck, Dorothea]. "Shakespeares Sonette." *Penelope: Taschenbuch für das Jahr 1826*. Ed. Theodor Hell. Leipzig: J.C. Hinrich, 1826.
[Tieck, Dorothea]. *Die Leiden des Persiles und der Sigismunda von Miguel de Cervantes Saavedra: Aus dem Spanischen übersetzt. Mit einer Einleitung vom Ludwig Tieck*. Leipzig: Brockhaus, 1837.
[Tieck, Dorothea]. *Shakespeares Sonette in der Übersetzung Dorothea Tiecks*. Ed. Christa Jansohn. Tübingen: Francke, 1992.

Secondary

Apel, Friedmar. *Sprachbewegung: Eine historisch-poetologische Untersuchung zum Problem des Übersetzens*. Heidelberg: Winter, 1982.
Apter, Emily. *The Translation Zone: A New Comparative Literature*. Princeton: Princeton UP, 2006.
Arac, Jonathan. "The Impact of Shakespeare." *The Cambridge History of Literary Criticism*. Vol. 5. Ed. Marshall Brown. Cambridge: Cambridge UP, 2000. 272–96.
Blätter für literarische Unterhaltung 1.71 (12. Mar. 1842).
Blätter für literarische Unterhaltung 2.14 (17. July 1826).
Brentano, Clemens. *Godwi*. Stuttgart: Reclam, 1995.
Brisset, Annie. "Alterity in Translation: An Overview of Theories and Practices." *Translation Translation*. Ed. Susan Petrilli. Amsterdam: Rodopi, 2003. 101–32.
Byron, George Gordon. *The Major Works*. Ed. Jerome McGann. Oxford: Oxford's World Classics, 2000.
Cardwell, Richard. *Reception of Byron in Europe*. London: Continuum, 2005. 2 vols.
Cervantes, Miguel de. *Los trabajos de Persiles y Sigismunda*. Ed. Carlos Romero Muñoz. Madrid: Cátedra, 1997.

Cervantes, Miguel de. *The Trials of Persiles and Sigismunda*. Trans. Celia Richmond Weller and Clark A. Colahan. Berkeley: California UP, 1989.

Chamberlain, Lori. "Gender and the Metaphorics of Translation." *The Translation Studies Reader*. Ed. Lawrence Venuti. New York: Routledge, 2000. 314–30.

Curran, Stuart. "The Sonnet." *Poetic Form and British Romanticism*. Oxford: Oxford UP, 1986. 29–55.

Damrosch, David. *What Is World Literature?* Princeton: Princeton UP, 2003.

Ebert, Friedrich. "Walter Scott und seine deutsche Übersetzer." *Überlieferungen zur Geschichte, Litteratur und Kunst der Vor- und Mitwelt*. Vol. 2.1. Dresden, 1826. 161–200.

Ezell, Margaret J.M. *Social Authorship and the Advent of Print*. Baltimore: Johns Hopkins UP, 1999.

Flotow, Luise von. "Feminist Translation: Contexts, Practices, and Theories." *TTR: Traduction, Terminologie, Rédaction* 4.2 (1991): 69–84.

Flotow, Luise von. *Translation and Gender: Translating in the Era of Feminism*. Ottawa: Ottawa UP, 1997.

Der Freimüthige 118 (14 Jun. 1804).

Gallagher, Catherine. *Nobody's Story: The Vanishing Acts of Women Writers in the Marketplace 1670–1820*. Berkeley: California UP, 1994.

Godard, Barbara. "Theorizing Feminist Discourse/Translation." *Translation, History and Culture*. Ed. Susan Bassnett and André Lefevere. London: Pinter, 1990. 87–96.

Goethe, J.W. "Cain: A Mystery by Lord Byron." *Ueber Kunst und Alterthum*. Vol. 5. No. 1. *Sämtliche Werke*. Vol. 22. Ed. Anne Bohnenkamp. Frankfurt a.M.: Deutscher Klassiker Verlag, 1999. 40 vols. 52–56.

Goethe, J.W. *Die Leiden des jungen Werthers*. *Sämtliche Werke*. Vol. 8. Ed. Waltraud Wiethölter. Frankfurt a.M.: Deutscher Klassiker Verlag, 1994. 40 vols.

Goethe, J.W. *Wilhelm Meisters Wanderjahre*. *Sämtliche Werke*. Vol. 10. Ed. Gerhard Neumann und Hans-Georg Dewitz. Frankfurt a.M.: Deutscher Klassiker Verlag, 1989. 40 vols.

Grazia, Margreta de. *Shakespeare Verbatim: The Reproduction of Authenticity and the 1790 Apparatus*. Oxford: Clarendon P, 1991.

Habicht, Werner. "The Romanticism of the Schlegel-Tieck Shakespeare and the History of Nineteenth-Century German Shakespeare Translations." *European Shakespeares: Translating Shakespeare in the Romantic Age*. Ed. Dirk Delabastita and Lieven D'Hulst. Philadelphia: J. Benjamins, 1993. 45–54.

Hahn, Barbara. *Unter falschem Namen: Von der schwierigen Autorschaft der Frauen.* Frankfurt a.M.: Suhrkamp, 1991.

Hannemann, Britta. *Weltliteratur für Bürgertöchter: Die Übersetzerin Sophie Mereau-Brentano.* Göttingen: Wallstein, 2005.

Hook-Demarle, Marie-Claire. "Reading and Writing in Germany." *A History of Women in the West.* Vol. 4. Ed. Geneviève Fraisse and Michelle Perrot. Cambridge: Belknap, 1993. 145–65.

Huyssen, Andreas. *Die frühromantische Konzeption von Übersetzung und Aneignung.* Zürich: Atlantis, 1969.

Kemp, Friedhelm. *Das europäische Sonett.* München: Wallstein, 2002. 2 vols.

Kittler, Friedrich. *Discourse Networks 1800/1900.* Trans. Michael Metteer with Chris Cullens. Stanford: Stanford UP, 1990.

Klopstock, F.G. "Vom deutschen Hexameter." *Gedanken über die Natur der Poesie: Dichtungstheoretische Schriften.* Ed. Winnfried Menninghaus. Frankfurt a.M.: Insel, 1989. 60–156.

Kord, Susanne. *Sich einen Namen machen: Anonymität und weibliche Autorschaft 1700–1900.* Stuttgart: Metzler, 1996.

Levine, Suzanne Jill. *The Subversive Scribe: Translating Latin American Fiction.* Minneapolis: Greywolf, 1991.

Lotbinière-Harwood, Suzanne de. *The Body Bilingual: Translation as Rewriting in the Feminine.* Toronto: Toronto UP, 1991.

Messner, Sabine u. Michaela Wolf. *Mittlerin zwischen den Kulturen—Mittlerin zwischen den Geschlechtern? Studie zu Theorie und Praxis feministischer Übersetzung.* Graz: Institut für Translationswissenschaft, 2000.

Messner, Sabine u. Michaela Wolf, ed. *Übersetzung aus aller Frauen Länder: Beiträge zu Theorie und Praxis weiblicher Realität in der Translation.* Graz: Leykam, 2001.

Mole, Tom. *Byron's Romantic Celebrity: Industrial Culture and the Hermeneutic of Intimacy.* Basingstoke: Palgrave, forthcoming.

Mönch, Walter. *Das Sonett.* Heidelberg: Kerle, 1955.

Nicoletti, Antonella. *Übersetzung als Auslegung in Goethes West-östlichem Divan.* Tübingen: Francke, 2002.

Piper, Andrew. "Rethinking the Print Object: Goethe and the Book of Everything." *PMLA* 121.1 (Jan. 2006): 124–38.

Plato. *Phaedrus.* Trans. Alexander Nehamas and Paul Woodruff. Indianapolis: Hackett, 1995.

Purdy, Daniel. "Sophie Mereau's Authorial Masquerades and the Subversion of Romantic Poesie." *Women in German Yearbook 13.* Ed. Patricia Herminghouse and Sara Friedrichsmeyer. Lincoln: Nebraska UP, 1998. 29–48.

Sand, George. *Indiana*. Ed. Pierre Salomon. Paris: Garnier-Frères, 1962.

Schwarz, Gisela. *Literarisches Leben und Sozialstrukturen um 1800: Zur Situation von Schriftstellerinnen am Beispiel von Sophie Mereau-Brentano, geb. Schubart*. Frankfurt: Lang, 1991.

Simon, Sherry. *Gender in Translation: Cultural Identity and the Politics of Transmission*. London: Routledge, 1996.

Sybel, Heinrich von, ed. *Erinnerungen an Friedrich von Uechtritz und seine Zeit in Briefen von ihm und an ihn*. Leipzig: Hirzel, 1884.

Tgahrt, Reinhard. *Weltliteratur: Die Lust am Übersetzen im Jahrhundert Goethes*. Marbach: Deutsche Schillergesellschaft, 1982.

Voß, J.H. *Homers Odüßee übersetzt von Johann Heinrich Voß*. Hamburg, auf Kosten des Verfassers, 1781. Reprint 1881.

Wägenbauer, Birgit. "Die Vermarktung der Gefühle: Fanny Tarnow (1779–1862)." *Beruf: Schriftstellerin. Schreibende Frauen im 18. und 19. Jahrhundert*. Ed. Karin Tebben. Göttingen: Vandenhoeck u. Ruprecht, 1998. 160–89.

"Weil ich der raschen Lippe Herr nicht bin": Oral Transgression as Enlightenment Disavowal in Kleist's *Penthesilea*

Heather Merle Benbow

Kleist's *Penthesilea* so shocked contemporary readers that the writer insisted: "She really did eat him, Achilles, out of love." Indeed, the oral aspect of Penthesilea's destruction of Achilles is sometimes overlooked, an omission this article seeks to address. I argue that by radically conflating oral appetites, the figure of Penthesilea disavows Englightenment culture in three respects: the ideal of feminine modesty; aesthetic values that posited woman as an object of appreciation rather than an agent of aesthetic taste; and the Enlightenment's social contract, which subordinated bodily appetites to the interests of the community. (HMB)

> *Complicated taboos and prohibitions surround the sensual pleasures of the mouth. In fact, the mouth appears to be the organ where the tightest controls are placed on women's behaviour, where women's sensual life is most closely policed.*
> —Rosalind Coward (118)

Scholars have often interpreted the late-eighteenth-century domesticated ideal of femininity as a reaction to the Enlightenment's discourse of emancipation and its perceived threat to the patriarchal order (Bovenschen; Stephan; Duden "Eigentum"). As feudal power structures were contested and rearranged, women invoked notions of freedom and equality and demanded the same rights as bourgeois men. The image of the dutiful bourgeois wife and mother was subsequently mustered, particularly in late-eighteenth-century and early-nineteenth-century literature, in defense of gender hierarchy. Such sources reasserted the "natural" subordination of women to men in spite of lofty Enlightenment and revolutionary ideals. Oral modesty provided a key aspect of this reasserted feminine ideal. Heroines of Enlightenment literature and conduct books used the organ associated with speech, consumption, and sexual desire sparingly. Where man spoke publicly, woman avoided the glare of a public profile; where he freely indulged a hearty appetite, she had a dainty appetite; where he acknowledged his sexual appetites, she moderated hers. Heinrich von Kleist's Amazon queen, Penthesilea, provides a shocking example of female oral excess that breaches oral taboos in a public spectacle of cannibalism.

Contemporary scholarship often reads *Penthesilea* as a critique of the Enlightenment's sublimation of female sexuality (Rigby; Schindler), its disembodied aesthetics (Chaouli), or the way in which it allowed for the rationalist nation state's denial of embodiment and emotion (Kluger). Some scholars regard the figure of Penthesilea as "transgressive" or taboo-breaking (Brandsteller; Rigby; Wilson; Kluger). Most of these critiques of the play address the difficulty of reconciling rationalist principles with female embodiment, for Penthesilea subverts an abstract Enlightenment rationality by indulging her physical inclinations. The Amazonian practice of amputating the right breast usually receives explicit critical attention, but not the equally important oral aspect of Penthesilea's corporeality. It is, after all, the mouth that is the site and the tool of Penthesilea's transgression. The play's impact upon audiences and scholarship would surely not have been so great without the taboo of feminine orality.

In this article I will reflect on Penthesilea's rampant orality, most blatant in her amorous consumption of Achilles, and how it disavows Enlightenment values. Penthesilea's oral excess amounts to a repudiation of the feminine ideal of Kleist's day. She represents the flip side of the Enlightenment's purification of the feminine, particularly in the figure of the obliging wife, graceful housewife, and selfless mother. Not only does the appetitive Amazon queen indulge her oral functions by conflating kisses with bites, thereby problematically linking feminine sexuality with the oral, she also challenges the Enlightenment's view of woman as the object of aesthetic appreciation, not the agent of aesthetic taste. Moreover, Penthesilea's oral transgression symbolically renounces Enlightenment values more generally. Her "dogged" pursuit of her love object (and canine epithets are everywhere in *Penthesilea*) via oral appetites represents the very antithesis of reason in the eyes of her sister Amazons and the Greeks. By indulging her oral desires, Penthesilea departs from reason and disavows the Enlightenment's social contract, which subordinates sexuality and other appetites to the interests of the community.

"Desires [...] like an unleashed pack of hounds"

Penthesilea's appetite dominates the teichoscopic descriptions of her by both Amazons and Greeks. Penthesilea's urgent longing for Achilles robs her of her capacity for reason. She pursues him on the battlefield "as if on fire with wanting" and "as if bereft of judgment" (15).[1] Penthesilea appears as a dog, a wolf, and a hyena, animals seemingly with no function but the fulfilment of their appetites: "A raving beast she is, a mad hyena!" (16). Portraying woman's sexual appetites in canine terms conflates sexual and gastronomic appetitivity; Penthesilea's sexual pursuit of Achilles resembles that of a predator on the hunt: "No grim-eyed she-wolf can select her prey / And track it down, not with such hunger-heat / Through forests decked with snow, as does this maid / Pursue Achilles through our serried ranks" (10).

Penthesilea and her seemingly irrational appetites—"ravenous and wild for prey" (128)—stand in stark opposition to the conventional femininity of Kleist's day. Thomas Laqueur links the gender conservatism of the late eighteenth century to a distinct shift in the understanding of the female body, which was robbed of its previously limitless capacity for desire: "Women, whose desire knew no bounds in the old scheme of things, and whose reason offered so little resistance to passion, became in some accounts creatures whose whole reproductive life might be spent anesthetized to the pleasures of the flesh" (3). This new sexual modesty was but one aspect of a broader development that associated femininity with a lack of overt oral desire. Sexual, gastronomic, and intellectual appetite are all linked via their association with the mouth. Semantically, the connections are clear in terms such as *Muttermund* (literally "mother's mouth") to describe the vagina, in the notion of "hunger" for knowledge, and in the eighteenth-century concern that women "devoured" too much lowbrow literature.[2]

Modesty in all areas was a centerpiece of late-eighteenth-century bourgeois femininity. One pedagogue, Joachim Heinrich Campe, (1746–1818) dubbed modesty "the crown of the female character" (179, trans. mine). This crowning feminine virtue dictated not only sexual, but also appetitive restraint. For Jean-Jacques Rousseau (1712–78), "feminine tastes" were synonymous with eating "sparingly" (358). Intellectual and social modesty also dictated women's reluctance to make a spectacle of themselves in the public sphere. Significantly, Kant characterized Enlightenment itself in oral terms as speaking in one's "own person" ("Enlightenment" 57). Eighteenth-century men of letters railed against women such as Emilie du Châtelet (1706–49) and Anne Dacier (1654–1720), who offended feminine modesty by engaging in masculine scholarly pursuits. Thus the doctrine of feminine modesty, exemplified by an orally passive biology, justified the exclusion of women from the Enlightenment's emancipatory opportunities in the public sphere (Laqueur 152).

This exclusion, though, belied persistent anxieties that an archaic feminine voraciousness might re-emerge and disrupt this late-Enlightenment doctrine of feminine modesty. Prior to the Enlightenment, female physiology conjured excessive appetite and malevolent powers. The female body, especially its "voracious openings," mouth and vagina (Duden, *Woman* 166), were then seen as demonic, threatening, and powerful.[3] Illuminating the dark recesses of the female body with the light of reason did not entirely eradicate its demonic power.[4]

Critics have long recognized Penthesilea's sexual transgression, noting that, as the Other to reason, woman can only be included in the Enlightenment project in a sublimated and purified form.[5] Criticism has also focused on the play's problematization of speech, regarding Penthesilea's conflation of "kisses" and "bites" (*Küsse* and *Bisse*) as a "short circuiting" of violence and sexuality (Schindler 194) or as a failure of rational communication (Mehigan 15–17). Certainly this focus on the political, communicative, and sexual implications of Penthesilea's "confusion" of word and deed is justified. But I wish here to consider orality more broadly as a territory that disavows late-Enlightenment values, for Penthesilea's grotesque conflation of oral appetites makes her transgression more than the sum of its parts. Since late-Enlightenment culture denies feminine sexuality and its oral connotations, the play conceives Penthesilea's capitulation to sexual desire in oral terms.

The widespread mythology of the *vagina dentata* also conflates women's oral and sexual appetites, and this is evident in early-nineteenth-century Germany. Carl Gustav Carus (1789–1869), portrayed nymphomania as an affront to the idea of feminine modesty. In his *Lehrbuch der Gynäkologie* of 1820 he describes it as "Nymphomania, Andromania, Furor uterinus" ("Mutterwuth, Manntollheit"; 216, trans. mine). It is, he notes in a tone redolent of both pity and horror:

> A sad disease which scorns the morality and modesty of female nature and, for this reason, presents a most adverse impression, and which reveals itself in an excessively erupting drive for sexual lust that almost or completely overpowers reason and conscience. (216–17, trans. mine)

This condition undermines a feminine sexual modesty based on "morality and modesty," and reveals sensuality conquering reason. Orality's central importance in this sensory mutiny manifests itself in the onset of the illness, characterized by "Lecherousness (Salacitas) where [...] the body outwardly reveals an excited sensuality (the flushed face, the bleary eyes, the deeply reddened opened lips and so forth)" (217). The "excited sensuality" of Carus's nymphomaniac recalls Penthesilea on the hunt for Achilles, "Her lips all flecked with foam" (124), making a meal of the space between them: "She sucks into herself the hindering air!" (20). Carus's description brings together gastronomic and sexual desires when he notes that the "[c]onsumption of high-nutrient and at the same time heat-generating food and drink [...] cause congestion in the sexual organs" (220). Thus, given a taste of "heating" food (associated with sexual pleasure), the woman may demand the object of her appetite in excess, or perhaps, as Penthesilea does, cannibalistically conflate the objects of her appetites.

When criticism of *Penthesilea* focuses on communication, sexuality, violence, and an Enlightenment critique, the fundamentally oral nature of Penthesilea's transgression recedes into the background. Some critics even delicately circumvent the issue, for example, referring to Penthesilea's cannibalistic act merely as "tearing at Achilles's flesh" (Bridgham 68). Yet Penthesilea confuses not only generic violence with sexuality, or speech with sexuality, but also gastronomic hunger, that other taboo feminine appetite. Penthesilea's capitulation to grotesque and excessive appetites represents her estrangement from her kind:

She's in a frenzy now among her dogs,
Her lips all flecked with foam, calling them sisters (124).

And throws—throws herself on him, oh Diana!
With the whole pack, and pulling at his crest,
For all the world a dog with other dogs
[...]
Into his ivory breast she sinks her teeth.
She and her savage dogs in competition,
Oxus and Sphinx chewing into his right breast,
And she into his left [...]. (127-28)

During this cannibalistic act, Achilles comments on Penthesilea's deadly confusion of appetites. Recalling the orgy that Penthesilea had promised him, he asks, "Penthesilea! My bride! What are you doing? / Is this the rosy feast you promised me?" (127-28). Reflecting on her devouring of Achilles immediately afterward, Penthesilea echoes his ironic questioning: "Did I kiss him to death?" (145). As the extent of her act dawns on her, Penthesilea initially views it as a mere rhetorical mistake. Addressing Achilles's corpse, she asserts:

> By Artemis, my tongue pronounced one word
> For sheer unbridled haste to say another;
> But now I'll tell you clearly what I meant:
> This, my beloved, just this, and nothing else.
> [She kisses him.]
> [...]
> So it was a mistake. A kiss, a bite,
> The two should rhyme, for one who truly loves
> With all her heart can easily mistake them.[6] (145)

It is, of course, not merely the rhyme in German between *Küsse* and *Bisse* that misleads Penthesilea, causing her "mistake," but also the convergence of appetitive taboos upon the mouth. Strong associations of the oral with both eating and sexuality have survived even the eighteenth-century purification of femininity: "Terms of endearment frequently refer to food: honey, sweetheart, peach, sugarplum [...]. Do we detect a note of cannibalism here? Certainly. Something about the sensations of sexual familiarity seems to evoke memories of food" (Coward 87). This association figures centrally in Penthesilea's confusion of word and deed: "And with this mouth, these lips that swell with love— / Oh made for such a different service than—!" (144).

The Amazons' horror at Penthesilea's oral indulgence prompts them to contrast Penthesilea as canine with the virtuous picture of womanhood they recall: "So fine a maiden, Hermia! So modest! / So deft at every art and handicraft! / So lovely when she danced, and when she sang! / So good a mind! Such dignity and grace!"[7] (128). This portrayal teems with Enlightenment connotations of female virtue: modesty, accomplishment in the feminine arts, physical beauty, dignity, and grace.[8] What Penthesilea repudiates through oral desires becomes explicitly clear. Carus's anxious pathologizing of female sexuality and the oral body becomes for Kleist the destruction of virtuous femininity.

Kleist's contemporaries may have shared the horror of the Amazons in witnessing this destruction. The author himself, and modern feminist readers, surely do not. Kleist seemingly gleefully emphasizes the extent of Penthesilea's act: "She really did eat him, Achilles, out of love. Do not be shocked, it is quite readable" (qtd. in Sembdner, *Sämtliche Werke* 796, trans. mine). He also has his heroine suggest that the act is not so absurd as his contemporaries would believe, for sexual and gastronomic desire share common bodily and metaphorical ground:

> How many a maid will say, her arms wrapped around
> Her lover's neck: I love you, oh so much
> That if I could, I'd eat you up right here;
> And later, taken by her word, the fool!

[...]
You see, my love, that was never my way.
Look: When *my* arms were wrapped around your neck,
I did what I had spoken, word for word;
I was not quite so mad as it might seem. (*Penthesilea* 145–46; emphasis in original)

Indeed, despite the Amazons' and Greeks' uncomprehending condemnation, Penthesilea is far from "mad" when she links gastronomics and sexuality, for the two are repeatedly linked in the gender paradigm explored here. Penthesilea provides an uncomfortable reminder of the female body as the abode of powerful and threatening forces, a body which "like an oven, could bring forth and take life" (Duden, *Woman* 8). Penthesilea reanimates a pre-Enlightenment notion of unrestrained female appetites when she eats Achilles, apparently out of a lack of oral restraint: "my tongue pronounced one word / For sheer unbridled haste to say another" (145). ("Weil ich der raschen Lippe Herr nicht bin"; *Penthesilea* 426.)

"The burning wish to possess him"

Reactions to *Penthesilea* in Kleist's lifetime were notoriously damning. His Amazon queen, this "breastless Penthesilea" (qtd. in Sembdner, *Lebensspuren* 179, trans. mine), was condemned as "a monster" (qtd. in Günzel 268, trans. mine). The contemporary reception of the play makes it difficult to disentangle judgments made on aesthetic and social grounds. Contemporary critics of Kleist wrote of their struggle with his indigestible prose and their own feelings of nausea, disgust, and shock (Sembdner, *Lebensspuren* 233–36). Kleist's contemporaries were thus so shocked by the play that they were themselves unable to separate their aesthetic critique from their disquiet at Penthesilea's transgression of gender norms. With its "unnatural images" (qtd. in Sembdner, *Lebensspuren* 234, trans. mine) the play represents an unacceptable departure from idealized portrayals of the feminine: "Women [...] one can hardly call them."[9]

These contemporary responses to the play suggest that *Penthesilea* challenges not only the gender norms of Kleist's day, but also prevailing aesthetic standards.[10] The play subverts an aesthetic consensus that emerged, not coincidentally, in the context of the social upheaval of the Enlightenment, just as gender norms were being reasserted (Klinger 193). The emergent binary aesthetic system converged on two always already gendered categories: the beautiful and the sublime. Aesthetic theory figured in the late-eighteenth-century normalization of gender inequality, with its distrust of feminine appetites of various kinds.

In his essay "Observations on the Feeling of the Beautiful and the Sublime" Kant affirmed gendered aesthetics with the appellation "the fair sex" ("das schöne Geschlecht"; 78). Here he describes how all aspects of woman—her appearance, her virtues, her understanding, even her faults—give effortless expression to the feeling of the beautiful.[11] In a section entitled "Of the Distinction of the Beautiful and Sublime in the Interrelations of the Two Sexes," Kant offers his views on the controversial theme of women's education, linking his analysis to Rousseau's dismissive treatment of girls' education in *Émile* (Klinger 194). Kant thus cleverly subsumes a salvo against women's emancipatory striving into his purportedly natural aesthetic categories. In this notorious attack on the scholarly women of the eighteenth century, Kant describes the female scholar as an "Amazon" (*Observations* 94).[12] Kant backs this insult by joining aesthetic standards with natural gender: "whatever one does contrary to nature's will, one always does very poorly" (*Observations* 95). No wonder Kleist's *Penthesilea* failed to delight Kleist's contemporaries, the heirs to aesthetic standards built on a bedrock of gender hierarchy.

Penthesilea clearly exceeds the feminine role as the beautiful object of masculine appreciation. In making Achilles the object of her aesthetic, sexual, and gastronomic appreciation, she subverts the gender hierarchy inherent in eighteenth-century aesthetics. When Penthesilea, "like a hunter" (127), seeks Achilles, her "prey" (10), the Greek hero recalls more Burkean weakness and feminine beauty than the masculine sublime:

> But now [...]
> He stops, and turns his slender neck, and listens,
> And bolts in terror, stops, and bolts again:
> Almost like a young deer that, from afar,
> Hears the grim lion's roar among the cliffs.
> He cries: Odysseus! With constricted voice,
> And shyly turns his head, cries: Diomede!
> And wants to flee and still rejoin his friends [...]. (126–27)

While the play portrays Achilles in uncommonly tender terms, its descriptions of Penthesilea lack anything that might serve the feminizing discourses of beauty from Kant or Burke. Instead, Penthesilea's abhorrent actions, her irrational desires, and her proximity to her hounds characterize her throughout.

Penthesilea subverts the beautiful nature of her sex and casts off the eighteenth-century's idealizing aesthetic discourses like a halo. Goethe, the creator of Ottilie, one of German literature's more modest and orally passive heroines,[13] finds Penthesilea's challenge to the security of aesthetic and gender binaries particularly challenging: "She is of such wondrous kind [*Geschlecht*] and moves in such a foreign realm that I require time in order to understand" (qtd. in Sembdner, *Lebensspuren* 180, trans. mine). Contemporary reviews of the play bristle with the epithet "disgust" (*Ekel*) and foreground Kleist's abandonment of classical aesthetic standards:[14]

> According to the theory of the aesthetics of antiquity, tragedy stimulates fear and compassion; their place here is occupied by shock, abhorrence, and disgust. (qtd. in Sembdner, *Lebensspuren* 234, trans. mine)

> He insults taste and upsets delicate feeling [...]. Anything disgusting must never become an object of the fine arts. (qtd. in Sembdner, *Lebensspuren* 236, trans. mine)

Penthesilea's double transgression of both aesthetic and gender norms evokes disgust, the sentiment touted in the eighteenth century as the very antithesis of both aesthetic beauty and idealized femininity. For Kant, disgust radically departs from the Enlightenment ideal of "the fair sex": "Nothing is so much set against the beautiful as disgust [...]. On this account no insult can be more painful [...] to a woman than being called *disgusting*" (*Observations* 83; emphasis in original).

Winfried Menninghaus has theorized disgust as complementary to discourses on love, desire, and appetite as "forms of intercourse with a nearness that is wanted" (1). Penthesilea exploits the porous boundaries between these forms of closeness in her confusion of kisses and bites, in the process moving away from femininity and love into an area beyond the gender dichotomies intended to contain women. According to Menninghaus, the eighteenth century celebrates "the codification of the aesthetic body as free from everything potentially disgusting" (15).[15] It is hard to imagine a more vigorous repudiation of this ideal than the foam-lipped Penthesilea dining on her lover. After attaining the object of her lust, Penthesilea consumes Achilles, collapsing the very concept of distance that underpins aesthetic appreciation.[16] Menninghaus points out that distance is crucial to the exercise of aesthetic judgment. By contrast, the experience of disgust, apparent in the visceral contemporary responses to Kleist's drama, requires proximity: "Disgust figures primarily as an experience formed from the senses of contiguity or proximity: something tastes disgusting [...]; something feels disgusting

[...]; something smells disgusting [...]. What excites disgust must be nearby—indeed this proximity is an essential part of the feeling of disgust" (Menninghaus 39).[17] When Penthesilea observes Achilles from a distance, the language of physical hunger characterizes her admiration: "With every hoofbeat / She swallows, as if ravenous, one more piece / Of ground still separating her from him—" (20). Chaouli sees in these lines not only orality's contamination of aesthetic taste, but also the consumption of "the very concept of distance" inherent in the distinction between Kantian aesthetics and gastronomy (129).

Penthesilea displays a violent affinity with Kant's most "limited" bodily sense and an incapacity to maintain the distance required for aesthetic judgment. Kant's categorization and hierarchization of the five senses, from the "inner," "subjective" senses (taste, smell) to the "outer," "objective" senses (sight, hearing, touch), underscores the importance of distance in aesthetic judgment, and, as I shall now show, the ability to uphold this distance is subtly attributed to the male gender. Kant prefers the outer senses because they enable the subject to perceive objects as separate from the self (*Anthropology* 43). This hierarchy of degraded "inner" senses demonstrates a disdain for orality. Taste and her sister, smell, represent sensuality in a way that makes aesthetic judgment impossible. Because sight operates at the greatest distance from the object being perceived, it is considered the most precious sense.[18] Because touch requires physical proximity to the object, it is regarded by contrast as "limited." Kant subtly genders the gaze itself when he describes it as noble (*edel*): "The sense of sight, while not more indispensable than the sense of hearing, is, nevertheless, the noblest (*edelste*), since, among all the senses, it is farthest removed from the sense of touch, which is the most limited condition of perception" (*Anthropology* 43). In Kant's *Observations* essay, which subsumes all feminine attributes under the adjective "fair" (*schön*) he describes the male gender as "noble": "if it were not required of a noble disposition to decline honorific titles [...]" (*Observations* 76). Significantly, Kant uses the same adjective to describe male virtue as he does for sight, that sensory tool most crucial to aesthetic judgment. So while the feminine is always the object of aesthetic scrutiny, i.e., *schön,* the aesthetic gaze itself is characteristically masculine or *edel*. Penthesilea reverses this dichotomy when she usurps the masculine aesthetic gaze, but in a horrifyingly feminine way, incorporating it into her visceral appetites, craving proximity to the object of her admiration, and making Achilles into a fearful, slender-necked deer. Bewildered by Penthesilea's transgressive behavior, Goethe is said to have once quipped: "Women, even the most cultivated, have more appetite than taste" (qtd. in Riemer 247, trans. mine). His comment betrays an enduring sense of the feminine as irredeemably oral. In confirming Goethe's pessimism, Kleist's play opposes the aestheticization of femininity that seeks to redeem it from its oral appetites. As I will argue, though, it goes even further and uses Penthesilea's disavowal of Enlightenment femininity and aesthetics to challenge the Enlightenment's idea of reason as the basis for human society.

"A sovereign nation founded"[19]

Penthesilea's indulgence of her oral appetites sets her apart from and allows her to renounce the rational organization of Amazon society. The Greeks' horror at Penthesilea's actions is matched only by the Amazons, who appear in the play as a mirror image of Greek rationality. Attempts by the Amazons to bring Penthesilea to her senses prove useless: "But she seemed not to hear the voice of reason" (48). Most of the action in Kleist's tragedy takes the form of military battle, which ensures the continuation of Amazon society since they capture the men required for procreation. Penthesilea disrupts the entire undertaking when she prioritizes her sexual whim over the continuation of the Amazon nation. War is, of course, usually a masculine undertaking, and Kant associates it in aesthetic terms with the (masculine) sublime in his *Critique of Judgment*:

> Even war has something sublime about it if it is carried on in an orderly way and with respect for the sanctity of the citizens' rights. At the same time it makes the way of thinking of a people that carries it on in this way all the more sublime in proportion to the numbers of dangers in the face of which it courageously stays its ground. (*Judgment* 122)

Unlike the social fortitude that follows from orderly and respectful warring, extended periods of peace tend to degrade the moral character of the nation, reducing people to "base selfishness, cowardice, and softness" (122).[20] A warring posture provides an essential component of the masculine rectitude required to confront relations with women.[21] According to Rousseau, for the family to represent a "little fatherland" (326), women's abundant desires must be subdued. For stimulating one of the feminine oral appetites might provoke others. For example, to educate woman and appease her "hunger" for knowledge encourages sedition in the sexual sphere: "our clumsy systems of education have made women so deceitful, and have so over-stimulated their appetites, that you cannot rely even on the most clearly proved affection; they can no longer display a preference which secures you against fear of a [sexual] rival" (393–94).

When Kleist lets the Amazons loose on the battlefield, the ensuing chaos seems to feed off this notion of women as an unruly force. The Greeks and the Trojans engage in battle when the Amazons suddenly intervene, although they seem to be fighting for neither side. This inexplicable complication of battlefield binary relations causes consternation among the Greeks: "And now begins / A struggle, friends, such as had not been fought / Since Gaia loosed the Furies on this world" (8). Moments earlier locked in battle against each other, the Trojans and the Greeks now unite to oppose the Amazons:

> A Trojan hides, hard-pressed by Amazons,
> Behind a Grecian shield, the Greek defends
> The Trojan from a girl, it seems as if
> Argos and Troy were suddenly allied,
> In spite of Helen's capture, to contend
> Against the onslaught of a common foe. (9)

The two male armies put aside their differences to oppose their common enemy and threat to civilization—an army of women who seem not to understand the conventions of war:

> I thought till now that Nature knows but force
> And counterforce, and no third power besides,
> Whatever quenches fire will not bring water
> Seething to a boil, nor vice versa.
> Yet here appears a deadly foe of each,
> Upon whose coming, fire no longer knows
> Whether to trickle with the floods, nor water
> Whether to leap with heaven-licking flame. (8–9)

The Amazons are the incongruous third party to a dualistic battle. This warring tribe of women, whose social laws Achilles describes as both "unfeminine" and "unnatural" (92), represents an affront to the eighteenth century's natural gender hierarchy. Yet in their disruption of gender norms, the Amazons share much with the rationalist stance of the Greeks and the Trojans. They have rationalized the role of sexuality in their society, strictly regulating gender roles and relations between men and women. They have indeed reduced the other gender merely to its reproductive function. The Amazons are not a third sex, as implied by the speech above, but mirror the patriarchal societies of the Greeks and the Trojans.[22] The Amazons do not undermine the notion of the rationalist state by virtue of their gender, for they rationalize individual desires as much as the male patriarchal states. Indeed, they exceed the Greeks in their horror at Penthesilea's transgression.

Kleist foregrounds the Amazons' loyalty to an Enlightenment concept of nationhood when he describes his nation of women as "a sovereign nation" (94) or "Ein Staat, ein mündiger" (389). While Kant sees women as unwilling to embrace Enlightenment maturity (*Mündigkeit*[23]), Kleist portrays a nation of women who pursue emancipation on rationalist terms. As such they also subordinate the body to the maintenance of social coherence, exemplified in their practice of amputating the right breast (389). Described by one scholar as "perversely patriarchal" (Rigby 151, 164), the Amazons seem the very archetype of a nation founded on the principles of the social contract. According to the social contractarians, citizens would give up certain freedoms in order to enjoy the commonweath's protection. As feminist political theorists have argued, this commonwealth was always conceived in terms of a disciplined and decidedly masculine "body politic." This body politic cannot accommodate a female body characterized by "voracious openings," by inward and outward flows (see Jones 81–82; Pateman 96). Yet in their pursuit of a masculine posture, evident in the amputated breast to accommodate the bow and arrow and the strict limitations placed on desire and fecundity, the Amazons create their own disciplined body politic.

The Amazon nation follows closely the historical trajectory dreamed up by the social contractarians. They even have their own founding myth: "Where now the Amazonian nation rules, / There lived before, obedient to the gods, / Warlike and free, a tribe of Scythians, / Equal to any nation on the earth" (92). This condition recalls the "state of nature" imagined by social contractarians. The Hobbesian *bellum omnium contra omnes* appears in the Amazon myth with the arrival of the Ethiopian King, Vexoris, whose army slays the entire male population:

> And with them died the splendour of the world.[24]
> The victors insolently set up house
> In our own huts and, as barbarians will,
> Fed themselves on the fruit of our rich fields,
> And, to allot us our full measure of shame,
> Forced us to tender them a loving welcome;
> They tore the women from their husbands' graves,
> And dragged them off to share their loathsome beds. (93)

In an ironic play on social contract theory, the Amazons founded their disciplined nation, their Enlightened "women's state," in response to the disorder represented by sexually avaricious men. Except for their gender, the Amazons conform in all other ways to the expectations of commonwealth citizens; the rationalization of reproduction in the "Festival of Roses" hold desire and fecundity in check. For the Amazons, sexual intercourse is but an annual event in which only select women participate, and not with partners of their choosing. Within a rationalist arrangement that makes individual sexual desire a taboo, Penthesilea transgresses Amazon law when she seeks out Achilles for herself. More than a mere inclination, the violence of her oral indulgence catastrophically repudiates the regulation and perpetuation of Amazon society. As Prothoe points out to Penthesilea, her pursuit of Achilles threatens to undo what the Amazons have achieved in the battle: "You will not win the son of Peleus, ever: / Instead [...] / The Youths we took in battle and hold captive, / The prize of such incalculable pains / And peril, will, by your lunacy, be lost" (36). When Penthesilea concedes to her lust for one man and indulges it in such a literal fashion, she briefly ruptures the rationalist Amazonian containment of the body and its capricious desires. In recklessly giving in to her oral drives—a heady mix of sexual, aesthetic, and gastronomic appetites—Penthesilea renounces her membership in a society founded on their containment. Even when she realizes she has annihilated the object of her desire, she refuses to return to the fold of Amazon society. Regarding her dead lover, she declares: "I hereby disavow the law of women / And I shall follow him, this youth" (146).

Conclusion

Kleist's depiction of this boundlessly appetitive heroine reanimates a masculine anxiety that the late Enlightenment's "stultifying praise" (Duden, "Eigentum" 126, trans. mine) of an aestheticized, self-abnegating, muted femininity was unable to salve. Kleist depicts the rationalist social contractarians' worst fears: that a man might relinquish the protection of civil society in order to indulge his desire, and that a woman might emerge from the intimate realm and disrupt the order of civil life with her oral excess. Jones writes in a critique of Hobbes that "threats to the body politic are represented as virtually cannibalistic, castrating actions of murderous women" (90). These threats fuse sexual and alimentary excess in the female oral body. When Kleist insists, "She really did eat him," the threats become real for horrified bourgeois readers. In *Penthesilea* the novelty of a matriarchal state reveals the absurdity of a civil society based on the rationalist negation of desire, and the notion of "the fair sex" becomes sullied by cannibalistic desire.

This article has documented a repudiation of the late Enlightenment's notion of a femininity "not much troubled with sexual feelings"

(Laqueur 3). Kleist dramatizes the failure of an ideal of femininity in which orality is quashed in favor of oral modesty. The political, gender, and aesthetic codes inspired by Enlightenment rationalism are shown in *Penthesilea* to be fragile constructs. Moreover, Kleist seems to prefer Penthesilea's morbid departure from rationality to the containment of sexuality and oral drives practiced by the Greeks and the Amazons. Nor can Penthesilea's pursuit and consumption of Achilles be understood as the victory of romantic love over the rationalization of sexuality. The grotesque figure of a cannibalistic Penthesilea could hardly be farther removed from the ideal of femininity upon which the romance narrative depends.

Kleist responded to his "Kant-Krise" with a sense of despair and with the conviction that "to act is better than to know" (qtd. in Mehigan 12, trans. mine). And he chose a transgressive female figure to represent "[his] innermost being [...] at once the complete filth and brilliance of [his] soul" (*Werke und Briefe* 797, trans. mine), endowing her with oral appetites that collapse the Enlightenment's neat polarities: female/male, appetite/taste, and love/lust.[25] In Penthesilea's disavowal of Enlightenment rationality a persuasive account of late-Enlightenment hypocrisy emerges that denies the desires of the body, yet invokes biology to perpetuate a "natural" gender hierarchy. Penthesilea herself is entwined in this hypocrisy. Having desirously but unsuccessfully pursued Achilles all over the battlefield, she is dismayed that plans for the "Festival of Roses" have begun without her chosen partner. Concerned only that she be able to participate in the orgy with Achilles as her partner, she roundly condemns the desires of her sister Amazons, who have acted with more restraint than she was able to muster, and in precisely those terms in which they have characterized her transgression: "A curse upon desires that, in the breast / of Mars's chaste daughters, bay like an unleashed pack / Of hounds" (56).

Notes

[1] All English quotations from *Penthesilea* are from the English translation; German quotations are from the German Sembdner edition, both of which are listed in the bibliography.

[2] I have explored elsewhere the connection between the various oral appetites (see Benbow).

[3] Barbara Duden's analysis of early-eighteenth-century women's medical histories, in which the female body appears to house an abundance of oral appetites, shows just how radically the Enlightenment's demure

feminine ideal reinscribed earlier notions of feminine embodiment (*Geschichte* 20–21). Pre-Enlightenment folk ideology attached mysterious and often malign powers to the female body: "Vermöge ihrer eigenen Periodizität und Fruchtbarkeit verkörpern die Frauen Mächte, deren Beistand das Dorf erwartet und fürchtet. Die Frauen begleiten die Übergänge des Lebens, den Eingang und Ausgang [...]. Ihr Körper beherbergt ja die Kräfte und Stoffe, die Gutes wie Böses bewirken können, das Blut, die periodischen Flüsse, die Afterbürde, das Kindswasser, und schließlich die 'Mutter,' die einem Ofen gleich hervorbringen und umbringen kann" (Duden, *Geschichte* 20–21).

[4] As Silvia Bovenschen explains, "Der Spuk einer schlecht domestizierten, die rationalistischen Konzepte gefährdenden Weiblichkeit verschwand jedoch nicht [...], er lebte untergründig fort" (83).

[5] See Rigby 148–49. See also Inge Stephan, who, in a reading of *Penthesilea* in the context of revolutionary images of Amazons, acknowledges the "uralte Männerängste vor der verschlingenden, kastrierenden Frau" (114) that are expressed in Penthesilea's consumption of Achilles. Stephan Schindler sees *Penthesilea* as the repudiation of the eighteenth-century disciplining of the "angeblich größeren Begierden" (200) of woman: "Hinter den Bestimmungen der bürgerlichen Frau als moralisch-reproduktives Wesen lauert das Schreckengespenst der wollüstigen Frau" (201), which undermines the idealized, passionless femininity of Enlightenment's collective imagination. Female sexual and political activity are intertwined in these analyses, in which the eighteenth-century domestication of femininity serves the dual purpose of disciplining an apparently threatening feminine sexuality (Schindler 200) and defusing emancipatory desires (Stephan 99–101).

[6] "Ich habe mich, bei Diana! bloß versprochen, / Weil ich der raschen Lippe Herr nicht bin; / Doch jetzt sag ich dir deutlich, wie ich's meinte: / Dies, du Geliebter war's, und weiter nichts. / (Sie küßt ihn)" (426). "[...] So war es ein Versehen. Küsse Bisse, / Das reimt sich, und wer recht von Herzen liebt, / Kann schon das eine für das andre greifen" (*Penthesilea* 425).

[7] "Solch eine Jungfrau, Hermia! So sittsam! / In jeder Kunst der Hände so geschickt! / So reizend, wenn sie tanzte, wenn sie sang! / So voll Verstand und Würd' und Grazie!" (414).

[8] Only the term "Verstand" in the German original (see above) is incongruous in a description of female virtue. As will be argued later, in this regard (the valuing of reason) Amazon society exceeds the qualities attributed in the eighteenth century to female nature.

[9] Sembdner, *Lebensspuren* 181. Jean Wilson identifies a tradition of reception, beginning with Goethe, which reacts to the play's threat to the

Enlightenment's gender norms by describing Penthesilea as unwomanly and even inhuman (194).

[10] See Brandstetter: "Sie stammt, wie Goethe sagt, in der Tat aus einem 'wunderbaren Geschlecht.' Hier artikuliert sich auch eine Verwirrung der 'Gattungs'-Grenzen,—ein 'gender trouble'—das Kleist [...] als Grenzüberschreitung zwischen den Markierungen eines 'sichren Geschlechts' bezeichnet. Er vergleicht es mit dem Verharren in einem unmarkierten Bereich zwischen Wasser und Land, als eine amphibische Existenz" (190).

[11] Cornelia Klinger writes that "Kant subsumes woman's essence, her entire being, under the category of the beautiful" (194).

[12] On the use of the term in the French context, see Stephan.

[13] See my discussion of the novel *Die Wahlverwandtschaften* (Benbow).

[14] See, in particular, Chaouli, but also Schindler for analysis of the motif of disgust in criticism of the play.

[15] Menninghaus identifies the gendered nature of disgust, noting, however, that the commonly invoked motif of disgust, used repeatedly by Kant and his contemporaries, is the old woman (84).

[16] Chaouli's 1996 essay pioneered this approach to the play. Chaouli's argument can be substantiated by Menninghaus's subsequent study of disgust, which forms part of my summary of Chaouli's argument here.

[17] For Kant, aesthetic judgment must be cleansed of bodily perception if taste is to advance beyond the "barbaric" level: "Der Geschmack ist jederzeit noch barbarisch, wo er die Beimischung der *Reize* und *Rührungen* zum Wohlgefallen bedarf" (*Urteilskraft* 77; emphasis in original). Michel Chaouli has pursued the consequences of *Penthesilea's* provocation to disgust via an analysis of Kant's aesthetics and comes to the conclusion that Penthesilea's "mistake" threatens the Kantian distinction between barbaric and aesthetic taste (128).

[18] In her feminist analysis, Schott has found in Kant's aesthetics a "hostility toward the body": "By emphasizing observation as the primary mode of knowledge, the perceiver achieves a distanced relation to his or her own body. In the act of looking we are less aware of our body than, for example, in the act of touching" (103).

[19] "Ein Staat, ein Mündiger" (*Penthesilea* 389).

[20] Genevieve Lloyd argues that Kant's idealization of war celebrates a victory over nature: "The special reverence associated with the soldier comes from his supposed perception of death as a 'might that has no dominion.' War is associated with a kind of autonomous selfhood that escapes domination by mere nature" (67). Nancy Hartsock argues that the disorder of a feminine-identified nature must be defeated in war in order to establish the *polis*: "Most fundamentally, the establishment of the polis takes place through a process of domesticating and subordinating the dangerous

and threatening female forces that surround what is to become the political community. [...] [F]or the warrior in battle, these were the forces of a hostile 'nature'" (190).

[21] As Carole Pateman has observed in relation to Rousseau: "[Émile] is told to put duty before desire and to leave Sophie, his betrothed, and travel abroad. A man must prepare for marriage like a soldier preparing for battle. The tutor (Rousseau) tells Emile [...] that 'a man does not exercise for battle in the face of the enemy but prepares himself for it before the war. He presents himself at the battle already fully prepared.' [...] Women's bodies are so opposed to and subversive of political life that Rousseau has Emile learn about citizenship before he is allowed to know the delights of being a husband" (98).

[22] As Ruth Kluger explains, "Kleists mythologischer Frauenstaat ist sozusagen der Staat in Reinkultur. Gewiß ist er extrem, aber er ist nicht pervers. Er verlangt ein ungewöhnliches Maß an Anpassung und Selbstaufgabe" (137). Similarly, Wolf Kittler argues the Amazon nation does not represent female independence, because it is founded upon a loyalty to a generation of murdered husbands (182).

[23] The term "Mündigkeit," although etymologically speaking not related to the term "Mund," surely evokes this association for most readers, and perhaps even for Kant himself.

[24] "Das ganze Prachtgeschlecht der Welt ging aus" (*Penthesilea* 388).

[25] It must be conceded that, while Kleist may have had his doubts about the disembodied reason advocated by Kant and other *Aufklärer*, its marginalization of women hardly seems to have been one of his explicit concerns. Thus, Kleist's Enlightenment critique in Penthesilea can lend itself to readings that downplay its challenge to gender norms and even posit it as a reactionary reassertion of patriarchal values (for example, Bridgham). There is, however, also a feminist tradition that critiques the play and looks beyond Kleist's apparent hostility to female emancipation for interpretive tools (for example, Stephan; Wilson).

Works Cited

Angress, Ruth. "Kleist's Nation of Amazons." *Beyond the Eternal Feminine: Critical Essays on Women and German Literature*. Ed. Susan L. Cocalis and Kay Goodmann. Stuttgart: Hans-Dieter Heinz, 1982. 99–134.

Benbow, Heather Merle. "Goethe's *Die Wahlverwandtschaften* and the Problem of Female Orality." *Body Dialectics in the Age of Goethe*. Ed.

Marianne Henn and Holger Pausch. Amsterdam: Rodopi, 2003. 315–32.

Bovenschen, Silvia. *Die imaginierte Weiblichkeit: Exemplarische Untersuchungen zu kulturgeschichtlichen und literarischen Präsentationsformen des Weiblichen.* Frankfurt a.M.: Suhrkamp, 1979.

Brandes, Ernst. *Betrachtungen über das weibliche Geschlecht und dessen Ausbildung in dem geselligen Leben.* 1787. 3 vols. Hanover: Gebrüder Hahn, 1802.

Brandstetter, Gabriele. "'Eine Tragödie von der Brust heruntergehustet': Darstellung von Katharsis in Kleists Penthesilea." *Heinrich von Kleist und die Aufklärung.* Ed. Tim Mehigan. Rochester, NY: Camden House, 2000. 186–210.

Bridgham, Fred. "Emancipating Amazons: Schiller's Jungfrau, Kleist's Penthesilea, Wagner's Brünnhilde." *Forum for Modern Language Studies* 36.1 (2000): 64–73.

Burke, Edmund. *A Philosophical Enquiry into the Origin of Our Ideas of the Sublime and Beautiful.* 1757. London: Routledge and Kegan Paul, 1958.

Campe, Joachim Heinrich. *Väterlicher Rath für meine Tochter: Ein Gegenstück zum Theophron.* 1789. Ed. Ruth Bleckwenn. Vol. 3. *Quellen und Schriften zur Geschichte der Frauenbildung.* Paderborn: Verlag M. Hüttemann, 1988.

Carus, Carl Gustav. *Lehrbuch der Gynäkologie, oder thematische Darstellung und Behandlung eigenthümlicher gesunder und kranker Zustände, sowohl der nicht schwangeren, schwangeren und gebärenden Frauen, als der Wöchnerinnen und neugeborenen Kinder. (Erster Theil).* 2 vols. Vol. 1. Leipzig: Gerhard Fleischer, 1820.

Coward, Rosalind. *Female Desire.* London: Paladin, 1984.

Chaouli, Michel. "Devouring Metaphor: Disgust and Taste in Kleist's Penthesilea." *The German Quarterly* 69.2 (1996): 125–43.

Choluj, Bozena. "Auf den Körper schauen und hören: Zur Körperproblematik in Heinrich von Kleists *Penthesilea* und *Die Marquise von O...*" *Beiträge zur Kleist-Forschung* 16 (2002): 103–16.

Cullens, Chris and Dorothea von Mücke. "Love in Kleist's *Penthesilea* and *Käthchen von Heilbronn.*" *Deutsche Vierteljahrsschrift für Literaturwissenschaft und Geistesgeschichte* 3.2 (1989): 461–93.

Duden, Barbara. *Geschichte unter der Haut: Ein Eisenacher Arzt und seine Patientinnen um 1730.* Stuttgart: Klett-Cotta, 1987.

———. *The Woman beneath the Skin.* Trans. Thomas Dunlap. Cambridge: Harvard UP, 1991.

―――. "Das schöne Eigentum: Zur Herausbildung des bürgerlichen Frauenbildes an der Wende vom 18. zum 19. Jahrhundert." *Kursbuch* 47 (1977): 125–42.

Günzel, Klaus, ed. *Kleist: Ein Lebensbild in Briefen und zeitgenössischen Berichten*. Stuttgart: Metzler, 1985.

Hartsock, Nancy M. *Money, Sex, and Power: Towards a Feminist Historical Materialism*. Boston: Northeastern UP, 1983.

Horkheimer, Max, and Theodor W. Adorno. *Dialektik der Aufklärung: Philosophische Fragmente*. 1944. Ed. Rolf Tiedemann. Vol. 3. *Theodor W. Adorno: Gesammelte Schriften*. Frankfurt a.M.: Suhrkamp, 1984.

Jones, Kathleen B. *Compassionate Authority: Democracy and the Representation of Women*. London: Routledge, 1993.

Kant, Immanuel. *Kritik der Urteilskraft*. 1790. Ed. Felix Gross. Vol. 6. *Immanuel Kant's sämtliche Werke in sechs Bänden*. Leipzig: Inselverlag, 1921.

―――. *Critique of Judgment*. 1790. Trans. Werner S. Pluhar. Indianapolis: Hackett Publishing Company, 1987.

―――. "Beobachtungen über das Gefühl des Schönen und Erhabenen." 1764. Ed. Felix Gross. Vol. 1. *Immanuel Kant's sämtliche Werke in sechs Bänden*. Leipzig: Inselverlag, 1921. 6–67.

―――. *Observations on the Feeling of the Beautiful and Sublime*. 1764. Trans. John T. Goldthwait. Berkeley: U of California P, 2003.

―――. "Beantwortung der Frage: Was ist Aufklärung?" 1784. Ed. Felix Gross. *Immanuel Kant's sämtliche Werke in sechs Bänden*. Leipzig: Inselverlag, 1921. 161–71.

―――. "What is Enlightenment" 1784. *Kant: Political Writings*. Trans. H.B. Nisbet. Cambridge: Cambridge UP, 1991. 54–60.

―――. "Anthropologie in pragmatischer Hinsicht." 1798. Ed. Felix Gross. Vol. 1. *Immanuel Kant's sämtliche Werke in sechs Bänden*. Leipzig: Inselverlag, 1921.

―――. *Anthropology from a Pragmatic Point of View*. 1798. Trans. Victor L. Dowdell. Carbondale: Southern Illinois UP, 1978.

Kittler, Wolf. *Die Geburt des Partisanen aus dem Geist der Poesie: Heinrich von Kleist und die Strategie der Befreiungskriege*. Freiburg: Rombach, 1987.

Kleist, Heinrich von. *Penthesilea: Ein Trauerspiel*. 1808. Vol. 1. Ed. Helmut Sembdner. München: Carl Hanser, 1961.

―――. *Penthesilea: A Tragic Drama*. 1808. Trans. Joel Agee. New York: Michael di Capua Books and Harper Collins, 1998.

―――. *Heinrich von Kleist: Sämtliche Werke und Briefe*. 1800. Vol. 2. Ed. Helmut Sembdner. München: Carl Hanser, 1961.

Klinger, Cornelia. "The Concepts of the Sublime and the Beautiful in Kant and Lyotard." *Feminist Interpretations of Immanuel Kant*. University Park: Pennsylvania State UP, 1997. 191-211.

Kluger, Ruth. *Frauen lesen anders: Essays*. München: Deutscher Taschenbuch Verlag, 1996.

Lange, Sigrid. "Kleists 'Penthesilea.'" *Weimarer Beiträge* 37.5 (1991): 705-22.

Laqueur, Thomas. *Making Sex: Body and Gender from the Greeks to Freud*. Cambridge, MA: Harvard UP, 1990.

Lloyd, Genevieve. "Selfhood, War and Masculinity." *Feminist Challenges: Social and Political Theory*. Ed. Carole Pateman and Elizabeth Grosz. Sydney: Allen & Unwin, 1986. 63-76.

Mehigan, Timothy. "Kleist, Kant und die Aufklärung." *Heinrich von Kleist und die Aufklärung*. Ed. Timothy Mehigan. Rochester: Camden House, 2000. 3-21.

Menninghaus, Winfried. *Ekel: Theorie und Geschichte einer starken Empfindung*. Frankfurt a.M.: Suhrkamp, 1999.

———. *Disgust: Theory and History of a Strong Sensation*. Trans. Howard Eiland and Joel Golb. Albany: SUNY P, 2003.

Pateman, Carole. *The Sexual Contract*. Cambridge: Polity P, 1988.

Riemer, Friedrich Wilhelm. *Mitteilungen über Goethe*. 1841. Ed. Arthur Pollmer. Leipzig: Insel Verlag, 1921.

Rigby, Catherine E. *Transgressions of the Feminine: Tragedy, Enlightenment and the Figure of the Woman in Classical German Drama*. Winter: Heidelberg, 1996.

Rousseau, Jean-Jacques. *Émile*. 1762. Trans. Barbara Foxley. London: Dent, 1974.

Schindler, Stephan K. "Die blutende Brust der Amazone: bedrohliche weibliche Sexualität in Kleists Penthesilea." *Kleists Erzählungen und Dramen: Neue Studien*. Ed. Paul Michael Lützeler und David Pan. Würzburg: Königshausen & Neumann, 2001. 191-202.

Schott, Robin May. *Cognition and Eros: A Critique of the Kantian Paradigm*. Boston: Beacon P, 1988.

Sembdner, Helmut, ed. *Heinrich von Kleist: Sämtliche Werke und Briefe*. Vol. 2. München: Hansen, 1961.

———. *Heinrich von Kleists Lebensspuren: Dokumente und Berichte der Zeitgenossen*. Frankfurt a.M.: Insel, 1984.

Shell, Susan Meld. *The Rights of Reason: A Study of Kant's Philosophy and Politics*. Toronto: U of Toronto P, 1980.

———. *The Embodiment of Reason: Kant on Spirit, Generation, and Community*. Chicago: U of Chicago P, 1996.

Stephan, Inge. "'Da werden Weiber zu Hyänen...': Amazonen und Amazonenmythen bei Schiller und Kleist." *Aus dem Verborgenen zur Avantgarde: Ausgewählte Beiträge zur feministischen Literaturwissenschaft der 80er Jahre*. Ed. Hiltrud Bontrup and Jan Christian Metzler. Hamburg: Argument, 2000. 96–117.

Wilson, Jean. "Transgression and Identity in Kleist's *Penthesilea* and Wolf's *Cassandra*." *Women in German Yearbook 16* (2000): 191–206.

The Photographic Enactment of the Early New Woman in 1890s German Women's Bicycling Magazines

Beth Muellner

The studio photographs of women bicyclists sent in by the readers of the German women's bicycling magazines *Draisena* and *Die Radlerin* in the latter half of the 1890s are read as evidence that an Early German New Woman was busy defining emancipation independently from the organized women's movement long before the New Woman of the 1920s. The photographic evidence of the magazines helps elucidate the terms "emancipation" and the "New Woman" in relation to bicycling and corrects historical scholarship that too easily conflates these terms with sport and the German women's movement, primarily due to the ubiquity of turn-of-the century bicycle advertisements. (BM)

Late nineteenth-century women bicyclists were viewed as independent, youthful, and emancipated, and were inscribed in the popular imagination as such through the proliferation and public display of advertising posters, postcards, and stamps. While European and American advertising suggests that bicycling was synonymous with women's emancipation, a number of historical and contemporary sources connect the sport with the German women's movement. In the 1897 publication *Der Radfahrsport in Bild und Wort* (The Sport of Bicycling in Picture and Word), editor Paul Salvisberg calls women's bicycling an almost compulsory activity in the modern women's movement.[1] In their 1992 book on German women's bicycling, historians Gudrun Maierhof and Katinka Schröder argue that women active in various factions of the women's movement unequivocally supported bicycling. But in reality, only a small number of women in the moderate German women's movement approved of bicycle use for females. If one considers that only four percent of Berlin's overall population even owned a bicycle in 1900, a closer examination of the bicycle as an emancipatory vehicle becomes necessary. Part of my purpose here is to clarify the meaning of emancipation and to analyze the sweeping allusions of the German Women's Movement to German women's bicycling in the 1890s. As historian Dörte Bleckmann concludes, while bicycling cannot be aligned with organized women's struggles for education, work, and voting rights, if one explains emancipation through the study of individual women's stories of emancipation, the bicycle was indeed an important vehicle for those who could afford one. As evidence of what I call the Early New Woman who emerged in the 1890s, my analysis focuses on photographs of women bicyclists in the German women's bicycling magazines *Draisena* (Draisena) and *Die Radlerin* (The Woman Cyclist) from the latter half of the decade. While the popularity of bicycling for women first reached its zenith in the 1890s and in 1896 more women's bicycles were produced than men's, the sport remained a matter of heated debate among religious leaders and medical doctors in the popular press throughout the decade. Frequent caricatures of women bicyclists in publications such as *Simplicissimus* depicted them as either Amazonian *Mannweiber* ("masculinized women") or idealized them as youthful and delicately feminine. But the evidence of numerous studio photographs of women bicyclists sent in by the readers of *Draisena* and *Die Radlerin* and published in each edition speaks to women's own strategies to envision and define an image of emancipation for themselves.

The richness of visual texts in the magazines provides a unique opportunity for readers to understand the Early New German Woman's interpretation of emancipation in the 1890s. Given the abundance of images produced in the nineteenth century with the development of lithographic and photographic technologies, it is easy to understand why cultural historians turn to visual artifacts in particular to interpret the past. The inventions of color lithography and the modern standard bicycle emerged more or less around the same time (1872), and lithographic artists and bicycle manufacturers were eager to show what their new machines could do. This development, coupled with poster artists' fascination with the bicycle, led to the creation of more color posters of the bicycle than any other product by the turn of the century (Franke 90). The texts in *Draisena* and *Die Radlerin* primarily covered such bicycling-related topics as health, fashion, etiquette, and technology, but the magazines also included regular commentary on and critical assessment of advertising images of the bicycle. Invoking the sensory overload of nineteenth-century visual stimuli that Stephan Kern discusses in *The Culture of Time and Space,* an 1898 cartoon in *Draisena* pokes fun at a male bicyclist's (mis)reading of an advertising poster (Figure 1). The cartoon playfully cautions against interpreting generic advertising images of emancipated bicycling women as reflecting the experiences of real women.[2] It plays on the male bicyclist's "short-sightedness" on many levels. In tipping his hat, he adheres to a traditional etiquette between the sexes that the Early New Woman might find charming but old-fashioned. The woman in the poster obviously does not respond, but neither may an actual modern woman. By adhering to traditional modes of behavior, the man loses control of the new technology—the bicycle—and also of his reading of the Early New Woman. In the man's assumption that the poster is actually a woman, *Draisena* reminds readers that the false representation and interpretation of women bicyclists can be hazardous. Because of such humor and other caricatures found in the magazines, readers might have studied the photographs of real women bicyclists all the more carefully. While the color lithograph offers little more than a one-dimensional print of a generic woman, photographs provide a more immediate representation of a historical "truth" and as such function differently primarily in regard to visual object's agency. But while nineteenth-century advertising images of bicycling women seem to have become icons of women's liberation and have been treated by scholars as important historical artifacts, the historical photographs of women bicyclists in particular have received no closer analysis except to embellish written histories of women's bicycling. No "truer" icons of modern womanhood serve as witnesses to history than the evidence of photographs.

Figure 1: Humor in Draisena

The articles in the German women's bicycling magazines *Draisena* and *Die Radlerin* focused on the relative newness of women bicyclists' public exposure and display. The nature of the static space represented in the magazines' studio photographs reflects a rather conservative approach to the display of the woman bicyclist by not depicting the sport in action. The magazines' women publishers situated women bicyclists within what Ruth-Ellen Joeres calls the "performance of propriety" in their modest representation of the "deviant" act of bicycling.[3] Indeed, the strategy of attracting both conservative and more liberal-minded women readers to the sport relied upon the acting out of various performances in print and image. By using professional photographic portraits, the editors of *Die Radlerin* and *Draisena* maintained some control over the promotion of bicycling as a serious and respectable activity for women. The majority of photographs in the magazines present meticulously dressed middle-class women and their bicycles. Although the higher number of studio photographs in the magazines was not necessarily tied to hobby photographers' limited access to the technology at the time, studios might have provided bourgeois women the kind of discretionary atmosphere they needed to allow themselves to be "taken."[4] While the magazines include the names of the various photographic studios next to the photograph itself, most names are only abbreviations. Thus it remains unknown whether or not the aesthetics promoted in studio portraits were controlled by mostly male photographers or if indeed women photographers also participated.[5]

The similarity between an advertising image (Figure 2) and studio photograph (Figure 3) reminds readers of the creative process behind visual representations and that the photograph, like the lithograph, can be considered a construction. However, instead of focusing on the art of photography or on the intentions of the photographer, I am influenced by Marianne Hirsch and Roland Barthes, who regard photographs as historical texts that speak in a complicated dialogue between past and present. Like Hirsch, I keep returning to the idea of a photograph as something that "has been" (Barthes's "ça a été"):

> The realists of whom I am one [...] do not take the photograph for a "copy" of reality, but for an emanation of *past reality*: a *magic, not an art.* [...] The important thing is that the photograph possesses an evidential force, and that its testimony bears not on the object but on time. From a phenomenological viewpoint, in the Photograph, the power of authentication exceeds the power of representation. (Barthes qtd. in Hirsch 6)

Figure 2: Bicycling Magazine Ad

Figure 3: Bicycling Magazine Photograph

The reader is confronted with an actual image staring back out of "the perpetual present: [...] a mutual look of a subject looking at an object who is a subject looking (back) at an object" (Hirsch 9). In contrast to flat, generic images in advertising, if one imagines the photographic referent as "looking out" of the photograph as much as the viewer is "looking in," the viewing and interpretation of photographs reveals a much more complex process. Viewing a photograph is not a one-way, linear experience—an important consideration in terms of challenging assumptions about gendered spectatorship, particularly regarding women's traditionally passive and/or objectified position. First, women viewers are empowered through the "past reality" of women bicyclists in photographs. In viewing the photograph as a visual artifact that speaks to the lived history of an individual woman and her choice to have a portrait taken with her bicycle, the photographic referent (the sitter) maintains a degree of individual agency.

The photographs present space for individual interpretations and fantasy for both the female spectacle/object and the spectator/viewer. Interpreting the photograph in a way that sees beyond images allows for a continuous dialogue with each viewer and generation. The viewer sees the subject-object's proud stature, her uniqueness, or the way the subject's neatly put-together bicycling costume may resemble the viewer's, the way the subject's gaze confronts or deflects the viewer, and the sitter's decision to either sit on or stand next to her bicycle. The sitter's choices are captured by the photograph and details—such as whether she crosses her arms or waves, or holds a whip or a flower, for instance—offer room for the viewer's individual interpretation of the sitter's self-representational decisions (Figure 4).

Figure 4: Frau Otto Koerner Chose to Sit

Carol Mavor offers insights into activating the subject and the viewer of the photograph from positions of passivity. The mobility of the photographic reproduction (an external landscape is viewed inside the parlor, for example) "permit[s] the reproduction to meet the beholder [...] in his own particular situation, [and] [...] reactivates the object reproduced" (221). Mavor refuses to give into the one-sidedness of photography, i.e., the "taking" of the subject by the photographer. Instead she focuses on the intransitive nature of photographs whose subject-objects "strike back at us with 'the will and the force of the sitter' [so that] just who is taking who [sic] becomes a moot point" (119). As with any photograph, we cannot truly know the circumstances of production. What we do know is that the photograph of Frau Otto Koerner (Figure 4) centers on her figure and the only-partially-visible bicycle in the lower right corner of the image. Wearing a suit with bowtie, boxy hat, and pants, she leans casually on a post and sits on a small stone barrier, legs openly crossed. The studio backdrop shows a column in the distance, and overall the photograph seems to capture her taking a break during a ride through a city park alone. She appears relaxed, but gazes toward the left. Despite her seeming modesty in not looking directly at the camera, the photograph most likely stirred interest, primarily due to the ongoing debate about pants or skirts for bicycling. Even the most outspoken bicycling advocates considered pants appropriate only for bicycling and nothing else. Frau Koerner's choice to wear pants for the photograph, not to mention the masculine position of her crossed legs, seems quite bold. But regardless of the viewer's regard of pants, the viewer contemplates the photograph on her own terms.

While photographic documentation provides important evidence of nineteenth-century women's mobility and can be used to allay claims that women's travel accounts were often fictionalized, these photographs give an imaginary space for projecting the ideals of emancipation according to individual preference.[6] The photographs in *Draisena* and *Die Radlerin* are offered within a specific context, and their interpretation depends upon various textual markers. The ultimate paradox of photographic portraits is that they represent both a specific social type and the private identity of the sitter; thus the reader can never truly "trust" what they see (Clarke). Such is the case with Frau Koerner, for example. How did her photograph come to be published in the magazine? Did she herself submit it? Viewers often affix photographs with a certain meaning, but such labels can lead to questions about what first appears as a visually stable identity on the surface. Upon closer inspection, titles affixed to photographic portraits place the image somewhere on the spectrum "between social sanctioning and private confusion"

(Clarke 85). Thus, the subtitles in the bicycling magazines given before or after the bicyclist's name, such as "From Our Gallery of Graceful Riders," "A High Protectress of the Sport of Ladies' Bicycling," or "Prize-Winning Amateur Acrobatic Bicyclist," give the image significance through its identification within codes of cultural and social status (Figure 5). While an image's title catalogs it according to a specific "type," the interior state of the private being remains through the inclusion of the sitter's full name and creates multiple interpretive possibilities.[7] Thus, whatever the physical presentation might mean, or whatever gesture the sitter offers (standing, sitting, waving, arms crossed, dress, pantaloons, smiling, turning away), the women depicted are automatically assigned significance in the world of women and bicycles through labels such as "graceful," "a protectress," or "prize-winning." But, as assured as these images may appear in their objective verification of a certain state, the façade they present also leads to a questioning of their static social world.[8] Is there any significance to Frau Anna Burkhardt's choice to sit on the bicycle (Figure 5) vs. Frau Otto Koerner's choice to next to it? Did Herr Koerner have a say in the matter?

"More than any other kind of photographic image, the portrait achieves meaning through the context in which it is seen" (Clarke 1). The context in which the photographs of women bicyclists were viewed is very specific—namely within the pages of a women's bicycling magazine. In this sense, the images have to be read against what is known (the printed text that frames them), as well as what is unknown (the historical context that motivated these women to have their images made permanent for later consumption).[9] The interest in, demand for, and production of the visual is presented as issuing directly from *Die Radlerin*'s readers:

> I have written up to now so much about women bicyclists that surely a few charming young women readers scold: "Oh, what use to me are all these words, I want to see some pictures!" Now, there is something to what she says, and the realization that a photograph makes an attractive women more interesting than one hundred lines of text has moved me to request the photographs of two outstanding young women bicycle disciples to be included in the *Radlerin,* and these have already been handed over to me willingly. (1897)

Both *Draisena* and *Die Radlerin* promoted the idea that the reader can actively participate in visually defining the woman bicyclist. From *Die Radlerin*'s inclusion of the address and owner of a company that specializes in small and price-worthy cameras for the bicyclist, to

Draisena's regular column "The Sport of Touring and Amateur Photography," women readers were encouraged to create their own photographs.[10] At the same time, however, while individual participation in visual representation was promoted, most photographs in the magazines came from professional portrait studios.[11] Like feminist historians of science and technology Ruth Oldenziel and Nina Lehrman, who see women taking on various tools of technology as "technological actors," the photographs document women's interest in the technology of the bicycle, but also their interest in and adoption of the technology of photography. It is the use of the latter technology that clearly illustrates how keenly aware these women were of the path-breaking nature of their status as cyclists.

Figure 5: Frau Anna Burkhardt "Gracefully" Poised in Action

The women in the bicycling photographs are an early-1890s version of the German New Woman. Although the New Woman has been well documented as a cultural phenomenon and historical reality between 1918 and 1933, many of the authors of Katharina von Ankum's important volume *Women in the Metropolis* emphasize that these women's liberation from traditional gender roles was already on the decline by the mid-1920s. The Early New Woman was busy making waves long before then. While historians do allude to the phenomenon of the Wilhelmine New Woman in regard to bicycling, such as David Ehrenpreis's 1999 article "Cyclists and Amazons," the emphasis is on caricatures and advertising. Others discuss the Wilhelmine New Woman as caught between the identities of the femme fatale and the femme fragile (Wittmann). I want to differentiate between these definitions of the term Early New Woman primarily in reading the existence of the photographs as a sign of women's own agency in constructing images of emancipation. The photographs offer evidence that they enacted emancipatory gestures— dressing differently and exiting the protected bourgeois sphere to bike in public *at their leisure*—which were independent gestures outside of organized women's efforts. They tended to their physical and mental selves, which can be recognized as emancipatory for women in every age. Moreover, they took the additional step to memorialize pleasure in the sport via photographs. The focus on bicycling demonstrates how women spent their leisure time before Siegfried Kracauer's 1920s observations of the "little shop girls" going to the movies. The focus on leisure to signify a new generation of women differs from the focus on women's labor efforts during World War I or the physical and social traits of younger women (bobbed hair, androgynous dress, unmarried, employed) as important markers of a modern woman. So how does the women's movement factor into the emergence of the Early German New Woman?

Prior to the last decades of the nineteenth century, moderate conservative members who adhered to rather traditional bourgeois ideologies regarding marriage and gender roles dominated the first generation of German women to organize. The number of women involved in the initial movement was relatively small; they came from upper-class families, had a university education, and often decided not to marry because of their "feminist" ideals. Their main interest was to change and improve the political and ideological conditions of women's lives in society. For a variety of reasons, including Bismarck's Anti-Socialist Law (1878–90), moderately conservative women prevented other factions of the wider women's movement from becoming members in the umbrella organization Bund Deutscher Frauenvereine (Federation of

German Women's Associations) formed in 1894. This excluded the interests of socialist, working-class, and radical factions of the movement.

The activities and work of the radical fraction sought to loosen the strict moral and sexual codes for women, and, as such, might seem more closely related to the interests of younger women. It is this group that is connected most readily with the New Woman of the Weimar time period. The women born after the first generation of organized German women were larger in number, uneducated, lower-middle class, and not particularly politically motivated. Because many emancipatory ideas were already present—women could work and study by 1908 and vote by 1918—younger women pursued interests that they felt benefited them personally, such as fulfilling their own sexual desires or delaying or avoiding marriage. Some historians regard the lack of political or economic force behind the more personal agenda of younger women as a failure vis-à-vis the community-building efforts of the original movement (Evans).

The New Woman can be connected to the Early New Woman primarily via their individual interpretation of emancipation through leisure activities. While some members of the radical fraction, such as Lily Braun, spoke out in favor of the bicycle, a sweeping endorsement of bicycle use for women by the German women's movement was not possible because of differences in agenda and membership. In general, the disconnect between older and younger generations, the political and economic conservativism during Germany's nation-building phase, as well as the incongruous interests of different factions of the women's movement created individual definitions and assessments regarding the impact of the bicycle. One area of disagreement was in the understanding of work versus leisure, a point that highlights use of the bicycle in the 1890s as a still mostly middle-class leisure activity.

Because of the debate over women's sexuality and social roles at this time, popular German language publications that promoted bicycling were careful to distance themselves from emancipatory ideas that would have seemed improper to more conservative bourgeois women. The handbook *Vademecum* (1897), published by the magazine *Wiener Mode* (Viennese Fashion), explains the relationship between the women's movement and women's bicycling as such:

> Above all, we recognize that the question about whether or not women should ride the bicycle has much in common with the general question of women's emancipation, even though the questions do not appear to belong together. "Emancipated women" take a stance only in regard to their aptitude for work and to their equality

with men in career opportunities, and concern themselves less with matters of mere pleasure. (qtd. in Bleckmann 142)

From this perspective, the women's movement in general seems to have presented itself as separate from the sport of bicycling, i.e., as a serious political endeavor versus a leisure activity. On one hand, one can detect in this comment the disdain for idle leisure that was ideologically imposed upon bourgeois women for much of the nineteenth century. On the other hand, socialist feminists would have had difficulty embracing the idea of leisure because it could be regarded as too bourgeois or capitalist. Therefore, they would also be unable to consider leisure as a serious emancipatory undertaking. It was only in the first decades of the twentieth century that women of the lower class were able to afford a bicycle, and frequently the sole purpose in purchasing a bicycle was to be able to seek and take on employment positions further from home.

Radical members of the German women's movement who spoke out on the controversial topic of women's sexuality remained cautious in associating leisurely or everyday activities such as bicycling with any notion that distracted from the more serious project of sexual liberation. One can also detect in the *Vademecum* quotation a slight disdain for "emancipated women" or for women active in the movement in general. After all, *Vademecum* was a publication devoted to the leisure activity of bicycling. That "emancipated women" could not bother themselves with "matters of mere pleasure" was meant as a jab at the caricatured uptight bluestocking. Ultimately, rather than associating the phenomenon of the bicycle with the various agendas of the German women's movement, the bicycle as a leisure activity could be interpreted as emancipatory on an individual level. Through a new self-consciousness that came about as the result of many societal changes, women undertook activities that led to their personal growth and development, and the bicycle was one of many instruments in this change (Bleckmann 150). Documenting one's life in photographs was another.

The individual pursuit of emancipatory experiences as exemplified by cycling is one feature that sets the Early New Woman apart from her predecessors in the organized women's movement. Of course the founding mothers of the movement had their own individual interpretations of emancipation, but what defines the women's movement has more to do with a joining of forces to reach specific goals rather than with the pursuit of individual interests. After all, they did not endorse bicycling for women as an organization. By and large, the goals of the organized movement dealt with work and education. The magazines *Draisena* and *Die Radlerin* offer important insight into how women's leisure experiences with bicycles reflect a period of transition for women. Inspired by the activities of the women's movement, but of a different political persuasion, the Early New Woman begins to forge ahead and on her own, deciding as an individual what suits her own notion of freedom, like bicycling. As Ehrenpreis concludes, positive images of bicycling women converted women "from political figures into commodities espousing the virtues of fashion, leisure—and consumption" (30).

For the most part, the magazines' layout and juxtaposition of the textual and visual allow multiple interpretations of emancipation for individual readers. In the humorous sketch, "My First Bicycle Excursion," in an 1898/99 publication of *Die Radlerin,* the married Frau Dr. Cäcilia Lederer recounts how her bicycle teacher abandoned her to her first public, solo ride. In preparation for her ride to the Prater, the author seems to exude confidence: "Truly cheekily did I pace the room, snapped on my gloves, so self-assured, as if to say, 'look at me, I have the courage to do this!'" Through this confessional mode, readers receive insight into Lederer's personal challenge and are made aware that emancipatory efforts do not come easily. Lederer's words "look at me!" remind the reader of women's self-consciousness and continuous self-vigilance as a spectacle in the public eye, the "as if" drawing attention to the performative aspect of the confidence she exudes.

The battle for self-actualization is fought in the performative space of the public and the private. While Lederer boasts in the privacy of her own room, she also confesses a desire to put an end to the "act." Instead of focusing on the visual accoutrements of what seems emancipatory and perhaps even too bold, suggested by the sister's disapproving comments that "the skirt was too short, the cap too crooked, the tie too red," Lederer follows through with her plan, inspired by personal pride and self-commitment. While the reader is made to understand that bicycling is always a public spectacle—"As the servant girl told me afterwards, at least fifty people were standing around watching me mount the bicycle"—Lederer's story also portrays the sport of bicycling as a space in which a more personal battle is fought: "my honor was at stake" (166). In keeping with women's individual interpretation of emancipation through bicycling, the author's reference to her honor can be interpreted as emancipatory in its reference to keeping a commitment to oneself, rather than in adhering to conservative, patriarchal, and/or bourgeois rules of femininity. This perspective revises the traditional notion of a woman's honor that regards men as its true protectors.

The visuals that accompany Lederer's story offer interpretive options for the more cautious-minded as well as for those willing to see the need for greater social risks to experience personal freedom. The story, which runs over four pages, begins under the photograph of a married couple standing next to their bicycles at a *Blumenkorso* ("flower pageant/parade") in the Rheinland. While there is no clear connection between the Rheinland couple and Lederer's text, organizing them in such a way on the magazine's page suggests to the reader that the story will be about a married couple. This would certainly be understood as a most appropriate way to undertake "a first bicycle excursion." On page two, the written text reveals that the author's escort is not her husband, but the bicycle teacher, and worse yet, he has accepted another "needier" student in place of the author. Lederer's frustration and disappointment motivate her to continue the excursion plans *on her own*. The images that balance the text on this page are ads of bicycles, bicycle seats, the Hammond Typewriter, and the "Neues Frauenblatt" (New Women's Newspaper). The juxtaposition of advertising texts that allude to consumer choices for women with the author's description of riding unaccompanied reinforces another aspect of women's independence: her role as consumer. The typewriter ad specifically seems to highlight women's paid work and the possibility of economic independence. For middle-class readers who might relate to the frustration of Lederer's struggle for emancipation—if only for an afternoon of bicycling in the park—the suggestion to acquire additional "tools" that better enable emancipation is empowering.

A center photograph that shocks visually and textually dominates the third page of Lederer's article (Figure 6). The photo's boldness is reflected in the image of the amateur bicycle artist Viola Ziemann of Hamburg balancing her bicycle's back wheel, front wheel high in the air. She wears striped pants gathered at the knee with white bows, a white ruffled shirt, and her long, black hair flowing openly down her back. Her eyes are directed almost defiantly at the viewer. The contrast of the female acrobat with Lederer's written account of personal bourgeois triumph acts to temper what might be read as a "deviant" solo excursion. Despite the wheelie-popping bicycling Amazon, Lederer's actions come across as quite innocent. The written narrative records Lederer's self-dialogue, reflecting both trepidation and exuberance ("O God, O God! [...] I must ride today to the Prater, come what may!"), her sister's jeers ("Ok, show me what you've got"), the spectators' observations as reported by the servant, and her departure for her courageous ride ("I was honored by several people out for a stroll with the usual cheers"). The comments emphasize the visual, repeatedly reminding the reader of the public spectacle of the solo woman bicyclist. Because the audience most likely consists of bicycling enthusiasts,

Lederer's story offers humorous inspiration and self-confidence to those seeking to assert their independence.

Figure 6: Frau Viola Ziemann Pops a Wheelie

The insertion of the Ziemann photograph pushes bourgeois readers to another level of desire and fantasy: the realm of celebrity and star worship. *Draisena* and *Die Radlerin* made frequent use of celebrity photographs, and portraits of various aristocratic women (who happen to endorse bicycling, but do not pose with their machine) were often placed on the title page of the magazine. Drawing on the cult popularity of some nobility, the magazines' editors hoped to make the sport even more attractive to the average middle-class reader. In the history of women's bicycling, aristocratic women and actresses were often the first to risk public visibility, primarily due to the fact that they could afford it, financially and socially, seeming to exist as they did beyond the boundaries of bourgeois rules and decorum.

The magazines also regularly include photographs of women bicycle acrobats, racers, and *Blumenkorso* participants. Integrating local celebrities, who were often *Blumenkorso* participants, and amateur sport stars in the magazines' visual spread convinced the average woman that, if the woman-next-door in the photograph could *perform* on a bicycle, she herself could attempt at least to *ride* one. Illustrating the multiple identificatory and interpretive positions for the female reader, the layout of Ziemann's photograph is positioned squarely between two triangle-shaped lithographs of men and women bicycling together on opposite corners of the page, creating a diagonal shape that borders the text on all sides. The photograph of the bold female acrobat counters the more generic lithographic images of men and women in the corners, both set against Lederer's written narrative of personal triumph. Readers can then choose to identify with either the bold photographic display of the acrobat, the more hetero-normative and neutral lithographs that hide on the sidelines, or with the smaller-scale, but still public actions of Lederer.

On the final page, readers are rewarded with a photograph of Frau Dr. Cäcilia Lederer herself (Figure 7). The author sits on a bicycle in a modest sporty dress and hat that contrasts Ziemann's acrobatic outfit and flowing hair. In the studio portrait, Lederer engages actively with the observer, smiling at and waving to the camera. To counteract the bold actions of her unaccompanied bicycle excursion, the caption reads, "From Our Gallery of Graceful Bicycle Riders." The text surrounding the photograph tells of her encounter with the male *Sportsgenosse* ("sports comrade") who accompanies her throughout the rest of her ride. Ending the article with the properly accompanied and appropriately dressed married woman (the caption also repeats the title "Frau Dr."), the magazine offers more conservative skeptics an attractive, well-dressed (skirted), and composed woman as role model.

Finally, despite the presence of textual messages that remind the reader of exterior hindrances—the teacher abandoning his pupil, her sister's constant nagging ("You riding alone to the Prater, have you lost your senses? Do you want to be brought home dead?"), etc.— the photograph of Lederer in a confident and relaxed pose reassures the reader that the solo excursion has done no harm. The photograph reflects the clothing and gesture of bourgeois femininity, and the bicycle's presence takes on the character of a prop. The reader must carefully examine the photograph of Lederer on the bicycle and might wonder how she balances on the bike, for her feet do not touch the ground. The reader hopefully recognizes in her "balancing act" the construction of emancipation and identifies Lederer's complicity in it, as she balances on a bicycle propped up by invisible wires. If the story recalls moments of emancipatory behavior—continuing her ride despite stares or comments, advertisements that suggest buying power or work opportunities, photographs of physically uninhibited female acrobats—the final photograph reminds the reader that neither the story nor the photograph are random, but borne out of Lederer's individual struggle to experience and document a particular kind of freedom.

Figure 7: Frau Dr. Cäcilia Lederer

In conclusion, using photography to represent women's attempts at "conquering" the bicycle, *Draisena* and *Die Radlerin* allowed their readers to interpret individually women bicyclists' versions of emancipation. The photographic referent in the bicycling magazines allows some subjectivity; the sitter's "performative" aspect extends to the reading of the photograph itself. "The structure of looking is reciprocal: photographer and viewer collaborate on the reproduction of ideology" (Hirsch 7). In understanding photographs as performative, i.e., as active rather than static images, readers gain insight into women's visual interactions and how they can be empowered in both subject and object positions. The evidence of bicycling Early German New Women in the photography of *Draisena* and *Die Radlerin* validates the claim that women were empowered to interpret and shape the image of emancipation on their own terms.

Notes

[1] "Das Damenradeln ist das Länder zwingende Moment in der modernen Frauenbewegung" (111). The rather archaic formulation here makes translation challenging. It is not clear to which "Länder" von Salvisberg refers given the awkward placement of the quote in the text. It stands alone as a subtitle for Amelie Rother's article on women's bicycling in von Salvisberg's edited book. All other translations are mine unless otherwise noted.

[2] Journalists and writers at the turn of the century too readily situated bicycling within the women's movement: "Für das weibliche Geschlecht bedeutet das Radfahren eine Etappe im Kampfe um seine Emanzipation," (Eduard Romberg in *Plaudereien eines Arztes über das Radfahren der Damen,* 1901). See also Eduard Bertz *Philosophie des Fahrrads,* 1900; Richard Leo, *Das weibliche Radeln: Eine wohlmeinende populär-medizinische Besprechung für Eltern, Erzieher, u.a.,* 1899; Eduard Goldbeck, "Umsturz durch Radsport," 1896; Carl Krauss, "Die soziale Bedeutung des Fahrrads," Patria. Jahrbuch der 'Hilfe,' ed. Fr. Naumann, Berlin-Schönberg: n.p., 1902, 117–32.

[3] Ruth-Ellen Joeres discusses ambiguous nineteenth-century "radicality": "Radicality may well have lurked behind eccentricity, but it can also be present in the *performance of propriety,* especially when that propriety is present in a woman who presents a modest appearance even if her activities tend to deviate from the expected gender role" (Joeres 117, my emphasis).

[4] The introduction of the Kodak roll film camera came in 1888 and led to an increase in image-making by amateurs and an overall democratization of photography (Stokes 194).

[5] The encouragement of women to become professional photographers was promoted in the woman's magazine *Die Frau* in the following articles: "Photoskulptur," Paul Schettler (Dec. 1899); "Die photographische

Lehranstalt des Lettevereins zu Berlin" (Feb. 1904); "Die Flucht in die Photographie," Franziska Mann (Dec. 1905); and "Die Berufsphotographin," Anna L. Plehn (Oct. 1906). Interestingly, in addition to being a bicycle enthusiast, radical feminist Anita Augsberg, along with her friend Sophia Goudstikker (1865–1924), opened a photo studio "Hof-Alelier Elvira" in Munich.

[6] Mills discusses various discourses particular to women's travel writing, such as the concerns of safety and believability, in chapters 4 and 5 of *Discourses of Difference*.

[7] Clarke discusses the photographic essay of the Weimar period, August Sander's *Menschen des 20. Jahrhunderts*, as the basis for his argument. Sander assigned generic titles such as "The Carpenter," "The Seamstress," and "The Gentleman," to describe studio photographs of anonymous people. "Susan Sontag felt that in his attempt to reflect a 'comprehensive taxonomy' of the German society, Sander 'unself-consciously adjusted his style to the rank of the person he was photographing'" (Clarke 86).

[8] The questioning of the way one reads the individual is prominent in the realist work of nineteenth-century writers such as Theodor Fontane or Gottfried Keller (in particular here, *Kleider machen Leute*).

[9] The juxtaposition of text and image is of importance when considering possible interpretations for each, as their positions reveal different types of relationships such as opposition, collaboration, and parallelism (Hirsch). While the concept "a picture is worth a thousand words" has credence in our cultural understanding, the power of language cannot be so easily dismissed. Indeed, the reading of an image must not be taken at "face value," but, as suggested, within the framework of a specific discourse. In cautioning against the lack of social context, Benjamin comments, "Wird die Beschriftung nicht zum wesentlichsten Bestandteil der Aufnahme werden?" ("Kleine Geschichte der Photographie" 93).

[10] The column started in 1898 and was edited by H. Schnauss, chief editor for the photographic journal "Apollo" in Dresden. Entitled "Die photographische Ecke," it covered various detailed aspects of photography for the bicyclist, including equipment, photo-taking tips, and film development on the road.

[11] If indeed amateur photography on bicycling tours was a popular hobby, without it being mentioned in magazine articles one would hardly come to the same conclusion through the choice of photographs displayed in these pages. Few reader-photographs appear, but this perhaps attests to women bicyclist's bourgeois modesty and avoidance of the "sin" of vanity.

Works Cited

Armstrong, Nancy. *Fiction in the Age of Photography: The Legacy of British Realism*. Cambridge, MA: Harvard UP, 1999.

Atkinson, Paul. "Strong Minds and Weak Bodies: Sports, Gymnastics and the Medicalization of Women's Education." *British Journal of Sports History* 2 (1985): 62–71.

Beduhn, Ralf. *Die Roten Radler: Illustrierte Geschichte des Arbeiterradfahrbundes "Solidarität."* Münster: Literaturverlag, 1982.

Benjamin, Walter. "Kleine Geschichte der Photographie." *Das Kunstwerk im Zeitalter seiner technischen Reproduzierbarkeit: Drei Studien zur Kunstsoziologie*. Frankfurt a.M.: Suhrkamp, 1974.

_____. "Das Kunstwerk im Zeitalter seiner technischen Reproduzierbarkeit." *Illuminationen: Ausgewählte Schriften,* 1955. Frankfurt a.M.: Suhrkamp, 1961. 148–84.

Berger, John. *Ways of Seeing*. London: Penguin, 1972.

Bleckmann, Dörte. *Wehe wenn sie losgelassen: Über die Anfänge des Frauenradfahrens in Deutschland*. Leipzig: Maxi Kutschera, 1999.

Bonnell, Marilyn. "The Power of the Pedal: the Bicycle and the Turn-of-the-Century Woman," *Nineteenth Century Contexts* 14.2 (1990): 215–39.

Bowlby, Rachel. *Just Looking: Consumer Culture in Dreiser, Gissing, and Zola*. New York: Methuen, 1985.

Bridenthal, Renate, et. al. *When Biology Became Destiny: Women in Weimar and Nazi Germany*. New York: Monthly Review P, 1984.

Briese, Volker, Wilhelm Matthies and Gerhard Renda, eds. *Wege zur Fahrradgeschichte*. Bielefeld: Bielefelder Verlagsanstalt, 1995.

Calif, Ruth. *The World on Wheels*. Toronto: Cornwall Books, 1983.

Clarke, Graham. "Public Faces, Private Lives: August Sander and the Social Typology of the Portrait Photograph." *The Portrait in Photography*. London: Reaktion, 1992. 71–93.

Clarke, Graham. *The Portrait in Photography*. London: Reaktion, 1992.

Ehrenpreis, David. "Cyclists and Amazons: Representing the New Woman in Wilhelmine Germany," *Women's Art Journal* 20.1 (1999): 25–31.

Evans, Richard. "The Concept of Feminism: Notes for Practicing Historians." *German Women in the Eighteenth and Nineteenth Centuries*. Eds. Ruth-Ellen Joeres and Mary Jo Maynes. Bloomington: Indiana UP, 1986. 247–70.

Foucault, Michel. *History of Sexuality Volume I: An Introduction*. Trans. Robert Hurley. New York: Vintage, 1978.

Franke, Jutta. *Illustrierte Fahrrad-Geschichte*. Berlin: Nicolai, 1987.

Frevert, Ute. *Frauen-Geschichte zwischen bürgerlicher Verbesserung und neuer Weiblichkeit*. Frankfurt a.M.: Suhrkamp, 1986.

Gehrhard, Ute. *Unerhört: Die Geschichte der deutschen Frauenbewegung*. Hamburg: Rowohlt, 1990.

Ginsberg, Madeleine. *Victorian Dress in Photographs*. New York: Holmes and Meier, 1982.

Gruver Garvey, Ellen. *The Adman in the Parlor: Magazines and the Gendering of Consumer Culture. 1880s to 1910*. New York: Oxford UP, 1996.

Heron, Liz and Val Williams. *Illuminations: Women Writing on Photography from the 1850s to the Present*. Durham, NC: Duke UP, 1996.

Hirsch, Marianne. *Family Frames: Photography, Narrative and Postmemory*. Cambridge, MA: Harvard UP, 1997.

Huyssen, Andreas. "Mass Culture as Woman: Modernism's Other." *After the Great Divide: Modernism, Mass Culture, Postmodernism*. Bloomington: Indiana UP, 1986. 44–64.

Joeres, Ruth-Ellen, B. *Respectability and Deviance: Nineteenth Century German Women Writers and the Ambiguity of Representation*. Chicago: U of Chicago P, 1998.

Kern, Stephan. *The Culture of Time and Space 1880–1918*. Cambridge: Harvard UP, 1983.

Kucich, John and Dianne F. Sadoff, eds. *Victorian Afterlife: Postmodern Culture Rewrites the Nineteenth Century*. Minneapolis: U of Minnesota P, 2000.

Lederer, Cäcilia. "Meine erste Radausfahrt." *Die Radlerin*, 1898: 165–69; 17 Aug. 1898: 401–04.

Lessing, Hans-Erhard. *Fahrradkultur: Der Höhepunkt um 1900*. Reinbek bei Hamburg: Rowohlt, 1982.

Lessing, Hans-Erhard. *"Ich fahr so gerne Rad..." Geschichten von der Lust, auf dem eisernen Rosse dahinzujagen*. München: dtv, 1995.

Maes, Jochen. *Fahrradsucht*. Köln: DuMont, 1989.

Maierhof, Gudrun, and Katinka Schröder. *Sie Radeln wie ein Mann, Madame: Wie die Frauen das Rad eroberten*. Zürich: Unionsverlag, 1992.

Mavor, Carol. *Pleasures Taken: Performances of Sexuality and Loss in Victorian Photographs*. Durham: Duke UP, 1995.

McPherson, Heather. *The Modern Portrait in Nineteenth-Century France*. Cambridge: Cambridge UP, 2001.

Miller, Michael B. *The Bon Marché: Bourgeois Culture and the Department Store, 1869–1920*. Princeton: Princeton UP, 1981.

Mills, Sara. *Discourses of Difference: An Analysis of Women's Travel Writing and Colonialism*. London: Routledge, 1991.

Mosse, George L. *Nationalism and Sexuality: Middle-Class Morality and Sexual Norms in Modern Europe.* Madison: U of Wisconsin P, 1985.

Paturi, Felix. *Die Geschichte des Fahrrads.* Stuttgart: ATVerlag, 1988.

Pfister, Gertrud, ed. *Frau und Sport: Die Frau in der Gesellschaft.* Frankfurt a.M.: Fischer, 1980.

Pinney, Christopher and Nicolas Peterson, eds. *Photography's Other Histories.* Durham, NC: Duke UP, 2003.

Rabenstein, Rüdiger. *Radsport und Gesellschaft: Ihre sozialgeschichtlichen Zusammenhänge in der Zeit von 1867 bis 1914.* Hildesheim: Weidmannsche Verlagsbuchhandlung, 1991.

Rappaport, Erika Diane. *Shopping for Pleasure: Women in the Making of London's West End.* Princeton: Princeton UP, 2000.

Riha, Karl, ed. *Das Fahrradbuch.* Darmstadt: Luchterhand, 1985.

Salomon, Eleonore. "Aus den Anfängen des bürgerlichen Frauenradsports in Deutschland." *Theorie und Praxis der Körperkultur* 14.3 (Mar. 1965). 199–206.

Salvisberg, Paul. *Der Fahrradsport in Bild und Wort.* Hildesheim: Olms, 1998.

Schenkel, Elmar. "Cyclomanie: Fahrrad und Literatur um 1900." *Literaturwissenschaftliches Jahrbuch* 37 (1996): 211–28.

Smith-Rosenberg, Carroll. *Disorderly Conduct: Visions of Gender in Victorian America.* Oxford: Oxford UP, 1985.

Stokes, Philip. "The Family Photographic Album." *The Portrait in Photography.* Ed. Graham Clarke. London: Reaktion, 1992. 193–205.

Timm, Uwe. *Der Mann auf dem Hochrad.* München: dtv, 1984.

Vademecum für Radfahrerinnen. Wien: Gesellschaft für graphische Industrie, 1897.

Von Ankum, Katherine. Ed. *Women in the Metropolis: Gender and Modernity in Weimar Culture.* Berkeley: U of California P, 1997.

Wittmann, Livia. "Zwischen Femme Fatale and Femme Fragile—die Neue Frau?" *Jahrbuch für internationale Germanistik* 17.2 (1985): 74–110.

Artist for Art's Sake or Artist for Sale: Lulu's and Else's Failed Attempts at Aesthetic Self-Fashioning

Kelly Comfort

Frank Wedekind's Lulu, of his plays *Earth-Spirit* (1895) and *Pandora's Box* (1904), and Arthur Schnitzler's Else, from the novella *Fräulein Else* (1924), are both examples of female performance artists given their construction of stylized and aestheticized selves. By comparing Lulu and Else, this essay reveals how women's performativity can either constitute a form of empowerment and self-affirmation or serve as a path toward commodification and consumability. Despite Lulu's and Else's initial attempts to achieve agency by fashioning themselves as artists or aesthetes, socioeconomic forces and the men who control them turn both women into aesthetic objects and salable commodities. (KC)

Frank Wedekind's Lulu, of his plays *Earth-Spirit* (*Erdgeist*, 1895) and *Pandora's Box* (*Die Büchse der Pandora,* 1904), and Arthur Schnitzler's Else, from the novella *Fräulein Else* (1924), are not artistic producers in the traditional sense, since they neither create concrete art objects nor base their professions on aesthetic talents. Both female protagonists can nonetheless be considered artists due to their construction of stylized and aestheticized selves. To understand the connection between Lulu, Else, and the figure of the artist it is helpful to examine how a turn-of-the-century strain of aestheticism, particularly Nietzsche's version in *The Gay Science,* redefined the artist's attributes by including professionals who do not create external artistic work. "The problem of the actor has troubled me for the longest time," Nietzsche observes. He then continues:

> I felt unsure (and sometimes still do) whether it is not only from this angle that one can get at the dangerous concept of the "artist"—a concept that has so far been treated with unpardonable

generosity: Falseness with a good conscience; the delight in simulation exploding as a power that pushes aside one's so-called "character," flooding it and at times extinguishing it; the inner craving for a role and mask, for *appearance*; an excess of the capacity for all kinds of adaptations that can no longer be satisfied in the service of the most immediate and narrowest utility—all of this is perhaps not *only* peculiar to the actor?

Such an instinct will have developed most easily in families of the lower classes who had to survive under changing pressures and coercions, in deep dependency, who had to cut their coat according to the cloth, always adapting themselves again to new circumstances, who always had to change their mien and posture, until they learned gradually to turn their coat with *every* wind and thus virtually to become a coat [...].

As for the *Jews,* the people who possess the art of adaptability par excellence, this train of thought suggests immediately that one might see them virtually as a world-historical arrangement for the production of actors, a veritable breeding ground for actors. And it is really high time to ask: What good actor today is *not*—a Jew? [...]

Finally, *women.* Reflect on the whole history of women: do they not *have* to be first of all and above all actresses? Listen to the physicians who have hypnotized women; finally, love them—let yourself be "hypnotized by them"! What is always the end result? That they "put on something" even when they take off everything.

Woman is so artistic. (316–17)

Nietzsche asks here whether falseness, simulation, and disguise are "perhaps not *only* peculiar to the actor," and in so doing, he invites us to assign the actor's attributes to a larger group of people for whom role-playing and acting come naturally. According to Nietzsche, the shared histrionic impulse of the lower classes, women, and Jews aligns members of specific class, gender, and religious groups not only with actors, but also with the figure of the artist. Two of the three categories clearly relate to Lulu and Else as women in precarious financial situations, while Else faces the additional burden of hiding her Jewishness. Nietzsche's expansive definition of actors and the link between them and the "dangerous concept of the 'artist'" underlie the present examination of the artist as a self-fashioned aesthete.

By comparing Lulu and Else as female performers who fashion themselves as actors, artists, and aesthetes,[1] I aim to illuminate how and why woman's performativity can either become a form of empowerment and agency or a path toward commodification and consumability. Just as art objects became commodified in turn-of-the-century consumer culture, so too do these female aesthetes become exchangeable or buyable commodities. Changes in the literary marketplace throughout the nineteenth century meant that art and the artist figure were no longer sacred or elitist. Industrial-capitalist society allowed market values—the laws of supply and demand, the notion of salability, concerns regarding production costs, and the ability of goods to be mass-produced and mass-consumed—to determine artistic worth. Simply put, artistic worth became devalued to make exchange value the determining factor of art. In *Theories of Surplus Value* Karl Marx argues that "capitalist production is hostile to certain aspects of intellectual production, such as art and poetry" (*Literature and Art* 28). Moreover, for turn-of-the-century women in particular, the fact that economic considerations contaminate aesthetic ones means that the female performance artist can easily become a commodified and consumable object. Because she produces herself as art, she is easily objectified. Thus, despite Lulu's and Else's attempts to achieve agency by fashioning themselves as artists, socio-economic forces and the men who control them turn both women into aesthetic objects.

Previous scholarship has neglected this aspect of Wedekind's and Schnitzler's female protagonists. In the seventies, critical attention to Schnitzler's *Fräulein Else* was mainly concerned with the protagonist's psychotic, neurotic, pathological, or morbid personality (Cohn, Beharriell). More recent readings from the eighties and nineties have focused on issues of vision, seeing, or surveillance (Anderson, Huyssen). My interpretation of the novella centers on acting and performativity, and thus shares a concern with certain critics for Else's literary and theatrical experiences (Aurnhammer), her "self-dramatizing tendency" (Yeo), and the overall importance of play, playacting, and drama (Raymond). It also examines her commodification and consumption, an aspect of the novella that has not yet been amply explored. My reading of *Fräulein Else* aims to show how Else's predicament and demise are not solely, or even primarily, the result of her position as bourgeois daughter, i.e., as a young, unmarried, middle-class woman, which has indeed been the most recent interpretive trend (Szalay, Huyssen). Rather, my comparison of Else with Lulu shows that despite their many differences, a similar fate ensures that both women ultimately become the commodified objects of male consumption, and thereby lose the initial agency and power that acting affords them.

While it is difficult to map the critical trends that relate to Wedekind's Lulu, one can locate five overarching interpretive tendencies over the last four decades: Lulu as (1) male fantasy and a projection of male desire; (2) "mythic persona in an archetypal mode" (Harris 44), i.e., as a reflection of Pandora, Eve, Lilith, Dionysus, Zarathustra, etc. (Littau, Jones, Weidl); (3) the incarnation of a masochistic female principle, some natural, lustful drive, an intrinsically destructive force, or the femme fatale par excellence (Willeke, Libbon, Midgley); (4) a deviant, degenerate, or a pathological figure (Gilman); (5) an actress (Boa), a construct (Hallamore), a multivalent character (Peacock), and a dandy-like figure (Finney). My interpretation of Lulu coincides with the last of these interpretive possibilities in that I consider her, at least initially, a protean actress and a dandified female aesthete. Given such beginnings, it is interesting to note how Lulu changes as a result of her interactions with society in general and the male characters in particular.

Before highlighting the parallels between these two views of the female performer, it is essential to note the gaping differences between Lulu and Else: the former's sexual experience, lower-class origins, public performances, and amorality versus the latter's virginity, upper-class background, sheltered upbringing, and moral considerations. In many ways, Else longs for the kind of liberated lifestyle that Lulu embodies, as evident in Else's self-narrated, yet secret fantasies. There are nonetheless striking parallels between these equally famous fictional women from the German-language tradition. Lulu and Else are both actresses in the broadest sense of the term; they fluctuate between self-affirmed visions of themselves as performers and self-critical notions of their fate as spectacles. Otherwise stated, they perceive their dual positions as artists and art objects, they are both forced into the role of commodity and prostitute by male figures, and they both die as a result of some form of "consumption," whether at the hands of Jack the Ripper in Wedekind's plays or through the consumption of a deadly dose of Veronal in Schnitzler's novella. This comparative reading thus examines how and why both female protagonists die in a tripartite transaction in which aesthetics, erotics, and economics converge.

As female aesthete, Lulu of *Earth-Sprit* self-consciously fashions herself as an artwork and invites her spectators to see her as such. Lulu constructs herself through a series of appearances, evident in her multiple names, costumes, and lovers. Although men continually try to give her a single name—Goll calls her Nelli, Schön suggests Mignon, and Schwarz prefers Eve—Lulu as Proteus refuses to be fixed or typecast. She becomes each new role she chooses, thus erasing within the world of the play the distance between actor and character. Rather than being separate from her performances, Lulu as actor exists only within them. Hence, Schwarz can respond, upon seeing Lulu in the pierrot costume, "Her whole body was as much in harmony with this impossible costume as if she had been born in it" (15). Likewise, Alwa can exclaim, while watching Lulu dance, "She was conforming strictly to her role" (64). Although Lulu's various lovers attempt to fix her in a given role, they cannot prevent her from changing forms and discarding them one by one, just as she does her many costumes.

Being so good at changing costumes and "so excited when [...] dressing" (71), Lulu of *Earth-Spirit* should be understood as an aestheticist ideal, a living example of art for art's sake. Based on this characterization, Lulu, always perfectly aware of herself, is the aesthete protagonist par excellence (19). Men might try to attain "an accurate picture" of her (49), or they might wish to see her, as Lulu speaks of Schön's misconception, as "an enchanting creature [...] with a heart of gold," but Lulu insists, "I'm neither the one nor the other. It's unfortunate for you that you think I am" (77). She cannot be defined by those external to her, nor can one speak of her true essence. Truth and hypocrisy become irrelevant terms once Lulu's appearances come to constitute her entire being. As she contends, "If men have done away with themselves for my sake, that doesn't reduce my *value*. [...] I've never in the world wanted to be anything but what I've been taken for, and no one has ever taken me for anything but what I am" (97, emphasis added). Here Lulu's "value" depends on her ability to overcome the splitting and alienation of the actress; being in her role, not estranged from it, proves empowering for her. What Judith Butler claims about gender identity and performance applies to Lulu in a more general way:

> If gender attributes and acts, the various ways in which a body shows or produces its cultural signification, are performative, then there is no preexisting identity by which an act or attitude might be measured; there would be no true or false, real or distorted acts of gender, and the postulation of a true gender identity would be revealed as a regulatory fiction. (180)

Lulu not only performs her gendered identity, but also "woman," "self," or in her case, "selves." Indeed, she exemplifies the female performance artist who purports to be herself in the act of performing. In this regard, she is what Jeanie Forte would call a "subject-performer" (257). On the one hand, Lulu's protean nature allows her to be anything and everything. On the other hand, her chameleon-like self-construction makes Lulu proud of never having wished to appear other than she is, namely because her state of appearing is always a state of being. Hence Schwarz, the artist who captures Lulu's variegated images in his paintings, can rightly assert that every day he feels as if he were seeing Lulu for the first time (39).

Lulu's mode of self-fashioning finds its philosophical parallel in Nietzsche's notion of "brief habits." A mode of self-formation based on brief habits responds to the conviction that life is bearable only as an aesthetic phenomenon. Despite the necessary ephemerality of each habit or, in Lulu's case, each role, it creates a feeling of endurance and wholeness; one is content and "desire[s] nothing else, without having any need for comparisons, contempt, or hatred" (Nietzsche 237). Yet even before one habit or role ends, another has already begun. Additionally, Lulu combines her series of roles and brief habits with a succession of masculine detours. Lulu, the actress who scripts her roles, turns herself into a spectacle and presents herself to a multitude of male onlookers. Wedekind's choice of a female seducer has led many critics to confuse Lulu's aestheticist self-poeticization with what they see as the willingness to be objectified by the male gaze. This interpretation establishes a "split between the male as active bearer of the look and the female as the passive receptor of it," and in so doing fails to see the powerful aspects of Lulu's performativity (Finney 91). A careful consideration of Lulu's detour method reveals that an occasional passivity can actually be in the service of one's active self-formation. Lulu's desire to be, as she claims, "good enough to eat," does not—at least not yet—imply complicity with consumption or woman's objectification (44). On the contrary, Lulu's role as actor is validated and her existence strengthened each time her spectators engage in observing her. Thus, even if being named by men and disappearing into roles seems too self-effacing to be protean or positively connoted, Lulu's role-playing ensures her power and survival throughout the entire first play. As Elizabeth Boa rightly asserts, "the way in which Lulu acts out men's desires does not necessarily signify lack of autonomy, for she consciously chooses to act and enjoys her own skill" (56). When Lulu sees herself as a pierrot in Schwarz's eyes or wishes she were a man when she looks in the mirror, she adds a narcissistic detour to her own general narcissism, thereby turning the passive act of being a spectacle into an active affirmation of her own being as constituted by acting and artistry. In short, Lulu determines and directs the male gaze, rather than being the passive recipient of it. It is not until *Pandora's Box* that, as Wedekind himself notes in the foreword to the second play, Lulu "plays an entirely passive role in all three acts" (103–04).

As such, Lulu's self-experimentation underscores her constructed and artistic nature, which opposes naturalistic interpretations of her as either "the primal form of woman" (Wedekind 11), or as "consisting of nothing but flesh and vulva" (Michelsen 55). Unlike characterizations of Lulu as a natural principle, I concur with critics who recognize Lulu "as the embodiment of artifice, carefully oiling, powdering, and dressing herself in an almost dandified manner" (Finney 90). It is, above all, Lulu's "cosmetic box" that serves as the main reference to the Pandora myth (Schuler-Will 31). In "Woman as Spectacle and Commodity: Wedekind's Lulu Plays," Gail Finney offers a similar interpretation of Lulu as a powerful artist and performer who represents "a type of the artist, her theatrical skills constituting a creative power otherwise denied to the sterile femme fatale" (90).

Although Schnitzler's Else appears neither on stage nor in portraits, she likewise represents an actor and artist in the Nietzschean sense due to her unceasing will to illusion, what Siew Lian Yeo terms her "self-dramatizing tendency" and her "literary-theatrical experiences" (18). At the outset of her monologue,[2] Else clearly constructs herself as an actress. Her first inner comment, "[t]hat was a rather good exit," establishes the theatricality of her character as she, like an actress, reflects on the quality of her performance (4). Else also concerns herself with the reception of her performance, evident in her next thought: "Did I nod back ungraciously or haughtily? I didn't mean to act that way" (6). Else's entire performance combines language-for-oneself and being-for-others, a combination that often requires her to double as other or to invent an imagined interlocutor in order to ensure that there is always an audience to watch her display.

Else is particularly aware of her dissimulation in the scene just before her interview with Herr von Dorsday, when she requests thirty thousand guilders to save her father from financial ruin. Else wonders, "What shall I wear? [...] At all events, I must look seductive when I interview Dorsday" (27). Her attractiveness will aid her, or so she assumes. Else believes that her multiplicity of roles will allow her to successfully persuade Dorsday: "I'll talk to Herr Dorsday of Esperies and I'll appeal to him, I, the haughty, the aristocrat, the Marchesa, the beggar-maid, the embezzler's daughter" (29). As Else explains, it is because of this protean cast that she is able to climb so well: "No one is a better climber than I am; no one has so much spunk. I'm a sporting girl. I should have been born in England, or else been a Countess" (29). Social-climbing via acting establishes the affirmative power of Else's will to illusion and links her with Lulu in obvious ways: both women clearly embody Nietzsche's conception of the artist as a social-climbing actor, on the one hand, and a histrionic woman, on the other hand. Moreover, both female protagonists represent the general tendency of women, both fictional and real, to use their bodies and acting skills to promote themselves.

Thus, whereas Else initially occupies a societal position above Lulu's humble beginnings, changes in her family's class status, coupled with their attempts to appear better off than they are, align her with Wedekind's protagonist. Else reminisces about the days when she and her family were better off, and pities herself as "the poor relative, invited out by her rich aunt" who, despite passing as an elegant young woman, is down to her last pair of silk stockings (6, 32). In fact, when she thinks of how her mother has been able to maintain the façade of wealth in the face of continual financial crises, Else comments, "Mother's really an artist," thus supporting Nietzsche's claim that the lower classes come to emulate the actor out of the necessity to keep up appearances (332).[3]

Acting out of necessity does not automatically undermine the agency and empowerment evident in my reading of Lulu in *Earth-Spirit*. Acting in the Nietzschean sense constitutes Lulu's mode of self-fashioning as well as her method of self-preservation. She has attained a life of "regal luxury" not only due to Schön's "superhuman efforts to advance [Lulu] in society," but also because of her own innate theatrical abilities and performative talents (43, 46). Given that "[s]he learnt how to change costumes when she was still a child," Lulu can change clothes more quickly without the help of her professional "dresser" (69). "If I hadn't known more about acting than they do in the theatre," Lulu reflects, "I wonder what would have become of me" (67). Unquestionably, Lulu's role-playing on- and offstage has taken her far. And even though acting saved her from poverty, Lulu refuses to see her talent solely as a result of sheer economic necessity.

Curiously, however, the Lulu tragedies do not sustain this privileged status of art, appearances, and surfaces. Beginning with Schön's death and Lulu's imprisonment at the end of the first play, and climaxing early in the second work, Lulu's art for art's sake becomes art for sale. This transition occurs most poignantly in act 2 of *Pandora's Box,* when the failed speculation on the Jungfrau shares[4] leads to Lulu's diminished wealth and prompts her lovers to turn into her employers and exploiters. Lulu and Alwa are "high and dry"; they "handed over" their last penny to purchase more Jungfrau shares and thus "no longer have any money" (133). Knowing of her imminent poverty, Rodrigo plans to turn Lulu into a magnificent trapeze artist, while Casti-Piani wants to become her "employment agent," a euphemism for being her pimp (133). In *Earth-Spirit,* Lulu as chameleon and performer manipulates men in a variety of ways and brings them to their downfall, but in the second play, men bring Lulu to her tragic end. Wedekind underscores this reversal in two ways: (1) by creating a growing rift between Lulu as aesthete and her portrait as art object, and (2) by eliminating Lulu's series of performances and casting her in the permanent role of commodity or object of exchange. As she becomes scripted by others, Lulu must recognize that she longer authors her own roles, nor does she maintain control of her spectators. Lulu goes from being her own master to being a slave. In fact, Geschwitz uses the term "slave" to refer to Lulu toward the end of the second play, the same word Else employs to describe Dorsday's treatment of her (138).

To understand the progression from art for art's sake to the commodification of art, a comparison between Lulu as self-fashioned aesthete and her portrait, a concrete art object, is useful. Unlike Wilde's *The Picture of Dorian Gray,* in which Dorian remains untouched by the hands of time while his portrait decays, Wedekind's Lulu plays emphasize the growing disparity between Lulu and a past performance, a former role, as preserved in the portrait. Lulu, not her painted image, undergoes a loss of value, what Walter Benjamin terms "*aura.*" Whereas Benjamin defines the "aura" as "that which withers in the age of mechanical reproduction," in Lulu's case it is she, and not her portrait, that undergoes loss (221). Because of her aging, her decay, and her numerous exchanges, Lulu herself erodes over time to a trace of her earlier beauty. To understand this transition, let us first consider act 1, scene 2 of *Earth-Spirit,* in which Lulu poses in her pierrot costume before three delighted spectators, her successive husbands Goll, Schwarz, and Schön. In this initial scene, Lulu appears as a "picture before which Art must despair" (19). Mounted atop the throne she herself, far more than her portrait, affords her onlookers a rare pleasure as they watch from their observation posts below (18). Here Lulu as artist and actor is celebrated. Alwa's and Schigolch's comments in the final scene of *Pandora's Box* on Lulu's relation to the portrait provide a striking contrast:

> ALWA. (comparing the portrait with LULU) In spite of all that she's been through since, the childlike expression in the eyes is still quite the same. (Pleasurably excited) But the dewy-freshness which was on the skin, the fragrant breath about the lips, the radiant whiteness of the brow, the bold splendour of the flesh on neck and arms—
> SCHIGOLCH. All that has gone into the dustbin. But she can confidently say 'That's what I once was.' No one into whose hands she falls today can form any conception of the glories of our youth.
> ALWA. (cheerfully) Thank God, one doesn't notice the advance of *decay* when one is constantly together. (Lightly) A woman blossoms for us precisely at the right moment to plunge a man into everlasting ruin; such is her *natural destiny.* (165, emphasis added)

Here Lulu's portrait provides the pleasure. Her ideal image becomes frozen and fixed in the art object, while she herself has been type-cast in the role of men's commodity, now curiously linked with her natural destiny and "mystified [...] into a supposed law of [woman's] nature" (Marx, *Capital* 771). Up until this point in the play Lulu has been "intoxicated with her own beauty, [...] idolatrously in love with it," but can now no longer stand to see her portrait and screams at Geschwitz, "Take that picture out of my sight! Throw it out of the window!" (69, 164). Clearly Lulu is now split and no longer one with her role. This splitting of self from object diminishes Lulu's power and leads to her alienation.

Along with this fragmentation comes Lulu's commodification. The reactions of other characters to her vis-à-vis her portrait foreshadow Lulu's new exchange value. Schigolch thinks the portrait will make an excellent impression on the clientele given that now "[t]he whole flat has a more elegant appearance" (164). Alwa, too, derives pleasure from the painting: "In the face of this portrait I regain my self-respect. It makes my destiny comprehensible" (164). These men derive use-value from the painting, and, more importantly, they come to see themselves as the owners of it and also of Lulu, a commodity from whose exchange value they intend to profit (Marx, *Capital* 179). The price or money form of a commodity stems from its inherent exchange value; Alwa traces in overtly passive language Lulu's exchange-value when he reminisces how "[t]he artist's wife became the wife of my lamented father. My father's wife became my mistress" (159). Here Lulu's masculine detours no longer signal an active subject; rather, Lulu becomes an object of possession, a commodity exchanged: the artist's wife, the father's wife, the son's mistress. Interestingly, all three of these men inhabit the artistic world as a painter, an editor and critic, and a playwright, respectively. Alwa establishes the male artist as Lulu's proprietor. Just as others have owned her portrait, so too might they own Lulu. Thus, while Geschwitz encounters a potential buyer for the portrait, Lulu, now forced into prostitution by her male-guardians, discovers her own price on the streets of London. Even the faithful Geschwitz admits that she was unwilling to sell Lulu's painting. Allowing Lulu to sell herself seems to be the preferred solution for her various "owners," who no longer see her as an empowered performative-subject, but merely as a sexualized body whose "work" or "sale" can turn them a profit.

We might ask, however, whether Lulu's acting has always bordered on prostitution, since she, at the young age of twenty, was already three times married and "had given satisfaction to an incredible number of lovers" (122). In stark contrast to "Fräulein" Else, "the young Lulu suffers not from a lack but from an excess of sexual knowledge" (Finney 85). Nonetheless, for both female protagonists there is an important distinction to be made between giving oneself and selling oneself. Interestingly, however, when the transition from Lulu as artist to Lulu as prostitute does occur at the end of the second play, the traits that made Lulu a successful aesthete are now cited as desired qualities for her new profession. For example, when Casti-Piani threatens to turn Lulu in to the police if she will not accept work as a prostitute, he insists that this new job well suits Lulu's "natural vocation" due to her "outstanding talent for languages" and her "heavy consumption in men" (133–35). Her "consumption" of men initially came from role-playing, yet when Lulu becomes "consumed" by men, it is because she has lost her ability to exist as actor, artist, and aesthete and has changed from active subject to passive object.

Wedekind's Lulu tragedies highlight the distinction between the empowered actress and the victimized prostitute, only to show how the latter usurps the position of the former. Lulu insists repeatedly that she would not make a good prostitute. "I cannot sell the one thing I've ever owned," she argues (136). Lulu likewise explains to Schön in act 2, scene 3 of *Earth-Spirit,* "I danced and was a model and was glad to be able to earn my keep in that way, but to love to order is beyond me" (49). Here, she shows agency given that she has loved her sex-partners, something prostitutes do not do. She reiterates the same notion—"I can't sell myself. That is worse than prison" (136)—while questioning Casti-Piani's plans for her: "Me, in a brothel?" (137). In these moments, the gulf separating the actress from the prostitute seems unbridgeable.

Yet despite her ability to escape from Casti-Piani, Lulu succeeds only by promising herself to both Schigolch and Geschwitz. The fine line between self-sanctioned and forced prostitution becomes blurred. Ultimately, Lulu *is* forced into prostitution by another set of male figures: Alwa and the mysterious father-figure, Schigolch. As Finney points out, "*Pandora's Box* presents us with one male character after another trying to 'cash in on' Lulu" (98). Still, in the final act Lulu again questions her ability to play the part of a prostitute, claiming, "I'd like to see the woman who could earn money with the rags I have on my body" (156–57). The donning of rags, a sign of Lulu's socio-economic position and *not* a new costume, disrupts the beauty of appearances and gives way to Lulu's material essence or bodily reality. Whereas Lulu was initially a body in representation or in performance, she now becomes a material body.[5] A series of roles, brief habits, and detours no longer constitute Lulu's essence. Instead she becomes one Lulu: the prostitute and object, not the actress and subject.

Wedekind foreshadows Lulu's tragic fate throughout the entire second play, in which Lulu no longer changes clothes, but rather exchanges them. In prison Lulu switches underwear with Geschwitz so as to contract cholera; in the hospital she trades clothes with Geschwitz once again in order to escape unnoticed; later, while in exile, she exchanges attire with Bob, the bellhop, to elude the police. The only "costume" mentioned in the second play is the humble garb Lulu wears as she makes her debut on the streets of London, "barefoot and in a torn black dress" (155). It is in this attire that Jack sizes up Lulu's body and determines that it is "well-made" and perfectly formed (173). Here she wears her "costume" out of necessity, not pleasure. Moreover, Lulu's discontentment with such a costume further underscores her splitting and contrasts starkly with her earlier disappearance into her roles. Any form of splitting, whether between her and the portrait or her and her costume, undermines Lulu's power. Now nothing but materiality, Lulu no longer represents a multiplicity of roles or a palimpsest of appearances, but simply a body, soon to become a corpse at the hands of the greatest male exploiter of turn-of-the-century Europe. As Littau aptly notes, when the serial killer Jack the Ripper kills Lulu, he also "kills her seriality" (902). Consequently, we see that once Lulu falls from her privileged position and undergoes a loss of wholeness and agency, she changes from female aesthete to exchangeable commodity.

In a strikingly similar manner, Schnitzler's protagonist is also threatened by men's attempts to convert her penchant for acting into a proclivity for prostitution. Interestingly, Else's histrionic sense of self allows her to interpret Dorsday's indecent proposal from the perspective of an actress. Dorsday tells Else that he wishes nothing more than "*to see*" her, since she will bring him much pleasure when she unveils (60–61), yet Else turns the act of unveiling into the possibility of a performance. Schnitzler's young female protagonist sees here an opportunity to demonstrate her theatrical abilities: "The moon hasn't risen yet. It'll rise only for the *performance,* for the *great performance* on the meadow" (82, emphasis added). The notion that an unveiling could be a "performance" suggests that, for Else, nakedness will be a new costume. The role of revealer is a part Else might enjoy playing: "I look forward to it. Haven't I longed for something like this all my life?" she muses (110). Viewing disrobing as a performance allows Else to transcend the notion of commodification. Her striptease can be an aesthetic or artistic act, and not merely an economic transaction.

Although Else can affirm the act of unveiling and revel in its eroticism, she cannot accept her audience, the single spectator who gazes at her as if she were his "slave" (82). Dorsday's presence hinders

Else's enjoyment and thwarts not only her erotic, but also her artistic enjoyment of this new performative role. Regarding the first of these tensions, that between the erotic and the ethical, it is important to note that most critics emphasize the confrontation between morality and desire in *Fräulein Else*. They note how Schnitzler's autonomous narrator oscillates between fantasies of the sexually liberated woman and the ideal bourgeois wife and mother, between one who enjoys herself sexually and one who feels shames over such enjoyment. Even before Dorsday's proposition, we sense Else's contradictory wishes and desires regarding marriage, motherhood, and fidelity. Such ambivalence should be understood as the product of upper-class Viennese society, which has shaped Else and created a paradoxical situation for her. It thus underscores what Aurnhammer notes as the difference between the societal role assigned to Else and the erotic dreams or wishes that she cannot completely repress (503).

Consequently, just as Dorsday's request triggers Else's sexual awakening, so too does it force her to censor her own desires in order to avoid becoming a slave or a prostitute. Else can only give herself if she chooses the object of her desire. Precisely for this reason, Dorsday is unacceptable. "No; I won't sell myself. Never. I'll never sell myself," Else exclaims. Then later: "Yes; if once I find the right man, I'll give myself" (68). Else insists that she choose the spectators of her performance, and she would rather "go to anyone else—but not him" (68). In a manner similar to Lulu, Else declares, "I'll be a wanton, not a prostitute" (68). The unveiling would not be as problematic if Else were in control of her own performance rather than the object of Dorsday's unrelenting gaze, of those eyes that will "stab" and "drill" their way into her (86). Once again, it is the split between subject and object that threatens to undermine the female performance artist's power.

Before replacing Dorsday, the undesirable, single viewer, with a group of people as a permissible audience, Else briefly becomes her own public as she performs before herself in private. This moment allows her to regain temporary control of the situation. In the famous mirror scene, Else attempts to define herself independently of society in general and male desire in particular. Gazing at her reflected image, she reveals her narcissistic desire:

> Oh, how pleasant it is to walk up and down the room, naked. Am I really as beautiful as I look in the mirror? Oh, won't you come closer, pretty Fräulein? I want to kiss your blood-red lips. What a pity that the mirror comes between us. The cold mirror. How well we'd get on together. Isn't that so? We need nobody else. Perhaps

there are no other people. [...] We merely dream of them. (105–06)

As spectator of herself, Else becomes both the subject and object of her own affection, particularly as her "pervasive self-address reaches a fitting climax" (Cohn 246). Now showing the "self-sufficiency" that Freud so famously attributes to beautiful, narcissistic women, Else compensates for "the social restrictions upon her object choice" and separates her ego from "anything that might diminish it" (Freud 70). Rather than being the object of Dorsday's voyeuristic desire, Else combines the active and passive extremes of voyeurism and exhibitionism as she enjoys both looking and being looked at. Like Lulu, Else seems here to be most in love with herself and her own beauty.

Nonetheless, we must also recognize the shortcomings of Else's perspective in the mirror scene, since she undeniably becomes a subject in this scene but still treats her body like a sexual object. Unlike Lulu, Else fails to become one with her role, since her splitting can easily be seen. We might ask then, along with Elisabeth Bronfen, whether Else "uses this histrionic self-display as her source of self-authorship, as the materialisation of her own fantasies," which would be akin to Lulu's positive self-construction in the first play, or whether "she stages an appearance that has nothing to do with her, that reduces her to the medium of another's fantasies" (282). We know that if Else discloses her own exhibitionist fantasies here, she also conforms to the voyeuristic desires of her culture. Else cannot fully eliminate the roles of object, other, and slave from her repertoire. She might appropriate the male gaze, but she still directs that gaze upon herself, thereby objectifying herself yet again. Narcissism is not necessarily liberating for her, whereas for Lulu it had the potential to be empowering.

Else does attempt to bridge the gap between subject and object when she says goodbye to her "dearly-beloved" mirror image and allows others to observe her naked body (111). Having decided "[i]f one sees me, others shall see me," Else chooses to disrobe publicly for a larger audience that will include, but not be limited to, Dorsday (103). Now Else will try to reassert her position as an artist, since disrobing for a man alone is prostitution, while disrobing skillfully and showing her beautiful body in public is art. Here I differ with other scholars about Else's reason for unveiling before a public rather than a private audience, for maintaining yet altering her original contract with Dorsday. According to Andreas Huyssen, Else "imagines how she might stage her naked body, seeking a way to make it a public event rather than satisfying Dorsday's private voyeurism, thus both fulfilling and negating the contract" (42). Anderson likewise asserts, "Fräulein Else attempts to challenge the external voyeur's control over her by exposing herself openly" (15). Cathy Raymond adds that Else "retain[s] a modicum of self-respect by disrobing publicly instead of only for Dorsday" (178). Yeo agrees that Else's "nakedness and eventual exhibition become almost a defiant assertion of her moral integrity [...], since she is fulfilling her exhibitionist inclinations in public rather than doing so 'discreetly' [...] as the *Sklavin* [slave] of Herr von Dorsday," and thus can act out the "'extreme' behaviour that she has only hitherto fantasized about" and still remain a virgin (22–23). While these arguments locate the growing tension between erotic desire and moral integrity that leads to Else's public unveiling and eventual suicide,[6] I wish to uncover an additional, but by no means incompatible or mutually exclusive reading. By focusing on the novella's ending I would like to emphasize how Else gradually abandons the artistic aspirations of the actress and settles for the role of art object. None of the aforementioned interpretations have recognized that the public unveiling provides an acceptable audience for the artist's new role. Whereas a sole spectator such as Dorsday likens the performance to prostitution, a public spectacle allows Else to justify her actions not only in moral but also in artistic terms.

Else suggests on several occasions that her true professional calling would be as an actress or artist. "I should have gone on the stage," she claims (29). "Everything would have been possible for you, Fräulein," says Fred to Else's corpse in one of her imagined dialogues or death dreams, adding "[y]ou could have been a *pianist,* or a bookkeeper, or an *actress.* There is no end of possibilities in you" (33, emphasis added). Else clearly blames her financial dependency on others' failure to support her theatrical talents: "They've brought me up only to sell myself one way or another. They wouldn't hear of acting. They laughed at me" (82). Unable to work as a professional actress, Else laments her inability to earn enough money to support herself and her family. She bemoans more than just her economic dependency and is also keenly aware of the fact that marriage is another form of slavery with similar demands and obligatory unveilings. Else begins to see her life as a series of unveilings and as continual servitude. "For whom will I have to strip next time," she wonders (66). Acting would have empowered her, despite the paradox of unveiling, whereas both marriage and prostitution "strip" Else of her agency.

Thus, in response to the predicament set in motion by her father and Dorsday's various requests, Else stages the performance before a larger public, one including her imagined and desired lover, the Filou, and thereby manages, at least in her own mind, to transform an economic exchange into an aesthetic act. Whereas Else formerly criticized Dorsday as the sole member of her public in part for his lack of theatrical talents—he "speaks like a poor actor" and "sounds like a book" (63, 61)—she now arranges a more appropriate audience from the hotel guests. Thus Else's theatrical conception of the event in the scenes directly preceding the public unveiling becomes very apparent. She insists that the "performance may begin" and even considers staging "a little rehearsal," one that would give new meaning to the phrase "dress" rehearsal, on the steps before heading downstairs (110, 112). On her way to what she calls the "[g]reat performance," Else must enter through the "[g]reen curtain over the door" that leads to the "*Spielzimmer*" or card room (112, 120).[7] As she takes center stage and prepares for her performance, she is keenly aware of her spectators, as well as the accompanying music, Schumann's *Carnival*. Else rejoices in the climactic moment of the unveiling: "How wonderful is it to be naked" (123). She also revels in the reaction her performance receives from Dorsday's wide-open eyes and the Filou's glowing eyes (124). In this moment Else is truly alive, despite her imminent death.

Else's naked body quickly becomes a corpse as her acting ceases and death begins. Unable to sustain her role as an actress, she will become simultaneously, as did Lulu, the prostitute and the inanimate art object on display. The transition from Else's exhibition to her deanimation underscores the notion that "once exhibited, the undressed body of superlative feminine beauty literally transforms into a corpse" (Bronfen 281). Elisabeth Bronfen explains that by dying, "a beautiful woman serves as the motive for the creation of an art work and as its object of representation" (71). She continues, "As a deanimated body, she can also become an art object or be compared with one" (Bronfen 71). Else does just this: she imagines herself becoming an art object and compares herself to one in various scenes throughout the novella. When dreaming up an alternative to Dorsday's indecent proposal, Else considers leaving a letter with the following testament:

> Herr von Dorsday has the right to see my body, my beautiful, naked corpse. So you can't complain, Herr von Dorsday, that I made false promises. You're getting something for your money. Our contract doesn't specify that I must be alive when you see me. Oh, no. There's nothing to that effect. So—a view of my corpse I bequeath to the *art dealer,* Dorsday. (90, emphasis added)

Else's explicit argument in this scene, as Bronfen astutely observes, is that "their contract does not stipulate that she must be a living sight, yet by inversion she implies that to be an object of aesthetic/erotic voyeurism, to have her nude body perceived as an artwork, is itself a form of death" (286). Instead of choosing a larger public for her performance, she decides here to negate the performance by changing artistic genres. No longer a living actress, she will play the part of the dead art object. This connection is underscored elsewhere in the novella when Else imagines what Dorsday might say at her funeral. She envisions his reaction to her death: "I must pay my last respects. Wasn't I the first one to disgrace her? Oh, it was worth the trouble, Frau Winawer. I've never seen such a beautiful body. It cost me only thirty million. A Rubens costs three times as much" (67). Here the price paid to "view" Else's beautiful body parallels that paid to view or own a painting. As an art dealer, Dorsday simply treats Else as he would a work of art. She is to be purchased from her current owner or male guardian, her father, and in the exchange process she loses her life of performativity and becomes frozen, inert, framed. Death allows Else to become both the aesthetic object that the art dealer demands and the commodity that her father needs. In the process aesthetic and economic concerns supersede moral and erotic ones.

Else comes to imagine her naked body not only as a corpse on display, but also as a representative work in the pictorial tradition. Indeed, Else the actress has an increasing interest in the plastic arts, beginning even in the famous mirror scene. While lost in self-absorption, she tells herself, "You're beautiful in the coat. Florentine ladies had themselves painted that way. Their portraits are hung in galleries and it is considered an honor" (110). Framed by the mirror, her image is held in place, fixed as is an art object. Later, on the verge of death, Else imagines another glimpse of the same mirror, only this time the framed image has changed to Cissy, Paul's secret lover, who is, in Else's imagination, "standing before the mirror." "What are you doing there by the mirror?" Else asks Cissy. "Isn't my picture still in it?" (136). Thinking that she will leave a trace of her beauty behind, like Lulu with her portrait, Else is shocked to find that no sign of her living self remains. Interestingly, whereas Lulu's death comes in the split between her performative and objectified self, Else, who once fed off of her double, now no longer intuits her "other," but rather the "others," or the audience that observes her death. Yet her public can only observe her as a dying body, not as a living, performative one.

To understand Else's choice of a public unveiling over a private one and of death over life, we must interpret Dorsday's request as implying both an artistic exchange and a sexual transaction. It is clearly no coincidence that Schnitzler assigns his antagonist the profession of art dealer, one who represents "the late bourgeois capitalist society and its mercantile law insofar as buying and selling are the lifeblood of this society" (Rey 63, trans. mine). He buys and sells art, while Else can only sell herself, the never-fully-realized artist turned art object, the failed actress turned prostitute. Just as Lulu's performativity gave way to her position as commodity and object of exchange, so too does Else fall victim to the market tendencies of the capitalist system that allow men and male artists to control both women and money.

The fates of both female protagonists point to the process of commodification that increasingly permeated nineteenth-century European culture but was especially evident regarding women, who have always been commodified to some degree. Hence, although Lulu's and Else's acts of artistic self-fashioning can occasionally be interpreted as forms of production that omit exchange and avoid alienation, the whole process is ultimately undermined when they lose control of their creations and become commodities exchanged by men. Rather than functioning as producers of images of protean femininity, these fictional performers become the inanimate artistic objects of male consumption, even if they do serve as prototypes of the powerful female performer one sees today in figures like Madonna. The commodification of art and women in turn-of-the-century European society accounts for this important and, as we have seen, tragic process of reversal.

Despite their desire for a series of roles and a constantly expanding wardrobe, Lulu and Else fail to "become," to use Nietzsche's metaphor, whichever coat they wear, namely because they eventually and literally lose their costumes, along with their attire and their lives. In spite of Caesar Ann Hallamore's insistence that Lulu is "a succession of clothes" and that she changes attire whenever something unpleasant happens, we must remember that she leaves the narrated world just as she entered it: barefoot, penniless, and in rags (199–200). Lulu's death and her corpse's dissection, together with Else's suicide and the exhibition of her body, signify that these women never succeed in replacing their physical bodies or natural cores with a permanent palimpsest of fictions, costumes, and roles. Lulu and Else's artistic aspirations are undermined by economic realities and male exploitation: Lulu becomes scripted by others as she prostitutes herself for Alwa and Schigolch and speaks English according to Jack the Ripper's "script"; Else internalizes the male gaze and becomes the inanimate object men desire her to be.[8] These literary works echo the Nietzschean conviction that an important connection exists between class status and economic dependency, on the one hand, and the need to be an "actor" or the need to be "adaptable," on the other hand. Yet Lulu and Else can neither sustain an elevated class position nor construct themselves through acting alone since, according to Wedekind's and Schnitzler's fictions, economic and erotic demands ultimately "outstrip" aesthetic ones (Nietzsche 317).

Notes

[1] To take Nietzsche's connection between the actor and the artist one step further, I wish to note that the equivalent of this combined term (actor-artist) might best be found in the figure of the aesthete.

[2] Dorrit Cohn defines the "autonomous monologue" as a "single narrative genre entirely constituted by a fictional character's thoughts," and she cites Schnitzler's *Fräulein Else* as one example of this narrative mode (218).

[3] Andreas Huyssen points out that Else and her family are likewise concerned with masking "by strategies of assimilation" the "precarious situation" of their Jewish background (41). Susan C. Anderson agrees that Else must engage in a "double monitoring of her role as woman and as assimilated Jew" (19).

[4] As the character Puntschy explains, the Jungfrau shares refer to stock options in the cable-railway that was to be built up the Jungfrau mountain. Lulu is one of several characters in the second play who erroneously saw these shares as an "opportunity [...] to make oneself a small fortune" (131). When the stock crashes, however, Lulu and her companions are left in a state of poverty. One should also note that the word *Jungfrau* means "virgin" in German, a word that seems wholly out of place in Wedekind's play.

[5] See Jeanie Forte's discussion of the relationship between the material body and the body in representation.

[6] David F. Kuhns offers an interpretation of Wedekind's Lulu tragedies that closely resembles traditional readings of Schnitzler's *Fräulein Else*. He posits that Wedekind "probed the very tension between erotic freedom and its repression, between healthy sensuality and its exploitative corruption" (53).

[7] Cathy Raymond likewise notes these same theatrical elements (the curtain, the "play" room), which are inserted into the novella just prior to Else's public unveiling.

[8] It is interesting to note that, unlike the situation of the male dandy, who "experiments with himself, makes new experiments, enjoys his experiments; and all nature ceases and becomes art," these female performers are unable to extricate their "nature" from their "art" insofar as their artistic and theatrical sides are never completely free from their corporeal nature (Nietzsche 303). Here we see evidence of the oft-noted distinction between the effeminate dandy and woman in that the dandy's adoption of the

stereotypically feminine traits of performance and adornment "paradoxically reinforce[s] his distance from and superiority to women, whose nature renders them incapable of this kind of free-floating semiotic mobility and aesthetic sophistication" (Felski 106).

Works Cited

Adorno, Theodor. "Letters to Walter Benjamin." *Aesthetics and Politics.* Trans. Ronald Taylor. Norfolk: Lowe and Brydone, 1977. 100–41.

Anderson, Susan C. "Seeing Blindly: Voyeurism in Schnitzler's *Fräulein Else* and Andreas Salomé's *Fenitschka*." *Die Seele...ist ein weites Land: Kritische Beitrage zum Werk Arthur Schnitzlers.* Ed. Joseph P. Strelka. Bern: Peter Lang, 1996. 13–27.

Aurnhammer, Achim. "Selig, wer in Träumen stirbt: Das literarisierte Leben und Sterben von *Fräulein Else*." *Euphorion: Zeitschrift für Literaturgeschichte* 77.4 (1983): 500–10.

Beharriell, Frederick J. "Schnitzler's *Fräulein Else*: 'Reality' and Invention." *Modern Austrian Literature: Journal of the International Arthur Schnitzler Research Association* 10.3-4 (1977): 247–64.

Boa, Elizabeth. *The Sexual Circus: Wedekind's Theatre of Subversion.* Oxford: Basil Blackwell, 1987.

Bronfen, Elisabeth. *Over Her Dead Body: Death, Femininity, and the Aesthetic.* New York: Routledge, 1992.

Cohn, Dorrit. *Transparent Minds: Narrative Modes for Presenting Consciousness in Fiction.* Princeton: Princeton UP, 1978.

Cornwell, Patricia. *Portrait of a Killer: Jack the Ripper—Case Closed.* New York: Berkley Books, 2003.

Duhamel, Roland. "Schnitzler und Nietzsche." *Amsterdamer Beiträge zur neueren Germanistik* 4 (1975): 1–25.

Eagleton, Terry. "The Author as Producer." *Marxism and Literary Criticism.* London: Metheun, 1976. 59–83.

Felski, Rita. *The Gender of Modernity.* Cambridge, MA: Harvard UP, 1995.

Finney, Gail. "Woman as Spectacle and Commodity: Wedekind's Lulu Plays." *Women in Modern Drama: Freud, Feminism, and European Theater at the Turn of the Century.* Ithaca: Cornell UP, 1989. 79–101.

Firda, Richard Arthur. "Wedekind, Nietzsche and the Dionysian Experience." *Modern Language Notes* 87.5 (1972): 720–31.

Freud, Sigmund. "On Narcissism: An Introduction." *General Psychological Theory: Papers on Metapyschology.* Trans. Cecil M. Baines. Ed. Philip Rieff. New York: Macmillan, 1963. 56–82.

Garelick, Rhonda K. *Rising Star: Dandyism, Gender, and Performance in the Fin de Siècle.* Princeton, NJ: Princeton UP, 1998.

Gilman, Sander L. "The Nietzsche Murder Case." *New Literary History: A Journal of Theory and Interpretation* 14.2 (1983): 359-372.

Hallamore, Caesar Anne. "Changing Costume, Changing Identity: Women in the Theater of Pirandello, Bontempelli and Wedekind." *Romance Studies* 20 (1992): 21-29.

Harris, Edward P. "The Liberation of Flesh from Stone: Pygmalion in Frank Wedekind's *Erdgeist*." *Germanic Review* 52 (1977): 44-56.

Huyssen, Andreas. "The Disturbance of Vision in Vienna Modernism." *Modernism/Modernity* 5.3 (1998): 33-47.

Jones, Robert A. "Frank Wedekind: Circus Fan." *Monatshefte* 61.2 (1969): 139-156.

Kuhns, David F. "Palimpsestus: Frank Wedekind's Theatre of Self-Performance." *New Theatre Quarterly* 12.45 (1996): 50-64.

Libbon, Stephanie E. "Frank Wedekind's Prostitutes: A Liberating Re-Creation or Male Recreation?" *Commodities of Desire: The Prostitute in Modern German Literature.* Ed. Christian Schönfeld. Rochester: Camden House, 2000. 46-61.

Littau, Karin. "Refractions of the Feminine: The Monstrous Transformations of Lulu." *Modern Language Notes* 110.4 (1995): 888-89.

Marx, Karl. *Capital: A Critique of Political Economy.* Trans. Ben Fowkes. London: New Left Review, 1976.

Marx, Karl and Frederick Engels. *Literature and Art.* Trans. anon. New York: International Publishers, 1963.

Michelsen, Peter. "Frank Wedekind." *Deutscher Dichter der Moderne: Ihr Leben und Werk.* Ed. Benno von Weise. Berlin: Schmidt, 1969. 49-67.

Midgley, David. "Wedekind's Lulu: From 'Shauertragödie' to Social Comedy." *German Life and Letters* 38.3 (1985): 205-32.

Moers, Ellen. *The Dandy: Brummell to Beerbohm.* London: Secker & Walburg, 1960.

Nietzsche, Friedrich. *The Gay Science: With a Prelude in Rhymes and an Appendix of Songs.* Trans. Walter Kaufmann. New York: Random, 1974.

Peacock, R. "The Ambiguity of Wedekind's Lulu." *Oxford German Studies* 9 (1978): 105-118.

Raymond, Cathy. "Masked in Music: Hidden Meaning in Schnitzler's Fraulein Else." *Monatshefte* 85.2 (1993): 170-88.

Rey, Williams. *Arthur Schnitzler: Die späte Prosa als Gipfel seines Schaffens.* Berlin: Schmidt, 1968.

Schnitzler, Arthur. *Fräulein Else: A Novel.* Trans. Robert A. Simon. New York: Simon and Schuster, 1925.

Schuler-Will, Jeannine. "Wedekind's Lulu: Pandora and Pierrot, the Visual Experience of Myth. *German Studies Review* 7.1 (1984): 27–38.

Szalay, Eva Ludwiga. "From Bourgeois Daughter to Prostitute: Representations of the 'Wiener Fraulein' in Kraus's 'Prozess Veith' and Schnitzler's *Fraulein Else*." *Modern Austrian Literature* 34.3–4 (2001): 1–28.

Wedekind, Frank. *The Lulu Plays and Other Sex Tragedies*. German Expressionism Series. Ed. J.M. Ritchie. Trans. Stephen Spender. London: John Calder Publishers, 1978. 7–175.

Weidl, Erhard. "Philologische Spurensicherung zur Erschließung der 'Lulu'-Tragödie Frank Wedekinds." *Wirkendes Wort* 35.2 (1985): 99–119.

Willeke, Audrone B. "Frank Wedekind and the 'Frauenfrage.'" *Monatshefte* 72 (1980): 26–38.

Yeo, Siew Lian. "'Entweder oder': Dualism in Schnitzler's Fraulein Else." *Modern Austrian Literature* 32.2 (1999): 15–26.

Marital Status and the Rhetoric of the Women's Movement in World War I Germany

Catherine Dollard

The rhetoric of the German women's movement regarding female marital status changed during World War I. Female marital status had been a central concern of the leadership of the women's movement prior to the war. Yet as female marital prospects diminished in the wake of the Great War, leading voices in the imperial German women's movement shifted their focus away from the problematic "surplus woman" and adopted a platform that emphasized female unity and patriotism. This rhetorical shift advanced a vision of a "maternal citizen" that would figure prominently in the divisive gender politics of the Weimar era. (CD)

The call for national mobilization at the outset of World War I recast the great social questions that had characterized the cultural, political, and social discourse of the *Kaiserreich*.[1] Discussions regarding the rights of laborers, the division of political power, the role of the military in society, the ownership of capital, and the composition of a healthy nation were channeled anew after the guns of August. The women's question was no less transformed in the time of the Great War. This article examines how the rhetoric of the German women's movement changed during the early years of the war, especially regarding the issue of marital status. While marital status and the role of single women in society were key to the women's movement prior to 1914, the outbreak of military hostilities brought about a marked shift in the language and agendas of women's rights advocates. As female marital prospects became increasingly shaky in light of the devastating battlefield casualties, the leaders of the German women's movement stopped talking about the plight of single women. This article seeks to explain how that transition occurred.

Myriad scholarly projects have examined the experiences of German women in World War I. In the last decade, literary studies have focused upon comparative analyses of female fictional responses to the war.[2] Recent works by historians have emphasized the gendered experience of both the home- and battlefronts.[3] Little work explicitly addresses the impact of World War I on the women's movement. While comprehensive histories of women's activism in Germany consider the period of the war, only one monographic treatment has specifically examined the impact of the war on the aims, nature, and rhetoric of the German women's movement: Sabine Hering's *Die Kriegsgewinnlerinnen: Praxis und Ideologie der deutschen Frauenbewegung im Ersten Weltkrieg* (War Opportunists: The Experience and Ideology of the German Women's Movement in the First World War).

Hering identifies three different groups of women's activists during the Great War: conservatives, moderates, and war opponents (7). Opponents based their resistance to the war on the principals of international pacifism. Leading female opponents of the war included Anita Augspurg, Lida Gustava Heymann, Helene Stöcker, and Clara Zetkin. Zetkin, one of the leading women of the German Social Democratic Party, opposed the war on the basis of international socialist ideals. Along with many orthodox Marxists, she saw the war as the outgrowth of capitalist competition (Quataert, *Feminists* 213). The latter three reformers opposed the war because of its horrific human cost, the inherent value of peaceful international relations, and an objection to the "male principles" that created war (Braker 107).[4] The purview of these war opponents extended beyond the particularities of both national politics and issues related to marital status. Their response to the war conformed to a prewar ideology that articulated a vision of equality-based feminism (Lischewski 117–21).

In contrast to the pacifists, conservatives and moderates shifted their views at the advent of the war. Hering argues that conservative and religious nationalists viewed the war quite differently from moderate leaders of the mainstream women's movement. She asserts that conservatives responded to the war with "absolute loyalty to the fatherland," while their counterparts developed a more strategic approach:

> The moderates maneuvered in the midfield. For them, "service to the homefront" was a means to an end: pushing forward the concerns of the women's movement. They systematically developed marching plans in order to facilitate the advancement of women into the world of work and spheres of political influence. The moderates epitomize [...] the prototype of the war opportunist [*Kriegsgewinnlerin*]. (Hering 7)

Hering's description of the moderate's wartime program, consisting of maneuvers, systematic planning, marching, and advancing, indicates how female activists adapted to the mode of war in order to pursue the goals of the women's movement. But her designating the moderates as the model of the *Kriegsgewinnlerinnen* raises more questions than it answers: were these women war profiteers or survivors? Were they canny tacticians who recognized that gains could be achieved in the midst of horrific circumstances or opportunists who were willing to make tradeoffs in order for the women's movement to survive? While Hering concludes that throughout the course of the war moderates had been "faithful to their prewar goals" (142), this article argues that, along with more conservative patriots, moderate advocates of women's rights abandoned their pre-1914 fixation on the plight of single women as one of the most significant justifications for the women's movement. In its place, these activists adopted a maternalist-nationalist rhetoric that argued for female advancement, regardless of marital status, on the basis of enhancing the German state and its culture through service. While the German women's movement became both more tactical and more inclusive in its argumentation during the war, such a shift also opened the door to a more *völkisch*[5] feminism that would have consequences well beyond the Great War.

Writings from two sets of female activists form the source basis of this argument. The first group is composed of leading moderate activists from the League of German Women's Associations (*Bund deutscher Frauenvereine*: BDF). The BDF was the largest women's association in Germany and the organizational stronghold of the mainstream women's movement. This paper examines the BDF's war yearbook of 1915, in which BDF leaders made the case for national allegiance. While each author took on different aspects of the female experience, the collective message offered by the BDF in 1915 was that of nation before all else.

Texts by Elisabeth Gnauck-Kühne and Lily Braun form the second category of evidence examined in this article. Both of these women loosely conform to Hering's categorization of "conservative" patriots, but in truth they are immensely difficult figures for historians to categorize.[6] Gnauck-Kühne had been one of the leading religious activists of her time, a founding member of both the national Protestant and, after a religious conversion in 1900, Catholic women's associations. Her purview extended beyond the realm of faith, however: Gnauck-Kühne studied economics and used her quantitative training to provide a statistical component to the women's question. Informed by social science training, Gnauck-Kühne also forcefully articulated the plight of unwed bourgeois women (*Deutsche*). But in 1915, she stopped identifying single women as the central concern of the women's movement and instead wrote about the ways in which the war revealed the errors of the former women's movement and provided a new mission for contemporary women.

Lily Braun was another important female activist who decried earlier forms of women's rights advocacy in the new patriotic age. Sabine Hering identifies Braun as a conservative based upon her "excessive war euphoria" (165), although designating Braun as a conservative is somewhat ironic. As a woman deemed "an orthodox Marxist with a few ideas of her own" (Meyer 61), Braun stood apart from the core of female Marxist activism embodied by Clara Zetkin and Luise Zietz (Quataert, *Feminists* 107–33). Prior to 1914, Braun wrote about a range of concerns, including the establishment of communal households for single women, the reform of female fashion, the decriminalization of prostitution, and the organization of employment agencies (Lischke 64). Yet her expansive agenda indeed took a conservative turn with the outbreak of war, when maternalist and nationalist rhetoric became the primary notes in her platform of social reform.

This paper examines in two parts how marital status disappeared from the rhetoric of the World War I women's movement. First, it provides a brief overview of the female surplus's importance to the imperial German women's movements. Second, it examines the wartime texts of female activists in order to determine how the rhetoric of leading women's rights advocates changed at the onset of war.

The Female Surplus of the Imperial Women's Movement

In arguing for the expansion of women's rights, the German women's movement prior to 1914 employed a particular reading of recent economic and social history. The advent of the modern age had forced women outside of the home, first because their traditional duties in the domestic sphere had been supplanted by commercial and technological advances, and second because middle-class men were taking longer and becoming more selective in marrying. Consequently, many perceived a surplus of unmarried women (*Frauenüberschuß*).[7] Explaining the bourgeois origins of this female surplus as well as educating and occupying its members engaged the leadership of the German women's movement.

Helene Lange, one of the most important figures in the early German women's movement and a leader of the BDF, was an empathetic spokesperson for women forced outside of the home. In an 1893 article, Lange described the term "woman" as connoting "an abundance of pictures and thoughts, [...] the poetry of the domestic hearth, the creative and protective mother, the faithful nurse and educator, [...] pictures of completely carefree grace" ("Wollen" 1). Only women of privileged classes had ever been so carefree. But Lange declared that these cozy images had been destroyed when "a callous hand brushed across the domestic hearth and millions of women were directed out into the world" ("Wollen" 1). The callous hand extended from the arm of industrialization, which Lange contended had displaced millions of middle-class females from their roles as domestic helpmates in the homes of parents, married brothers, and wealthier families seeking governesses or household managers. These forced outcasts comprised the female surplus. In her overture to women of the modern age, Lange decried the "bitter peril" that confronted single, middle-class German women.

Along with the broader German women's movement, Lange did not intend to leave the unwed in such a dire predicament. Together, the movement's publications, organizations, and leadership would bring about "a new time [...] in which the woman [...] would stand before great challenges, her horizons would expand, her view would deepen; when powers, which had so far slumbered, would uniquely unfold" ("Wollen" 2). Lange believed that the dilemmas faced by unwed women were unique to her own historical era. Along with other moderate leaders of the prewar German women's movement, she asserted that the *Kaiserreich* had been characterized by "the spiritual and economic plight of the girls 'of good families.' [...] One must consider: never, as long as there has been a German history, has the daughter of the socially leading circles worked for an outside employer for money—never, except in cases of personal misfortune" ("Fünfzig" 103). By emphasizing the plight of middle-class and elite young women, Lange and her fellow reformers, many of whom were single women themselves,[8] had found a powerful theme that would elicit the sympathies of those familiar with Gabriele Reuter's popular novel *Aus guter Familie* (*From a Good Family*). By stressing the trauma of enforced solitude, calling on history, directing her concerns toward the middle and upper classes, and evoking a beloved tragic heroine, Lange hoped to craft a movement borne out of necessity.

Evocations of unwed, displaced bourgeois women were tied to calls for extensive changes to education and the professions. Arguments for vocational options often hinged upon demographic displacement. Moderate activist Anna Pappritz argued that the futile search for a happy home spurred the need for more comprehensive preparation for life:

> Every girl longs to one day find the man to whom she can devote her love and trust. [...] Her own household, husband and children are [...] her natural life's work. [...] But not every girl's fate turns in such a way that it leads to a happy marriage. Many thousands as the unwed, relying only on themselves, must find their life's purpose in professional work. (*Hinaus* 4-6)

Every girl wanted to marry, but not every girl could. Alice Salomon, in describing the need to provide professional education for young bourgeois women, concurred: "Since nobody can forecast the future, nor that of a girl's life possibilities [...] [daughters must be educated for] occupations in which they will find employment through their work, in case they are not offered sustenance through marriage" ("Zölibat" 241). Moderate feminism responded by proposing careers that engaged maternal resources (teacher, social worker, *Kindergärtnerinnen,* nurse) and could change the world in the process. The *Frauenüberschuß* joined with the ideology of spiritual motherhood and the pursuit of professional and educational opportunities to establish a distinctive platform for women's rights.

Salomon's advocacy of vocational training targeted the bourgeois daughters of *Die Gartenlaube* (The Arbor).[9] Her call for female education echoed the BDF view that industrialization had been especially harmful for middle-class young women. In the BDF's reading of history, middle-class women simply were not accustomed to working outside of the home. At the same time, they also were more likely to gain greater leisure by the expanded availability of consumer goods. But leisure breeds sloth, or at least the suspicion thereof. Unmarried bourgeois women thus became the achingly visible victims of the modern age due to their inability to take on new forms of work, either through individual incapacities or structural prohibitions. The middle-class man was also unintentionally to blame: in "the unpropertied middle-class, the man only comes late to an income which allows him to establish a family" ("Zölibat" 242).

Faced with such challenges, women had to band together to seek relief. The movement "originated out of economic momentum, out of the plight for women created by the transformation of goods. As a result, the women's movement had to draw the necessary social, legal, political, and ethical conclusions, to seek the right means to establish a remedy" (BDF, *Pressbericht*). To this point, the BDF's explanation for the rise of the women's movement echoes socialism in its reading of economic change. But the BDF's bourgeois orientation emerges in its description of middle-class charity transformed into feminist activism: "Quite timidly, in the shadow and under the protection of church associations [...] the first women's associations [...] developed for charitable purposes which then gradually emerged into independent establishments for the purpose of material and spiritual elevation and the liberation of their own sex." Who led this movement? "Those who first set out on the path of self-help were naturally [...] the perhaps somewhat more independent bourgeois women" (BDF, *Darlegung* 5–6).

The socialist women's movement joined mainstream, moderate activists in linking the female surplus to the capitalist age, although they came to quite different conclusions about what the *Frauenüberschuß* portended. In an 1896 speech, Clara Zetkin argued that the surplus of women increasingly became a problem as capitalism advanced:

> For millions of women the question arose: Where do we now find our livelihood? Where do we find a meaningful life as well as a job that gives us mental satisfaction? Millions were now forced to find their livelihood and their meaningful lives outside of their families and within society as a whole. At that moment they became aware of the fact that their social illegality stood in opposition to their most basic interests. It was from this moment on that there existed a *Frauenfrage* [women's question]. (73)

Bourgeois women, both married and single, had not questioned their social and legal status as long as they found their "livelihood and meaningful life" in the private sphere. But Zetkin believed that social, legal, and marital status all became increasingly significant to the bourgeoisie as capitalism gradually eroded the haven of the middle-class home.

Conversely, Zetkin argued that the women's question as such simply did not emerge among the working-class. Capitalism created two different outcomes for proletarian women. First, it offered parity with men: "She became the equal of the man as a worker; the machine rendered muscular force superfluous and everywhere women's work showed the same results in production as men's work" (77). The second consequence of capitalism was oppression. Working women's economic dependence merely shifted from their husbands to their employers so that in the industrial age "the proletarian woman fights hand in hand with the man of her class against capitalist society" (77). The women's question among the proletariat thus was absorbed by the greater social question.

Another Marxist, Lily Braun, maintained that the financial requirements for marriage forced expectant middle-class brides to either hope for an inheritance or to actively pursue professional development so that they would be more attractive prospective brides: "Marriage, still today seen in bourgeois circles essentially as an institution to provide support, has become more and more unattainable for the growing number of girls without independent means" (*Frauenarbeit* 11). Braun's writing does not provide evidence of such "unattainability," but the way she casually cites the difficulty of marriage as "a fact" suggests that she had internalized the notion of a female surplus. The obstacles to marriage, however, were eased significantly in Braun's view when a woman entered into a profession; earning potential made for a fine dowry and also demonstrated that marriage was essentially a contractual institution.

Neither the BDF nor socialists ventured into demographic analysis. Other voices in the women's movement, especially religious-activist Elisabeth Gnauck-Kühne, took on this task. Gnauck-Kühne offered a summary of the origins of the woman's question:

> The social and economic relations of the present have [...] made marriages more difficult to attain, an occurrence which does not correspond to the conditions desired by nature. While for every 100 female births, there are 106 male births, the statistics count 104 women for every 100 men. This difference results in a substantial surplus of female population and [...] brings forth a crisis that has created a reforming movement in the world of women. [...] These facts are united in the slogan "*Frauenfrage*" (*Universitätsstudium* 2).

Yet the population crisis described by female activists did not, in fact, exist: women of all classes were marrying at basically the same rate in 1914 as they had fifty years earlier. The prewar surplus woman, then, was the product of imagined demography (Dollard 55–96).[10] This begs a question of origin: did female reformers make up the surplus to spur the need for change? Such an interpretation suggests tactics and manipulation that are unsupported by evidence. A far more plausible explanation for the prevalence of such rhetoric can be found in the expanding economy and intense urbanization of the *Kaiserreich*. These dynamic forces led to a perception of deeper, underlying causes that simply did not exist and thus to a limited reading of demographic events. Certainly, unmarried middle-class women were becoming far more visible at the turn of the century and debates surrounding citizenship, marriage, work, education, and sexuality made those unwed women a more dynamic and also problematic element of German society.

The plight of the surplus woman served three purposes in the women's movement of the German *Kaiserreich*: it offered a demographic description that provided urgency to calls for change; it served as a platform for reform of education, the professions, and the institution of marriage; and finally, it elicited sympathy for a group of middle-class women who through no fault of their own had been left outside of home, motherhood, and marriage.

World War I and the Paradox of the Disappearing Female Surplus

As soldiers West and East dug in and men began to be killed by the hundreds of thousands, European demography changed irrevocably, which became obvious to many. But knowing this fact was one thing; admitting it in calls for national patriotism and solidarity was quite another. In the writings of the German women's movement's leading figures in the early years of the war, social Democrat Luise Zietz had the clarity of mind and seeming disregard for jingoistic rhetoric to assert the basic demographic reality. Zietz wrote the following in 1916:

> The war has mightily increased the female surplus. Very many young, single or recently married soldiers have been killed and among the severely maimed, young men in their teens and in the best years of manhood are represented in greater numbers. Therefore the marital possibilities for girls are reduced to a not insignificant extent. (12)

The facts were straightforward, inarguable, and as might well be expected in such a tremendous conflict. Yet Zietz's articulation of these facts offers one of the only clear statements made by a leader of the prewar women's movements about the demographic realities of war and their consequences for females and their marital prospects.

With slaughter rampant across Europe, the surplus of unmarried women became a stark reality. During the course of the war, the number of marriages in Germany decreased significantly. In 1913, 252 marriages occurred for every 10,000 unmarried Germans over the age of fifteen; by 1916 that rate had dropped to 127 per 10,000, increasing to 156/10,000 by 1918. Among German females over the age of fifteen, the percentage of those unmarried rose from 34.7% in 1913 to 38.6% by 1918, representing a numerical increase of 1.3 million single women (Daniel 133). Facing the reality of an appallingly lethal war, it would have been fair to assume that women's rights advocates would continue to expand their discussion of the female surplus to foment calls for change. Yet evidence derived from texts on female wartime service written by key figures in the women's movement from 1914 to 1916 shows that this was not at all the case. The surplus single woman disappeared from the rhetoric of the German women's movement just when reason dictated that she ought to arrive. Three factors brought about this change: the celebration of unity occasioned by the war, the patriotic nationalism that resounded in wartime solicitations of women's work, and the vision of maternal citizenship that emerged along with calls for female service to the state.

Women United

In the history of the German women's movement, World War I occupies a transitional space between the Wilhelmine advocacy of expanded professional, educational, and legal rights, and the Weimar adjustment to suffrage, labor reconfiguration, and the tensions between democratic principles of egalitarianism and cultural and social limitations on gender equality. The wartime women's movement has often been characterized by the anticipation of "recompense and reward" in the form of postwar legal rights, especially suffrage (Frevert 162).[11] But this anticipation of payback for wartime contributions (and accompanying debates about female opportunism) emerges most strongly in the later war years (Hering 130–33). Expectations of postwar rewards for loyalty increased along with the horrific trials exacted by the war. Jean Quataert has noted a significant transition between the early war, when "a gendered war culture of patriotic duties extended deep into civil society," and the late war, when "soldiers and civilians alike had to make sense of the sacrifices asked of them. Then, the patriotic vocabulary of the August days, which had defined the sacrifices in the name of God, king, and fatherland, quickly faltered" (*Philanthropy* 272). Quataert identifies the "decisive turning point" as 1916, when "the army's voracious need for human and industrial resources was pushing Germany toward 'total war'" (*Philanthropy* 274).[12] Quataert's chronological reading of the war reflects the wartime rhetoric of the German women's movement in its early focus on unity (*das Volk*) and maternal citizenship and, from 1916 to the end of the war, its increasing engagement with the hope for postwar gains and the difficult realities of persevering through the conflict.[13]

Margaret and Patrice Higonnet have convincingly argued that "a study of war is truly productive for the study of women and social change, because war crystallizes contradictions between ideology and actual experience" (41). Such crystallized contradictions emerged in the disappearance of rhetoric surrounding the female surplus in light of wartime fatalities as well in the rise of maternalist patriotism as sons were sent off to die. The rhetorical shift of the early war foreshadowed coming contradictions between belligerent commitment in the wake of domestic privation and the anticipation of feminist rewards versus the reality of mixed results in the postwar epoch.

In its prewar incarnation, the female surplus had been presented as primarily a middle-class issue.[14] The Kaiser's call for "peace in the fortress" (*Burgfrieden*) at the outset of the war made such class-based interests seem unpatriotic (Fritzsche 51–66; Verhey 139–46, 160–81). Leaders of the women's movement shared this feeling as they repudiated endeavors that emphasized the needs of one group of Germans over another. They began to reevaluate the successes and to explore the failures of the antebellum women's movement. Chief among their criticisms was that the movement had been fragmented and misguided. The war itself had forced this reevaluation, leading women's leaders "in the most varied areas to relearn views that we held as irrevocable, to recognize it as essential to change and to make perspectives that we had long thrown overboard into our own intellectual property" (Levy-Rathenau 60).

Once most women began fighting for the same cause after 1914, the energy directed toward the betterment of single women received special critique in assessments of the prewar movement. Lily Braun provided a scathing commentary, asking of the prewar women's movement, "Were the ideas and ideals not enough to elevate women?" (*Frauen* 5). She believed that female activism had stagnated, achieving nothing of lasting value, "neither in supporting daughters not provided for in marriage, [nor] in the conquest of the *Gymnasium,* the universities and the professions [...] nor in political equality" (*Frauen* 6). Elisabeth Gnauck-Kühne looked at the unmarried and lamented, "And now of the single! The time-squandering of our female youth, and in no way only in the class of education and property, is a dismal chapter" (*Dienstpflicht* 19). These critics believed that the aimless struggle for equality could only amount to wasted effort:

> After the war the naked wrestling for a barren egalitarianism, — no ballot and no doctoral cap solves the women's question! — the struggle against the man who, despite all the still so fervid statements of opposition, is a basic element of the women's movement, dare still be upheld by only some hopeless representatives of dried-up old-maidenhood. (Braun, *Frauen* 45)

The unmarried were simultaneously identified as a source of women's woes and relegated to vicious stereotype.

Not all evaluations of the women's movement in general or of single women in particular were so cutting, but most moderates shared the same assessment of activism gone awry and of a cohort put to insufficient use. Gertrud Bäumer, leader of the BDF, wrote in 1915 that "the present war must lead women out of their isolated activities or fragmented associational lives. [...] That which has been achieved in these months may not be lost again" (5). Helene Lange, Bäumer's life partner and the vaunted spiritual head of the moderate movement, linked a unified women's movement to the essence of being German:

> We have now experienced that the common good of our Germanness [*Deutschtum*] is as great and essential as the particularities of each individual. [...] The spirit of oppositional action was a mental illness from long periods of peace and prosperity. We were conscious of this illness, and from all camps in the last years came the call for will, action, achievement, the battle cry against intellectualism. [...] But one does not make such an awakening of action with journals, programs, and congresses. (Lange, "Krieg" 18)

Lange, herself the editor of a journal and a presiding chair at many women's congresses, saw her life's work from a newly critical perspective once war broke out.

Braun pointed an accusatory finger at Lange's own BDF for the schism that existed between bourgeois and proletarian women. Yet uniting in the war effort made it possible to bridge the divide:

> For the first time the representatives of the bourgeois women's movement work hand in hand with those of the social democratic organization testifying to a great advancement [...] since those founding days of the BDF twenty years ago, from which the proletarian women's movement was explicitly held distant. (*Frauen* 21)

While some doubted how far the fledgling accord would go in making a contribution to the war effort (Gnauck-Kühne, *Dienstpflicht* 24), most female activists saw the *Burgfrieden* as rejuvenating and uniting organized German womanhood. In dispensing with old habits, moderates saw both women and Germany from a new political perspective:

> These days most surprisingly have shown how far the socialist train of thought, also in that of social democracy, is active in very wide circles. We all hold it as a natural duty to assist not only the relatives of those who fight in the field, but also those otherwise affected by war and its consequences. (Baum 35)

As they sought sisterhood in the new unity of women working for Germany, how could moderate women's rights advocates continue articulating their concern for such a small fragment of German society—that is, the unmarried women of the middle-class?

In striving to shrug off old "views that had been held as irrevocable," leaders of the German women's movement returned to some very traditional ground. Political, educational, and vocational campaigns that largely advantaged single women could no longer form the core arena of female advocacy. Women should gather together "not to demonstrate for the right to vote but instead to place themselves in disposal for the care of the ill and wounded," which would lead to an outpouring "of a long-suppressed female feeling that wants (only) helping and healing—every primitive feeling of her sex that a single word best portrays: motherliness [*Mütterlichkeit*]" (Braun, *Frauen* 11). In energetically accepting calls for a unified fatherland, female activists hastened the triumph of spiritual motherhood and left behind their prewar concerns for the unwed.

Women as Volk

The wartime writings of moderate leaders of the German women's movement convey enthusiastic patriotism. Gertrud Bäumer called for national loyalty: "Germany has been forced to defend with the blood of its men the fruits of its cultural strength. [...] We German women are a part of our land with every love and every hate." Passion would lead to action: "The deeper we feel the greatness of these actions, the higher our own duties as women must stand. [...] If already the lives of thousands must be given, the more beautiful and greater the mission to protect life, to preserve, to nurture" (8). Maternalism nestled comfortably within testimonials to the German wartime mission. In the discourse surrounding wartime service, homefront duties were glorified: "Is what we bring forth with our work then a sacrifice? No, it is a blessing to us [...] to serve our beloved fatherland as custodians and protectors of its material and cultural wealth which our brothers defend outside in the field with body and life" (Pappritz, "Nationaler" 33). Wartime service was configured by its advocates as all things good: a blessing and a duty, the next best thing to fighting on the fronts. For some women of the homefront, the ability to participate in the historical moment presented by war was no doubt a tremendous motivation. But for many others, work during the war was not a choice to elevate the spirit but a grave necessity conditioned by privation, scarcity, and—yes—absent men.[15]

If, prior to the war, unmarried women needed to work in order to replace the void left by marriage, during the war they simply were needed to work with no explanation necessary. Called upon to occupy men's positions in factory, field, and the professions, women had to do their part to fill the spaces left behind by killed or mutilated men (Salomon, "Probleme" 52). Because so many married women had to function as single women during the war, the previously firm connection between marital status and working life among middle-class women all but vanished in discussions of finding replacement workers.

The early war writings did not ignore the economic upheaval of the period, but poverty and need were overshadowed by the celebration of the civic unity that promised so much for the future. As Salomon observed, this "blazing national enthusiasm" seemed to offer "great possibilities to women. As the men of all classes stand together in the field and feel that they are a community, so the social work of these days brings together women of all parties, all confessions" ("Probleme" 59). Patriotic emotion provided the key for preserving and enhancing the German *Volk*. The nuanced nature of the BDF's prewar "sober and functional approach to nationalism" was "played down" after the outbreak of hostilities, and a conviction regarding the greatness of German *Kultur* emerged (Schaser 257, 258).

The enthusiasm of the early war months caused Bäumer to review the history of women's activism and to lament its internationalist tendencies:

> The word "sisters" for women of other countries was natural for us. [...] [Yet] in interactions with the others we were all the more deeply conscious of our own essence; [...] we experienced that which has well been termed German cultural distinctiveness: the particular knack that we Germans bring to the intellectual work of the world. (3)

Bäumer's wartime nationalism contrasted strikingly with her prewar belief that "it is in the nature of certain intellectual movements not to be contained by national boundaries" (qtd. in Schaser 260).[16] Before the war, as Angelika Schaser has argued, "internationalism and nationalism were not mutually exclusive" in the agenda of the German women's movement (260). Yet after 1914, Germanic distinctiveness served as the cornerstone of the BDF's support of the war. Internationalist tendencies amounted to subversive pacifism, and moderates would not be found in such a camp. German *Kultur* had created envy throughout the world, and jealousy of a superior civilization had led to belligerence: "In this mirror of world envy we saw our Germany with its flourishing cultural strength which in peaceful conquest had attempted to create space for itself in the world. Truly not to the disadvantage of humanity, for whom the German achievements [...] have brought immeasurable cultural advancement" (Lange, "Krieg" 7). Lange's belief that the world should welcome German *Kultur* rivaled that of most national newspapers and patriotic organizations.

A conflict over the destiny of civilized society naturally had very deep consequences for each individual—man or woman—who now understood himself or herself to be members of a "great, steady, inherently joined community of work and effort, against which an entire world had raised itself in enmity. Each now at once saw his existence [...] as a link in a chain, a threatened part of the whole" (Lange, "Krieg" 17). These links created the united national community; as constituent parts, women could no longer identify marital status—or even gender itself—as a relevant topic. The success of the war effort and sacrificed lives were the only things that counted. In the first years of the war, single women had not been forgotten; they simply no longer merited discussion even as their numbers rose. Lange wrote, "We feel our Germanness as a condition and foundation of all other blessings, as our united common internal strength—all must be expended in order now to strive for its value, for its future existence" ("Krieg" 17). As a result, the iconographic surplus woman no longer mattered. As the women's movement let go of this prewar catalyst for change, they adopted a vision of female citizenship that provided an empowered position in the early years of the war (Reagin 187). But that strength would be fleeting. As Margaret Higonnet has argued, assessments of wartime gains tended to emphasize "visible but isolated material changes. The evidence points to ideological mechanisms limiting the transformation of gender lines" (33). Such a limiting ideology manifested itself in the vision of maternal citizenship that women's rights advocated during the First World War.

The Motherly Citizen

The literature surrounding women's service to the war effort repeatedly asked how and where the women should best serve the German cause. Jean Quataert's study of female patriotism asserts that the late *Kaiserreich* was a period in which female "patriotism became instinctual, located essentially in the routines of family life and childbearing" (*Philanthropy* 263). During the war Lily Braun melded her advocacy of the maternalist spirit with the sacrifices of German men in war: "If the dead could talk, our dead, they would elevate themselves and call to us, 'How can you my mother, you my wife not want to prove as my blood [that you will] devote everything for the greatness to come—even in death to serve life?'" (*Frauen* 51). Note how the dead beckoned to mothers and wives, not sisters. Maternal ties alone summoned those ghostly cries. Braun was interested in precisely this essential link. For her, maternalism manifested itself in a gut-feeling that emerged at the outbreak of war: "All thinking and actions of women were immediately subjected to the natural female instinct that broke through with elemental power—the instinct that intellectualism had seemed almost to dissolve"

(*Frauen* 12). Braun sought to do away with the minutiae of the women's movement and to rise above the pedestrian bureaucracy of university entrance and job training. Those had been the concerns of women who had lost touch with their essence, women who had been numbed by a prosperous civilization into forgetting primordial concerns.

The onset of the war had demonstrated that "the women's movement was in danger of petering out. The war leads it [...] to fresher waters. The return of the woman to the primitive feelings of her sex also further produces their corresponding ability to contribute" (Braun, *Frauen* 45). War provided women with a mission that the fragmented, intellectualized women's movement could not: "Now it is the women who have to [...] return themselves to the highest law of nature, through the strong, conscious will of motherhood" (53). Such a vision left no room for the concerns of unwed women. Single women were subsumed within a maternalist community of citizens, providing both sustenance through the grim war years as well as hope for the victorious future.

Mandatory service to the state offered one avenue for maternalist endeavors. Elisabeth Gnauck-Kühne argued that a mandatory year of service would provide benefits for German society as a whole by infusing it with the maternal essence and training each German girl needs "for her female calling" (*Dienstpflicht* 24). Such service would ensure that females' contributions to the nation equaled men's (19–20). While calls for compulsory service long preceded the war, the age of hostilities brought new energy to such proposals. Discussions of mandatory service absorbed the forms of rhetoric that had surrounded the prewar female surplus: women needed to be occupied lest they become dilettantes; if their own homes and families did not preoccupy them, they needed training to become able workers rather than casual volunteers. And the war certainly invoked the necessity of such training. Class-based assumptions still pervaded discussions of compulsory service (after all, working-class women had no chance of becoming dilettantes or casual volunteers), but various kinds of social stratification were muted under the wartime demand for unity.

The proposed obligation would have lifelong implications, with one's name being added to a list of future conscripts after completing a year's worth of service (*Dienstpflicht* 33). Gnauck-Kühne recognized the centrality of marriage to her program, but noted:

> The unmarried is and remains a person of the national community, the more solitarily she stands in life, all the more she can be such. Then the great national community becomes her family; in the event that she has a vocation [...] young trainees become her child, or she bestows maternal care and maternal love to the

orphaned or the off-track. [...] To be female means to be like a mother. The most female woman is the most maternal female, whether she is virgin or wife. (*Dienstpflicht* 34-35)

Single women were thus made distinct not by their mass numbers but by their singular ability to serve *Volk* and fatherland. Unwed women who prior to the war had served as rhetorical evidence of a national crisis could be transformed into a national resource. Contributions to the war effort would demonstrate the female capacity for citizenship, and these contributions would come from both single and married women alike.

After 1918, Germany's defeat channeled wartime maternalist-nationalist rhetoric in two quite different directions. First, the cultural icon of the New Woman reacted against both the surplus woman of the *Kaiserreich* and the maternal citizen of the Great War. Atina Grossman has described the New Woman as representing "both a blurring of traditional gender roles and a polarization of gender experience during the war: men in the trenches and women on the home front." The New Woman described sexual subversives like "the intellectual with a Marlene Dietrich-style suit and short mannish haircut" as well as "the young white-collar worker in a flapper outfit." Marital status hardly configured this modern female, since she might be "the young married factory worker who cooked only one warm meal a day [...] and tried with all available means to keep her family small" (156). The overdrawn lines of this stereotype helped to fuel reactionary politics that sought to eradicate the trailblazing New Woman and replace her with the patriotic *Hausfrau* and her hardworking, pure daughter.

This second appropriation of maternalist-nationalist rhetoric furthered rather than repudiated female patriotism. While the New Woman certainly reflected the experience of some German women of the Weimar era, she was more a cultural construction than lived reality.[17] As Susanne Rouette has asserted in a study of early Weimar labor and social policy, the gender politics of the postwar emphasized "talents considered 'natural' to women: as wives, homemakers, and particularly as mothers. [...] Such desires and demands could serve as justification for a conservative reconstruction of gender relations" (51).[18] Linking motherhood to citizen's rights served as a continuation of prewar maternalism. Rouette finds that the "gender stereotypes (of early Weimar) returned to a program of femininity within which, in the course of the nineteenth century, 'motherliness' had been granted a central status" (63). But a simple—yet crucial—change from the prewar women's movement's view of motherliness had taken place during the early years of the war: single women had been rhetorically removed from the ranks of the maternal. This did not mean that the women's movement abandoned all concern for the unwed. But the new view of female civic place did result in the bourgeois women's movement calling in November 1918 "for women's participation as 'mothers and citizens' in 'building Germany's future'" (Rouette 63).[19] By embracing the maternal citizen, the women's movement presented a vision of womanhood that was more *völkisch* and timeless than the surplus woman, who had been both a victim of circumstance and a reason for change.

Scholarship on the Weimar women's movement is marked by descriptions of its disappointments and paralysis, its generational conflict and lost sense of purpose.[20] The ungrounded nature of Weimar feminism certainly rests partly in the dialectical opposition of the New Woman and the maternal citizen. Ute Frevert has adeptly summarized the tension:

> The [women's] movement had no answer to the question of how the 'new woman' could resolve the conflict between modern occupational demands and traditional family ties. [...] Instead, it offered women another role: that of dutiful, selfless, conciliatory members of an idealized *Volksgemeinschaft* [community of the German people]. (203)

This dutiful, selfless construction of womanhood achieved its central place in the language of the women's movement during the early years of World War I. In envisioning a German victory, the rhetoric of a strong and united wartime women's movement articulated a patriotic and heavily gendered vision of shared service to the nation.[21] In the light of German defeat, an unsure and fractured postwar women's movement faced and in part helped to create a heavily gendered vision of national service that glorified masculine sacrifice (Quataert, *Philanthropy* 302) and increasingly understood calls for female rights as individualistic and unpatriotic (Harvey 20–26). The wartime shift away from the surplus woman and toward maternalist-nationalist rhetoric helped to create the divisive gender politics of the Weimar era. By predicating female advancement upon women's inclination and ability to serve the nation in a time of conflict, women's rights advocates during the war abandoned their earlier emphasis on the plight faced by the unwed and advanced a feminism that appeared to be more unified, useful, palatable, and patriotic. This approach to women's rights left a very real void, however, when the postwar women's movement carved a new identity in an era that ultimately brought them "to echo the ideas of the Right" (Harvey 6).[22]

Conclusion

War is a creative force both despite and because of the upheaval it brings. In the light of August 1914, women's lives and the women's movement faced new pressures and exigencies, but also new opportunities. Antebellum feminist advocates had looked upon middle-class single women as a group in need. The war recast these women, both in rhetoric and action, as important to social stability rather than as threats to the prevailing order, as essential rather than superfluous, as citizens rather than a burden. The raging conflict and its domestic disruption formed a crucible in which a former social dilemma could become a source of civic strength.

Recognizing the intrinsic potential in an era of patriotic fervor and social upheaval, women's rights advocates responded to the onset of war by advancing a vision of female citizenship based upon women's maternal character. Anna Pappritz articulated this emphasis on citizenship by asserting that the work of the BDF was most consequential "when it [taught] its members to feel like responsible citizens of the state with the duty to dedicate their ability to work not only in the narrow circle of family, but also to fatherland and *Volk*" (Pappritz, "Nationaler" 33). The onset of war led female activists to argue that women had to earn recognition by demonstrating their capacity for citizenship, rather than by jockeying for rights on the basis of damage done to them via social and economic change. They believed that such jockeying had been a critical mistake made by the fragmented pre-1914 women's movement. The war provided the opportunity to demonstrate female civic strengths, and thus the prewar emphasis on marital status was exchanged for a wartime vision of national citizenship. As the twentieth century progressed, a feminism that moved beyond the contextual categories of demography or national allegiance would prove an elusive goal for the moderate leadership of the German women's movement.[23]

Women—married and unmarried, of means and indigent—were essential to the functioning of German society. War made this evident in ways that in peacetime begged explanation. In the antebellum *Kaiserreich,* the notion of a female surplus provided one such explanation: the changing economy had pushed surplus women outside of the home, thus they had to be educated and given useful work. Yet war—in every way but demographically—erased the female surplus. Prior to 1914, a lack of female vocational training meant that single women would falter. In wartime, a lack of female vocational training meant that Germany would falter. The Great War changed single women from a group that German society had to do something about to a category that Germany would not survive the war without. Single women were no longer on the front lines and the central object of the German women's movements; instead, Germany was on the front lines and all women, wed and unwed, were called to duty.

Notes

This article is a revised and extended version of a paper first presented at the conference on "The Gentler Sex: Responses of the Women's Movement to the First World War" sponsored by the Institute of Germanic & Romance Studies at the University of London (8-9 Sept. 2005). I am very grateful to the *Women in German Yearbook* reviewers for their extensive and very helpful comments. Unless otherwise identified, all translations are mine.

[1] The *Kaiserreich* refers to the German Empire, established in 1871 after the Franco-Prussian war and lasting until German defeat in 1918.

[2] Byles's *War, Women and Poetry* offers a history of British and German female poets and writers in both world wars; O'Brien's *Women's Fictional Responses to the First World War* focuses on the Great War.

[3] Davis's *Home Fires Burning* and Daniel's *The War from Within* explore the wartime experience of working-class women; *Home/front,* ed. Hagemann and Schüler-Springorum, assesses the gendered nature of military conflict; *Behind the Lines: Gender and the Two World Wars,* ed. Higonnet, et al., offers an international perspective.

[4] On German female pacifism, see Braker; Lischewski 100–97; on socialism and pacifism, see Evans.

[5] "*Völkisch*" connotes a specifically German patriotism that invokes an idealized vision of a mythic past rooted in the German countryside, language, and folk culture.

[6] Hering employs the term "conservative" to denote the intermediate position of the moderates: "The former trisection: socialists—moderates—radicals disintegrated in August 1914 widely on the basis of the polarization between supporters and opponents of the war. Thus a third group emerged on the scene as part of the patriots: the conservatives, who it is important to identify here in order to make clear that the patriotism of the moderates [...] is not depicted as the sole and above all not the most extreme adversaries of the radical and socialist war opponents" (7).

[7] On the female surplus, see Bussemer 23; Dollard; Frevert 118–23; Hackett 40–66; Kuhn 37–100; Mazón 51–52; Reagin 99–122.

[8] While some married women played formative roles in the women's movement, in terms of publications and leadership positions, the most visible activists were unmarried women, including Anita Augspurg, Ottilie Baader, Gertrud Bäumer, Lida Gustava Heymann, Mathilde Lammers, Helene Lange, Marie-Elisabeth Lüders, Marianne Menzzer, Bertha Pappenheim, Anna Pappritz, Alice Salomon, Auguste Schmidt, Franziska Tiburtius, and Luise Zietz.

[9] On the bourgeois orientation of *Die Gartenlaube,* see Belgum.

[10] Demographic discussions of a prewar *Kaiserreich* female surplus tended to emphasize urban populations and the standing female population surfeit, a surfeit that had existed for centuries in Western Europe largely as a result of the longer female lifespan. Many *Kaiserreich* accounts of the female surplus speculated projected a change based upon the increasing urbanization that characterized imperial Germany and did not examine the surplus over time. Such an inquiry reveals fairly consistent gender ratios and marriage rates during the imperial period.

[11] On the expectation of the women's movement for political gain, especially suffrage, after the war, see Hering 122–37; Frevert 162; Harvey 6; Reagin 200; Quataert, *Philanthropy* 82, 300.

[12] On 1916 as the central turning point in the German civilian view of the war, see Chickering 65, 76–82.

[13] On the impact of the extraordinary distress of the war period on the rhetoric of the women's movement, see Davis 207–08; Gerhard 307; Quataert, *Philanthropy* 272, 300; Reagin 199.

[14] On the bourgeois cast of the female surplus see Greven-Aschoff 46–47; Gnauck-Kühne, *Soziale* 8, 26; Hartmann; Prinzing 550–53; Vely, Wildenthal 6.

[15] See Daniel 189–207 and Davis 24–92 for a discussion of the impact of domestic privation on women.

[16] Bäumer, Gertrud. "Frauenbewegung und Nationalbewußtsein." *Die Frau* 20 (1912/13): 387.

[17] On the New Woman as cultural icon, see Meskimmon, *We Weren't Modern Enough,* as well as the edited collections, *Women in the Metropolis,* ed. von Ankum; and *Visions of the "Neue Frau,"* ed. Meskimmon and West.

[18] Rouette argues that this "conservative reconstruction of gender relations" was most clearly manifested in early Weimar labor and social legislation that led to a "restoration of the gender-hierarchical division of labor" (59).

[19] Rouette cites here the Petition of the Federation of German Women's Associations to the Reichstag, 4 Nov. 1918, qtd. in Wex.

[20] On disappointment, see Reagin's chapter "A Movement Adrift" (203-19); Schaser notes the minimization of "female national tasks" in early Weimar (262). On paralysis, see Harvey's account of the movement as "immobile" (2) and facing "senility" (8); Frevert's view of a movement both "harmless and predictable" (171) and "confused and contradictory" (203); Gerhard's description of a leadership "timid and evasive" (377). On generational conflict, see Frevert (198, 201), Gerhard (370-72) and especially Harvey's article that describes the older bourgeois movement, which, "in seeking to bridge the generation gap [...] felt it necessary to change their language and reshape the presentation of their ideas" (24). On lost purpose see Reagin 203-08 and Rouette 66.

[21] On the strength of the early wartime movement, see Frevert 160-62; Reagin 187-94; Schaser 258-62.

[22] On the rightward shift of the Weimar movement, see Rouette on a "backward-looking utopia" (64); Harvey on the movement's increasing compromises (24-28); and Reagin's chapter "Growth on the Right," (221-47).

[23] Heineman's *What Difference Does a Husband Make?* finds that deep into the post-World War II era in both East and West Germany, "marital status continued to determine the contours of women's lives" (236).

Works Cited

Ankum, Katharina von. *Women in the Metropolis: Gender and Modernity in Weimar Culture*. Berkeley: U California P, 1997.

Baum, Marie. "Volkskraft zur Kriegszeit." *Kriegsjahrbuch des Bundes Deutscher Frauenvereine (BDF)*. Ed. Elisabeth Altmann-Gottheiner. Berlin: B.G. Teubner, 1915. 33-41.

Bäumer, Gertrud. "Die Frauen und der Krieg." *Kriegsjahrbuch des BDF*. 2-8.

Belgum, Kirsten. *Popularizing the Nation: Audience, Representation, and the Production of Identity in* Die Gartenlaube, *1853-1900*. Lincoln, NE: U of Nebraska P, 1998.

Braker, Regina. "Bertha von Suttner's Spiritual Daughters: The Feminist Pacifism of Anita Augspurg, Lida Gustava Heymann, and Helene Stöcker at the International Congress of Women at the Hague, 1915." *Women's Studies International Forum* 18 (1995): 103-11.

Braun, Lily. *Die Frauen und der Krieg*. Leipzig: S. Hirzel, 1915.

———. *Frauenarbeit und Hauswirtschaft*. 1901. *Selected Writings on Feminism and Socialism: Lily Braun*. Ed. and trans. Alfred Meyer. Bloomington: Indiana UP, 1987. 55-101.

Bund deutscher Frauenvereine (BDF). *Eine Darlegung seiner Aufgaben und Ziele und seiner bisherigen Entwickelung.* Frankenberg: Lothar Riesel, 1900. Vol. 5 of *Schriften des Bundes Deutscher Frauenvereine.*

———. "Offiziellen Pressbericht über den Berliner Frauenkongress." Helene Lange Archiv-Bund deutscher Frauenvereine. Carton 77, Folder 310: 27 Feb.–2 Mar. 1912.

Bussemer, Herrad-Ulrike. *Frauenemanzipation und Bildungsbürgertum, Sozialgeschichte der Frauenbewegung in der Reichsgründungszeit.* Weinheim: Beltz, 1985.

Byles, Joan Montgomery. *War, Women and Poetry, 1914–1945: British and German Writers and Activists.* Newark: U of Delaware P, 1995.

Chickering, Roger. *Imperial Germany and the Great War, 1914–1918.* New York: Cambridge UP, 1998.

Daniel, Ute. *The War from Within: German Working-Class Women in the First World War.* New York: Berg, 1997.

Davis, Belinda. *Home Fires Burning: Food, Politics, and Everyday Life in World War I Berlin.* Chapel Hill: U of North Carolina P, 2000.

Dollard, Catherine. *The Female Surplus: Constructing the Unmarried Woman in Imperial Germany, 1871–1914.* Diss. U of North Carolina at Chapel Hill, 1999.

Evans, Richard. *Comrades and Sisters: Feminism, Socialism, and Pacifism in Europe 1879–1945.* New York: St. Martin's, 1987.

Frevert, Ute. *Women in German History: From Bourgeois Emancipation to Sexual Liberation.* Trans. Stuart McKinnon-Evans. New York: Berg, 1989.

Fritzsche, Peter. *Germans into Nazis.* Cambridge, MA: Harvard UP, 1998.

Gerhard, Ute. *Unerhört: Die Geschichte der deutschen Frauenbewegung.* Reinbek bei Hamburg: Rowohlt, 1990.

Gnauck-Kühne, Elisabeth. *Dienstpflicht und Dienstjahr des weiblichen Geschlechts.* Tübingen: J.C.B. Mohr, 1915.

———. *Die Deutsche Frau um die Jahrhundertwende: Statistische Studie zur Frauenfrage.* Berlin: Otto Liebmann, 1904.

———. *Die Soziale Lage der Frau.* Berlin: Otto Liebmann, 1895.

———. *Das Universitätsstudium der Frauen: Ein Beitrag zur Frauenfrage.* 3rd ed. Oldenburg: Schulzesche Hof-Buchhandlung, 1892.

Greven-Aschoff, Barbara. *Die bürgerliche Frauenbewegung in Deutschland, 1894–1933.* Göttingen: Vandenhoeck & Ruprecht, 1981.

Grossman, Atina. "The New Woman and the Rationalization of Sexuality in Weimar Germany." *Powers of Desire: The Politics of Sexuality.* Ed. Ann Snitow, Christine Stansell, and Sharon Thompson. New York: Monthly Review P, 1983. 151–73.

Hackett, Amy. *The Politics of Feminism in Wilhelmine Germany, 1890-1918*. Diss. Columbia U, 1976.

Hagemann, Karen and Stefanie Schüler-Springorum, eds. *Home/front: The Military, War, and Gender in Twentieth-Century Germany*. New York: Berg, 2002.

Hartmann, Eduard von. "Die Jungfernfrage: Schluss." *Die Gegenwart* 35 (1891): 131-34.

Harvey, Elizabeth. "The Failure of Feminism? Young Women and the Bourgeois Feminist Movement in Weimar Germany, 1918-1933." *Central European History* 28 (1995): 1-28.

Heineman, Elisabeth D. *What Difference Does a Husband Make? Women and Marital Status in Nazi and Postwar Germany*. Berkeley: U of California P, 1999.

Hering, Sabine. *Die Kriegsgewinnlerinnen: Praxis und Ideologie der deutschen Frauenbewegung im Ersten Weltkrieg*. Pfaffenweiler: Centaurus, 1990.

Higonnet, Margaret R. and Patrice L.-R. Higonnet. "The Double Helix." *Behind the Lines: Gender and the Two World Wars*. Ed. Margaret Randolph Higonnet, et al. New Haven, CT: Yale UP: 1987. 31-47.

Kuhn, Bärbel. *Familienstand Ledig: Ehelose Frauen und Männer im Bürgertum (1850-1914)*. Köln: Bohlau, 2000.

Lange, Helene. "Fünfzig Jahre Frauenbewegung." 1915. *Lebenserinnerungen*. Berlin: F.A. Herbig, 1930.

———. "Der Krieg und der deutschen Kultur." *Kriegsjahrbuch des BDF*. 14-19.

———. "Was wir wollen." *Die Frau* 1.1 (Oct. 1893): 1-4.

Levy-Rathenau, Josephine. "Die Lehren des Krieges für die Frauenberufsbildung." *Kriegsjahrbuch des BDF*. 60-68.

Lischewski, Heike. *Morgenröte einer besseren Zeit: Pazifistische Frauen 1892-1932*. Münster: Agenda Verlag, 1995.

Lischke, Ute. *Lily Braun: 1865-1916. German Writer, Feminist Socialist*. Rochester, NY: Camden House, 2000.

Mazón, Patricia. *Gender and the Modern Research University: The Admission of Women to German Higher Education, 1865-1914*. Stanford: Stanford UP, 2003.

Meskimmon, Marsha. *We Weren't Modern Enough: Women Artists and the Limits of German Modernism*. Berkeley: U of California P, 1999.

Meskimmon, Marsha, and Shearer West, eds. *Visions of the "Neue Frau": Women and the Visual Arts in Weimar Germany*. Brookfield, VT: Scolar P, 1995.

Meyer, Alfred. *The Feminism and Socialism of Lily Braun*. Bloomington: Indiana UP, 1985.

O'Brien, Catherine. *Women's Fictional Responses to the First World War: A Comparative Study of Selected Texts by French and German Writers.* New York: Peter Lang, 1997.

Pappritz, Anna. *Hinaus in das Leben: Ein Geleitwort für junge Mädchen.* München: J.G. Weiss'sche, n.d.

———. "Nationaler Frauendienst." *Kriegsjahrbuch des BDF.* 26-33.

Prinzing, Friedrich. "Heiratshäufigkeit und Heiratsalter nach Stand und Beruf." *Zeitschrift für Sozialwissenschaft* 5 (1902): 549-59.

Quataert, Jean H. *Reluctant Feminists in German Social Democracy, 1885-1917.* Princeton: Princeton UP, 1979.

———. *Staging Philanthropy: Patriotic Women and the National Imagination in Dynastic Germany, 1813-1916.* Ann Arbor: U of Michigan P, 2001.

Reagin, Nancy. *A German Women's Movement: Class and Gender in Hanover, 1880-1933.* Chapel Hill: U of North Carolina P, 1995.

Reuter, Gabriele. *Aus guter Familie.* 27th ed. Berlin: S. Fischer, 1931.

Rouette, Susanne. "Mothers and Citizens: Gender and Social Policy in Germany after the First World War." *Central European History* 30 (1997): 48-66.

Salomon, Alice. "Probleme der sozialen Kriegsfürsorge." *Kriegsjahrbuch des BDF.* 49-60.

———. "Die Zölibat der Lehrerin." *Die Welt der Frau,* supplement to *Die Gartenlaube* 16 (1910): 241-42.

Schaser, Angelika. "Women in a Nation of Men: The Politics of the League of German Women's Associations (BDF) in Imperial Germany, 1894-1914." Trans. Pamela Selwyn. *Gendered Nations: Nationalisms and Gender Order in the Long Nineteenth Century.* Ed. Ida Blom, Karen Hagemann, and Catherine Hall. New York: Oxford UP, 2000. 249-68.

Vely, Emma. "Die unverheiratete Frau in früheren Zeiten und heute." *Illustrierte Sonntags-Zeitung* 42 (1898/1899): 659-60.

Verhey, Jeffrey. *The Spirit of 1914: Militarism, Myth, and Mobilization in Germany.* New York: Cambridge UP, 2000.

Wex, Else. *Staatsbürgerliche Arbeit deutscher Frauen 1865 bis 1928.* Berlin: Herbig, 1929.

Wildenthal, Lora. *German Women for Empire, 1884-1945.* Durham, NC: Duke UP, 2001.

Zetkin, Clara. "Only in Conjunction with the Proletarian Woman Will Socialism Be Victorious." SPD Party Congress. 16 Oct. 1896. Rpt. in *Clara Zetkin: Selected Writings.* Ed. Philip S. Foner. New York: International Publishers, 1984.

Zietz, Luise. *Zur Frage der Frauenerwerbsarbeit.* Berlin: Paul Singer, 1916.

Cooking up Memories: The Role of Food, Recipes, and Relationships in Jeannette Lander's *Überbleibsel*

Heike Henderson

This article examines the role of food in Jeannette Lander's 1995 novel *Überbleibsel*. It considers the multifaceted connections between food, memory, and intercultural experiences. Special emphasis is placed on the rules of Kashrut and their impact on the narrator's culinary practice. The article further explores the relationship between the narrator's two great passions, cooking and writing. It also investigates the contradictions between the narrator's gourmet aspirations and weight-loss ambitions, and the power relations inherent in the process of cooking for others. Gender, while rarely mentioned by the author herself, plays an important role in all of these topics. (HH)

Food links people across geography and time and provides insights into the intersections of transnational, intercultural, and intracultural alterities. It plays a central role in both religious practice and everyday life, sustaining us physically and spiritually. And second to no other form of human expression, food embodies culture, generates memories, and initiates storytelling.

Food, memories, and cultural differences are the main topics in Jeannette Lander's 1995 novel *Überbleibsel: Eine kleine Erotik der Küche* (Leftovers: A Small Erotica of the Kitchen).[1] While describing the preparation of an elaborate meal, Lander contemplates her life as a Jewish-American woman who grew up in a black neighborhood in Atlanta, which is within predominantly Protestant America, and who, after many years in West Berlin, now lives in East Berlin. Lander reflects on food as a marker of difference and cultural alterity, but also as a means of coming together: "Cooking connects all of my worlds."[2] She examines the leftovers ("Überbleibsel") of her biography and the implications of cultural imprinting, social expectations, and religious rules. Recipes and relationships are called upon to investigate memories of the past and predicaments of the present.

Überbleibsel revisits many themes that Lander had started to explore in her earlier work. Her first three novels deal primarily with questions of Jewish identity and history. Because of its innovative structure and language, *Ein Sommer in der Woche der Itke K.* (A Summer in the Week of Itke K., 1971) in particular has received much critical attention.[3] Her subsequent work, especially the equally critically acclaimed *Jahrhundert der Herren* (Century of the Masters, 1993), moves away from Lander's prior focus on Jewish experiences and instead explores the colonial condition.[4] In all of these texts Lander's protagonists, like the one in *Überbleibsel,* vacillate between conflicting desires: the wish to belong vs. the wish to remain an outsider. As outsiders they are able to recognize structures not easily identifiable by those steeped in the culture. Already in a 1979 interview entitled "Unsicherheit ist Freiheit" (Insecurity Is Freedom), Lander referred to the enriching nature of the outsider's position: "I feel at home abroad [...] I enjoy the advantages of someone who cannot quite be categorized" (258).[5] Lander's reflections about the positive implications of minority status came long before they had been considered by most academics. Many years later, the protagonist in *Überbleibsel* still echoes this sentiment: "Away from home, I feel free. I am standing outside, observing from the sidelines" (40).[6]

For the first time since *Die Töchter* (The Daughters, 1976), published almost twenty years earlier, *Überbleibsel* foregrounds a Jewish protagonist. Although *Überbleibsel* does not carry any genre-specific categorization, the text contains many autobiographical elements. The narrator of the text is closely patterned after Lander herself.[7] Any details we learn about the life of the protagonist coincide with the life of the author, and while for the most part the narrator remains unnamed, at one point *Überbleibsel's* narrator mentions her father talking about his daughter, Jeannette (61). Lander herself, while refusing to categorize the text as either fiction or memoir, refers to it as an autobiographical novel: "This is the only book in all my writing up to now where I can say *every* word is autobiographical, where there is nothing in there that didn't happen or is not portrayed to the best of my knowledge" (Goozé and Kagel 21).

Überbleibsel, like all of Lander's books, was written in German, and for a German audience. Structurally less experimental than *Ein Sommer in der Woche der Itke K.,* it shares one important trait with Lander's first novel: whenever the protagonist remembers her parents, she switches into Yiddish. The memory of what her parents say is tied to the language in which they said it. For the reader, this literary device adds a strong *Verfremdungseffekt* (a Brechtian alienation effect) as well as a crucial sensory aspect. Similar to the effect of the detailed description of the food the protagonist is cooking (one can almost smell the delicious fare), the Yiddish language adds cultural depth and flavor. It brings to life an environment that most contemporary Germans have little experience with. It also undermines the traditional German reception of the "Jewish topic" restricted to the aftermath of the Holocaust.

Food plays a crucial role in *Überbleibsel,* and insights and perspectives from the interdisciplinary field of Food Studies can help to elucidate this text. As Carole M. Counihan asserts in her introduction to *Food and Gender: Identity and Power,* foodways are "an effective prism through which to illuminate human life" (1). The connections between food, memory, and intercultural experiences constitute the very center of Lander's autobiographical text. Carolyn Korsmeyer, in her seminal study, *Making Sense of Taste: Food and Philosophy,* insists that much of the importance of food is cognitive: It "has a symbolic function that extends beyond even the most sophisticated savoring" (103). This symbolic function is evident in narratives of eating as well: "Eating can signal gross indulgence and moral laxity or lusty participation in life's offerings. Attention to taste may indicate refinement of perception or silly preoccupation with superficial pleasures" (185). Lander's text succinctly illuminates this very gendered conflict between the desire to cook and eat well on the one hand, and culturally enforced body ideals as well as power relations inherent in the process of cooking for others on the other hand. The food she eats and serves is intimately related to and indicative of the narrator's construction of identity.

In her often-cited piece "'I Yam What I Yam': Cooking, Culture, and Colonialism," one of the few early explorations of the role of food in culture and literature, Anne Goldman observed that culinary memoirs "confound the line traditionally drawn between autobiography proper, where the subject is presumed to constitute herself as unique, and ethnography, whose postcolonial origin has situated the subject as representative of a culture" (189). By reading about *Überbleibsel*'s narrator and her culinary pursuits, we thus learn a lot not only about her as a person, but also about her cultural background and surroundings. Goldman has pointed out how such autoethnographic texts discourage cultural appropriation by "making ethnicity concrete, representing it as it is experienced by the individual, rather than invoking Culture as an abstraction" (189). Especially in regard to Jewish culture in Germany, this is of utmost importance. With the help of food, Lander thus continues and refines literary investigations of ethnicity and religion that characterized her earlier work.

Like any life-writing, Lander's text circles around the two poles of distinction and affiliation.[8] In *Reading Autobiography: A Guide for Interpreting Life Narratives,* Sidonie Smith and Julia Watson have identified five constitutive processes of autobiographical subjectivity: memory, experience, identity, embodiment, and agency, all of which are present in *Überbleibsel.* In the act of remembering, the autobiographical subject/narrator actively creates meaning from the past. The past thus gives meaning to the present, and the present necessitates a reconsideration and re-evaluation of the past. The subject is also constituted through her transcultural experience of geographical displacement. Cooking plays an essential role in Lander's discussion of cultural differences. It prompts her to reflect on cultural likes and dislikes, the availability (or lack thereof) of certain food items, and on different methods of preparing food. Frustrated about the limited availability of ingredients like curry leaf, coconut, and arrowroot, the narrator sighs, "We have not yet achieved the Asian level of cooking. We barely have reached the Italian level."[9] Having been exposed to different cultures and cooking styles, the narrator can make distinctions. The ensuing ranking turns the prevalent cultural preconceptions upside down.[10]

While discussing different styles of cooking and the availability of certain food items, Lander also compares distinctive German and American ideas about life, which provides a way to explain American culture to a German audience. In an interview, she describes this purpose as follows: "I wanted to create a tapestry of American life as I had known it, so that there would be more depth in the German picture of what America was like and what its people think" (Kraft and Lorenz 131). In *Überbleibsel,* Lander specifically mentions the following examples of cultural differences between Germany and the United States: the gigantic size of American supermarkets (24–26), the slow pace of life in the American South (26), the American belief in the power of positive thought (48), the American predisposition to view themselves as the center of the universe (50), American naiveté (52), the importance of shopping as a leisure time activity in the United States (76), the friendliness of American retail workers (77–78), and the ease of returning purchases in the United States (79–80). Lander sees it as her mission to rectify common stereotypes. She, for example, insists that sales clerks in the United States really smile, that it is not false pretense, as many Europeans believe: "They really smile. They don't paste on the smile, as Europeans usually believe."[11]

The narrator's identity manifests itself within collectivities, but it is an American collectivity of the past that determines her present German life. Memories of the past carry much more textual weight than the present-day storyline. While the narrator cooks dinner for present-day friends, there is very little interaction with and exploration of contemporary German issues and concerns. Instead, she reflects on the past, a past that for the most part took place outside of Germany. Lander paints a sometimes almost nostalgic picture of a different time and place, although she does recognize and verbalize the inconsistencies of life in the "old South." She misses the slower pace of life that allowed people to cook from scratch and pay attention to the food they were eating, but Lander recognizes the fact that, due to racial injustice, this slower pace of life did not apply to everybody: "One had time in the old South. In the old South, where those who ate were all white, and those who served were all black."[12] It is precisely her geographical and temporal distance that allows Lander to re-evaluate this time in her life, to compare, and to make sense of it. She recognizes the role these experiences played in her self-development, and she makes it her mission to explain them to a German audience with little knowledge of this time and place.

The narrator anchors her autobiographical subjectivity not only in geography and time, but also within her own body. Food and eating are central to our "experience of embodiment" (Lupton 1), and one way of taking control over the body is "to exert discipline over eating habits" (Lupton 16). My analysis of the contradictions between the narrator's gourmet and weight-loss ambitions will show how the narrator in *Überbleibsel* continually struggles to exert self-control over her body's desires. Any discussion of food explicitly points to the body as a site of autobiographical knowledge. Food becomes part of our own substance, or, as the well-known saying goes, one literally is what one eats.[13] What is eaten has the power to transform our bodies and thus ourselves, which is one of the reasons why so many cultural and religious rules concerning food and food taboos exist. Food and culinary practices possess the power to define boundaries between bodies and cultures.

Despite the narrator's refusal to be bound by any traditional strictures, her Jewish culinary heritage strongly influences her cooking and culinary reflections. The narrator sets her own practice of cooking against her mother's, a first-generation immigrant from Poland, and her older sister's, who follows the Jewish dietary laws of Kashrut. Because of their intricacies, kosher rules demand a cultural concentration on food. Lisë Stern, in her comprehensive guide to understanding Jewish dietary laws, describes the effect of Kashrut as follows: "Keeping kosher helps us pause and think about what we eat, and how we eat it, and elevates the act of eating into a spiritual as well as physical activity" (2). For Jews, the rules of Kashrut serve as a reminder of God and Jewish beliefs whenever one eats and also provide structure.

Although Lander's narrator decides to break the rules for kosher food, these rules nonetheless remain present: "The irrational rules and prohibitions of early childhood are very hard to erase. [...] If at all, one can only overcome them with the head, not with one's feelings."[14] While she extols the pork roast's delicious taste, the narrator also acknowledges that she has always had problems with pork: "Despite everything: I have had problems with pork roast from the beginning, I still have them with pork in general. I never totally overcame the prohibition of eating pork."[15] She especially has difficulties in finding uses for leftover pork: "To use leftover pork the same way Mom uses leftovers has always caused ambivalent feelings in me."[16] Residues of guilt mix with the freedom of transgression and self-determination, a feeling closely related to defiance, as she herself acknowledges.

In her youth, the narrator's adherence or non-adherence to the rules of Kashrut had already influenced the family dynamics. She reflects on her family's weekly visits to a restaurant. Every week, her father ordered a steak, immediately followed by ice cream for dessert, thus violating the rule of separating meat and milk products. Clearly the same rules that governed the choices of food at home did not apply to the restaurant. The narrator both follows suit and takes the violation even further by ordering shrimp cocktail, which she describes as "heavenly un-kosher,"[17] and bacon to put on her salad. She reveled in the feeling of transgressing religious rules, ever willing to counter criticism by debating the rules' inherent inconsistencies: "I really enjoyed pointing out other people's contradictions. The biblical laws of Kashrut provided many opportunities to do that, because they are marvelously illogical."[18] In sharp contrast to this behavior, her mother and sister ordered fish, considered a safe choice in a restaurant. In breaking the rules of Kashrut, the narrator thus tried to form an alliance with her father against her mother and her pious sister: "No, in the restaurant, Mom's kosher soul had no power over Tatte and me."[19]

Many years later, the narrator's own cooking exemplifies how her ethnic, religious, and gender identity informs every aspect of her daily life. While she rejects the strict rules of Kashrut, and even pities her religious sister, who will never be able to enjoy a roast with creamed potatoes (107), she does appreciate the mindfulness required of those who follow the laws of Kashrut. She herself has traded in the age-old religious rules of Kashrut for a contemporary mode of thinking closely related to the international Slow Food movement. Although Lander never directly refers to it, *Überbleibsel* can be read as a celebration of Slow Food. Founded in 1986 to protest the opening of a McDonald's in Rome, Slow Food now has chapters in over 100 countries. Its agenda is "to change the rules of the game so that taste, cultural identity and regional individuality are not assimilated into, and homogenized by, a global food culture devoid of diversity and pleasure" (Donati 228). This valuation of taste over convenience, as well as Slow Food's sometimes nostalgic approach to protecting tradition and rejecting commercial food, are more than evident in *Überbleibsel*. Voicing her frustration about the unavailability of fresh fowl, the narrator admonishes the storekeeper: "One cannot always eat frozen food. That's not healthy. [...] And it also does not taste good."[20] She argues for a mindfulness of eating that, in accordance with the Slow Food Movement, aims to "protect the pleasures of the table from the homogenization of modern fast food and life" (<http://www.slowfood.com>). By doing so, she effectively transforms the rules of Kashrut with which she grew up into a personal practice of cooking that shares many affinities with Slow Food.

The last of the five constitutive processes that Smith and Watson identify concerns agency, which they define as follows: "We need to consider how [...] people are able to change existing narratives and to write back to the cultural stories that have scripted them as particular kinds of subjects. Moreover, we need to consider how narrators negotiate cultural strictures about telling certain kinds of stories" (10). In *Überbleibsel,* the narrator assumes this type of agency. She writes against German stereotypes of Americans as careless consumers of fast food. Although she ultimately does confirm some stereotypes about Americans, her own sympathies for Slow Food locate her at the opposite end of the spectrum regarding the most persistent stereotype about Americans and food. In the same way that the American factor disrupts the traditional binary constellation of Jews and Germany, her eating habits, which ultimately go back to her Jewishness, refract the binary constellation of Germans and Americans.

Lander's narrator transforms culinary rituals, thereby resisting and rebelling against strict rules, while at the same time reclaiming parts of her heritage. The self in *Überbleibsel* is constituted and located with respect to a sense of family, community, and ethnic traditions. In *Überbleibsel,* cooking functions as "a metaphor for writing about and breaking tradition" (Blend 147).[21] According to Benay Blend, "reproducing a recipe, like retelling a story," requires the author to "maneuver between personal and collective texts, between an autobiographical 'I' and various forms of a political/cultural 'we'" (147), which Lander's text certainly does. Her narrator reclaims her culinary and cultural heritage, transforming and adapting it, and in doing so she assumes agency in the present.

Commenting on M.F.K. Fischer's culinary autobiography *The Gastronomical Me,* Anne Goldman observes how "writing literature and cooking dinner are represented as equally significant and equally satisfying forms of work" (169). The same could be said about Jeannette Lander's novel, where writing and cooking are complementary, since one originates in the mind and the other employs all the senses. In an interview for the *Women in German Yearbook,* Lander herself describes this connection as follows: "For me personally, cooking is absolutely necessary. If I am going to write, I have to cook. Because, you know, it's sensual: the thoughts that you are having, and looking for the right word and the next sentence. That goes on while you're doing something with your hands, something satisfying, something sensual. It's complementary. I need it" (Goozé and Kagel 21). Clearly, the sensory aspect of food in general and cooking in particular triggers memory; for Lander it fosters not only recollection, but also self-expression.

Writing and cooking are complementary, but they are also a lot alike. Lynn Z. Bloom, in her essay "Writing and Cooking, Cooking and Writing," describes them as "a messy mix of knowledge and improvisation, experience and innovation, and continual revision with a lot going on between the lines" (69). Of course they also both compete for one's time and dedication. While it is nice to escape to the sensual world of the kitchen when the writing process flounders, or to flee the manual labor of cooking and cleaning into the more cerebral world of literature and composition, there are times when both writing and cooking need to be done simultaneously. Lander's narrator seems at times consumed by these conflicting desires to both cook and write well: "Should I go into the kitchen? Should I not rather sit down at my desk and work? Write at least one page."[22]

She holds imaginary conversations with her mother in which she tries to explain her predicament and why she will not be able to keep her household up to her mother's standards: "'But Mom, I am writing,' I explain, striving for her understanding: 'If I were to complete every little household chore right away, I would always be cleaning and straightening up. One never finishes with that.'"[23] While seemingly at ease with her choices, the narrator still feels the need to justify her priorities. She knows that she does not fulfill traditional expectations of a spotless house; yet these expectations are so ingrained in her that she cannot help but feel inferior.

For Lander's narrator, the self is shaped and culture is transmitted through cooking *and* writing. She therefore invests a lot of emotional energy into both cooking and writing. While cooking a meal, she composes a story that explains, defines, and shapes a multifaceted and interconnected identity. Memories of family recipes compete with the seemingly endless possibilities and challenges of new recipes and new surroundings. Although Lander's narrator talks a lot about the ethnic Jewish food her mother used to make, the food she prepares herself is remarkably un-ethnic. Reading food as language, Sherrie Inness extrapolates how ethnic foods "create a powerful social language that speaks of cultural traditions and tastes that have been handed down from one generation to the next" (3). These foods become "strong markers of cultural and regional identity, conveying special feelings about belonging and place" (5). Lander's narrator seems conflicted between her desire to belong and her equally strong desire to transgress boundaries. She craves the cultural traditions of her family, but at the same time she refuses to be tied to them.

While Lander's narrator reminisces about family memories and cultural traditions, she resists being defined solely by her nationality, ethnicity, or religion. She constantly expands her repertoire of recipes and techniques, thereby increasing her range of available cultural expressions. And yet even the most un-ethnic food she prepares causes her to indulge in very ethnic memories. The narrator can break with or modify ethnic traditions regarding food, but she cannot break with her own past. Cooking food has the power to conjure up memories, and even a break with tradition does not negate tradition's role. In the words of Blend, "from the kitchen emanates not only food making but also ritual, tradition, and family history" (149). Eating habits are concrete symbols of cultural and personal identity and reconstruct cultural history, ground familial memory, and formulate individual authority (156). By simultaneously writing the self and representing the cultures within which that self takes shape, Lander's narrator claims her own subjective position and, at the same time, negotiates cultural stereotypes and expectations.

Connections between food, memory, and intercultural experiences and the complementary, but also problematic relationship between cooking and writing, make up two of the many layers imbedded in the text. Another layer consists of the relationship between the narrator's gourmet aspirations and her simultaneous weight-loss ambitions. On the very first pages of the text, the narrator describes her contradictory obsessions: losing weight and cooking extravagant, indulgent food. The text starts with the self-critical observation: "Actually I wanted to lose weight, but I had subscribed to this gourmet food magazine. I always want to lose weight. What kind of a life is that?"[24] She contemplates the difficulty of cooking tempting food that is low in calories, and how the seductive photos in this magazine tempt her to make homemade pasta with Gorgonzola cream sauce, which she knows she will regret the next morning when she steps on the scale. She ends this paragraph with a discussion of lust and reason, concluding with the heartfelt lament, "Oh why is pleasure not reasonable?"[25]

The magazine that causes these dilemmas is *Gourmet: The Magazine of Good Living*. Although it is an American magazine, the narrator has it sent to her house in Germany. The subtitle of *Gourmet* already implies its mission, which goes beyond providing recipes. It is a primer for the good life—for those of us who can afford it. Geared toward the upper-middle class, *Gourmet* discusses food, wine, travel, and restaurants, and copying its lifestyle requires large amounts of money and time. *Gourmet* celebrates an alluring, but mostly unachievable image of refinement and sophistication. As Leon Rappoport has pointed out in *How We Eat: Appetite, Culture, and the Psychology of Food,* gourmet pretensions are, however, increasingly accepted in our society as evidence of sophisticated cultural values (57). Jeremy MacClancy makes a similar point:

> These days it is not just OK, but almost *de rigueur,* for members of the aspiring middle classes to be foodies: to be knowledgeable about food and to cultivate an aesthetic sensibility towards it. [...] [F]oodies score conversational points by namedropping the best restaurants or by describing their latest visits to one of the culinary paradises. (209)

In her ground-breaking study, *Female Desire,* Rosalind Coward coined the term "food pornography" to describe the type of glossy food photos one encounters in culinary magazines and advertising. Coward's contemplations start with the observation that few activities rival relaxing in bed with a good recipe book (103). Jeannette Lander's narrator, who describes how the monthly issues of *Gourmet* magazine provide more than recipes and inspiration for her cooking, echoes this sentiment. She recalls a visit to her sister's house in Washington, DC, where she first encounters the magazine. After her sister and her husband go to bed, the narrator starts leafing through some back issues stored in the guest room. Reflecting on this first encounter, she reminisces, "Rarely was I so stimulated by reading."[26] *Gourmet*'s celebration of the "good life" awakens desire and allows her to indulge in vicarious pleasures. At the same time that she falls in love with the magazine, she wonders why her sister subscribes to it, since religious rules forbid her to make and eat many of the recipes. But maybe for her sister the visual gratification proves stronger than the recipes' limited usefulness. Later, the narrator continues to drop everything whenever the magazine arrives, and she describes how she goes back to bed and looks at the pictures. This behavior so resembles the consumption of sexual pornography that her husband Tony teases her, "Ah, your porn magazine has arrived."[27]

Unlike sexual pornography's mostly male audience, food pornography is explicitly geared toward women. It presents glossy pictures of food, perfectly prepared and presented. While at first glance food pornography seems to lack the illicit and naughty qualities of sexual pornography, Coward points out how even this kind of pornography cannot be consumed without guilt: "Because of pressures to diet, women have been made to feel guilty about enjoying food. [...] [A]t the same time as food is presented as the one legitimate sensual pleasure for women we are simultaneously told that women shouldn't eat too much" (103-04). Jeremy Iggers makes a similar point in *The Garden of Eating: Food, Sex, and the Hunger for Meaning*. Commenting on the link between sin and lust, the forbidden and the desired, he states, "Food has come to occupy the place in our consciousness once held by sex" (12). Accordingly, food has replaced sex as women's taboo subject: "In the fifties, good girls didn't have sex; today good girls don't have chocolate" (Iggers 110). While on the one hand we have more choices than ever regarding food, these choices are value coded and ultimately code their consumers: "What we choose makes us *naughty* or *good*" (Tisdale 4).

According to food sociologist Deborah Lupton, this binary opposition between good and bad food "is not simply a conceptual categorization, but involves the assigning of moral meaning to foods. 'Good' food is [...] indicative of self-control and concern for one's health, while 'bad' food is bad for one's health and on a deeper level of meaning is a sign of moral weakness" (27). Lupton goes on to explain how such distinctions are powerfully influenced by the cultural values of group membership. Religious rules offer a strict set of categorizations between what is good to eat and what is not. Less defined, but no less prohibitive, are the rules attached to gender. What popular Western culture deems good to eat for a man is not necessarily good for a woman, who is expected to adhere to a different set of guidelines regarding body weight and physical appearance.[28]

This double-edged view of food as cause of pleasure *and* guilt is certainly obvious in Lander's text. She constantly counts calories, and any contemplation of food she considers serving includes an evaluation of its richness and impact on her diet. She even wonders if she might possess the will power to serve high-caloric "Creamed Potatoes Bettle," part of a six-course menu, without eating any herself: "I know how good they taste, I don't need to eat them! I can just serve them, right? So the guests are impressed."[29] She regrets never being free from thoughts about her weight (36), and yet she cannot control negative thoughts whenever she contemplates food. Food causes her immense pleasure, but it also prompts self-doubt, guilt, and moral blame.

Discussing the role of food in film and fiction, Leon Rappoport has noted how "good women" are frequently "defined by the painstaking preparation of foods they serve to others but hardly eat themselves. 'Bad women,' on the other hand, tend to be shown as careless consumers" (52). The narrator's choice to prepare the wonderfully rich creamed potatoes for her guests, but abstain from eating them herself, reflects this sentiment. Women are urged to fulfill a role as nurturer by providing food for others. At the same time, they have to contend with external and internal pressures to fast and to conform to a mostly unattainable body image. These contradictory expectations are clearly noticeable in Lander's work. Interestingly, they come not from the outside, but from the narrator herself. She has internalized these expectations, and even while recognizing the absurdity of trying to fulfill these contradictory demands, she cannot escape their strictures.

For Lander's protagonist, eating well and writing well are connected. She traces her decision to give up fast food and pay attention to her weight to a single day when she was thirteen years old when she published her first poem in a newspaper.[30] On that day, she decided that the tongue, in both senses of the word, would be her means for living (29). Eating poorly or being overweight signifies a lack of discipline and quality, and this, she decrees, is not fitting for a writer: "I decided to bring discipline and quality into my life. After all it is not appropriate for a budding poet to accept her own contradictions, to eat poorly, to be fat."[31]

Looking back, the narrator still tries to live up to this original decree. Of course she now also realizes that eating well and, at the same time, losing weight can be hard to combine: "It was a paradox [...] between losing weight and eating well."[32] She strives for perfection in everything she does, and the food the narrator cooks and eats serves as evidence of her sophisticated cultural values, with her presentation of food mirroring and reflecting her presentation of self.

From this perspective, *Gourmet* becomes the harbinger of sin, which she already ascribes to the packaging of the "tempting" magazine that arrives every month in "innocent" yellow envelopes (20). Underneath this protective cover are the titillating photos that seem to jump out at the narrator. Rosalind Coward remarks that the "aim of these photos is the display of the perfect meal in isolation from the kitchen context and the process of its production. There are no traces of the hours of shopping, cleaning, cutting up, preparing, tidying up, arranging the table and the room which in fact go into the production of a meal" (104). Food appears immaculate and glimmering on fancy plates in perfectly arranged surroundings. It inspires viewers' wonder and makes them question, as the narrator's husband does, "How did they ever manage to do that?"[33]

While the narrator of *Überbleibsel* tries to recreate the perfectionism she encounters in these photos, she also carefully describes the many steps that go into the creation of a multi-course dinner. We learn about the hours involved in recipe selection, shopping, food preparation, and cooking. The narrator describes the pleasures she experiences cooking, but also those frenzied moments right before the guests arrive, aptly described as "moment of craziness"[34] when everything has to happen at once. The time crunch increases as the day moves on, which she captures in her style of narration. The pace literally accelerates, and any cooking mishap threatens to throw the narrator over the edge: "Now nothing, but really nothing at all is allowed to go wrong, otherwise it is like cars bumper to bumper on the freeway: a single small obstacle and everything breaks down."[35]

Despite sharing the frenzy of cooking with her readers, in front of her guests the narrator tries to obliterate the traces of hard work. She intends to make her cooking appear effortless in a Martha Stewart-like way: perfect without the messiness. Only her husband is privy to the amount of work necessary to impress her guests with ever more elaborate meals. This begs the question as to why she feels that she has to always up the ante and outdo herself each time. She wonders why she cannot scale back her menus: "I wish I had the strength of character to return to a simple style of cooking, although my guests by now expect these 'Gourmet' dinners."[36] Despite the toll that this perfectionism takes on her well-being, the narrator remains unwilling to step back, simplify the menu, or take any short cuts. She does not want to disappoint her guests' expectations or her own self-expectations.

Lander's narrator has very high standards that she applies to herself and to others. She disdains those who take shortcuts while cooking; remembering a time long ago in Atlanta when she actually bought baking mixes makes her shudder (24). Lander's narrator also has very strong feelings concerning the use of real stock. Using bouillon cubes would make her an accomplice in the loss of sensual perception; she wants to see, smell, and touch the bones that form the basis of the sauce she prepares (132). A purist who values taste over convenience, Lander observes, "I need to say what happens when you have to go back to scratch when you just cannot use one of these little bouillon cubes because it hurts your heart" (Kraft and Lorenz 135).[37] The smell of the stock that permeates her house while it cooks is a necessary and indispensable precursor to the taste of the finished sauce.

Despite her *Gourmet* aspirations, the narrator does not always cook such elaborate fare. For the narrator in *Überbleibsel,* the clever use of leftovers becomes a source of inspiration. Combining leftovers in just the right way, creating something new and as delicious as the original meal, is an art. She follows her mother's lead in using leftovers not out of a sense of duty, but as something to which to look forward: "[W]hat started as a use of leftovers, has become a purpose, to have leftovers."[38] The novel even ends with praise of leftovers. The narrator envisions how, after their guests have left, she and her husband will contemplate the leftovers they will enjoy the next day: "After they have left, we will pour ourselves a whisky. 'Mmmm,' he will say, and tomorrow, tomorrow we will have leftovers."[39] For the narrator, leftovers become an integral part of cooking, serving as well as a symbol for the leftovers of one's upbringing and cultural background. She even refers to the East Berlin neighborhood Prenzlauer Berg, where she currently lives, as a "leftover" from a different time that reminds her of Berlin in 1950, when she first arrived in the city (133–34).

The narrator's own use of leftovers manifests one of the many ways in which *Überbleibsel* pays homage to the narrator's mother. She praises her mother's cooking and credits her for her own cooking ambitions: "My culinary ambitions originated in Mom's good cooking, and her cooking was so good because she was never able to throw away anything."[40] Cooking connected her mother to her cultural heritage, and at the same time it helped her mother rise above her culture's limitations: "With her culinary art, my mother transcended the narrow limits of her origin. But her culinary art also connected her more deeply to her origin, because Yiddish moms have always strived to be their husband's pride, to experience his appreciation."[41]

The narrator codes her mother's desire to gain her husband's approval via cooking as a typical Jewish trait, and she places herself in the same tradition. She even speculates that a lack of recognition caused the failure of her first marriage and the success of her second: "My whole life, I was desperately seeking the recognition that I experienced between Dad and Mom. I think the lack of this recognition was the real reason for the failure of my first marriage, and I am sure its existence is the deeper reason for the happiness of my second marriage."[42] She craves the same recognition for her culinary skills that her mother received from her husband: "And now I am sitting here with my magazines, I am cooking elaborately, sometimes self-sacrificingly [...] becoming fatter, and all I want is to emulate Mom. I want Dad's satisfied and happy gaze."[43] Like her mother, she even refuses to let her husband help in the kitchen because she wants to earn his praise (23–24).

Both the narrator's own and her mother's situation show the act of cooking for others as one of power and control. On the one hand, cooking for family and friends is a labor of love and an expression of servitude: "That we should aspire to produce perfectly finished and presented food is a symbol of a willing and enjoyable participation in servicing other people" (Coward 103). By preparing and serving food to others, the narrator accepts a very gendered role of proper female behavior. To be sure, preparing an elaborate meal for friends differs from the daily obligation to put dinner on the table for one's family.[44] It allows much more room for artistic freedom and exploration. *Überbleibsel* shows how cooking can be a vehicle for artistic expression and sensual pleasure. And yet this type of cooking is also a service, one most often fulfilled by women, and is frequently accompanied by anxiety. Lander's narrator tries to impress her guests, and she expects to be judged for her cooking.

On the other hand, while cooking for others is an act of servitude, it also encompasses power. Beyond decisions of what to cook and how to prepare it, an accomplished cook, in particular, commands respect and admiration. Pierre Bourdieu has shown how the meals served on special occasions can be considered "an interesting indicator of the mode of self-representation adopted in 'showing off' a life-style" (79). Similarly, *Überbleibsel's* narrator uses her meals as an indicator of the self-image she wishes to present. Jeannette Lander's narrator clearly enjoys the admiration she garners with her cooking skills. When a friend asks her how she manages to cook the lamb to perfection, she offers only a very cursory description of her technique, prefaced with the statement, "[b]ut lamb is very simple."[45] Even her husband chides her for leaving out necessary steps:

> "I just find it dishonest," Tony insisted, "when you say 'very simple' and leave out everything that for you naturally is part of the process, but that somebody else does not know.... Then one tries. One does everything exactly as you described it. But of course it won't come out as good as yours, and you are the greatest."[46]

By withholding important steps, the narrator prevents others from copying her and "measuring up." While transforming the kitchen from a place of confinement to one of liberation and artistic expression, she simultaneously cements her superior position. Her relationship with her contemporaries is hierarchical, not reciprocal. She tries to dazzle and impress her guests by recreating the perfectly executed and staged food she encounters in *Gourmet*. Instead of fostering relationships with others through the exchange of recipes, she sets herself apart from and above the rest. Cooking an elaborate dinner for them is clearly an act of love, yet she determines the rules.

Lynn Bloom describes how for her "to write was to join the conversation of mankind, to cook [...] was to join the conversation of womankind" (71). Jeannette Lander's narrator refuses to join this feminine discourse exemplified in sharing recipes.[47] Instead, she participates in a more general human discourse. Lander herself articulates her intentions in *Überbleibsel* as follows: "I am describing methods of cooking, but actually, I am describing a state of being of people who like to cook, who love to cook and can do nothing which is halfway. But it's not a recipe" (Kraft and Lorenz 135). Life does not follow a recipe. Through her memories and reflections as well as through her cooking, she negotiates relationships with her past and her cultural background. Memories of her family's traditional religious and economic influences intermingle and interact with the "new world" inspirations of *Gourmet* cooking. These sometimes competing influences manifest themselves in her style of cooking and also in the recipes she uses. They are expressed in both her food and her writing, and it is the intimate connection between the two that makes this text so rich and multi-layered. Food takes center stage in *Überbleibsel,* becoming the catalyst for the narrator's discussion of past and present, self and others. Recipes build bridges and cause rifts, and food becomes the basis upon which relationships are formed and explained.

Notes

[1] All translations from the German are my own.

[2] "Das Kochen verbindet alle meine Welten" (40).

[3] Adelson, "Jeannette Lander's *Ein Sommer in der Woche der Itke K.* Jews and Other 'Others'" in *Making Bodies, Making Histories* provides the most sophisticated analysis of this novel. Adelson, "There's No Place Like Home," while primarily concerned with Lander's second novel *Auf dem*

Boden der Fremde (On Foreign Soil, 1972), examines the question of how to feel at home as a Jew in Germany.

[4] For interpretations of this novel see Adelson, "Imagining Migrants' Literature"; Adelson, "Interkulturelle Alterität"; and Shafi, "Between Worlds." Shafi, "Point of No Return" investigates paradigms of exile and loss in Lander's *Eine unterbrochene Reise* (An Interrupted Journey, 1996).

[5] "In der Fremde bin ich zu Hause. [...] Ich genieße die Vorteile des nicht ganz Einzuordnenden" (258).

[6] "In der Fremde fühle ich mich frei. Ich stehe außerhalb, beobachte vom Rande" (40). Lander's last novel, *Robert* (1998), is again situated in Germany. It is her first novel with a male protagonist, and it explicitly deals with the aftermath of the fall of the Wall. The language is saturated with contemporary German expressions like *Besserwessi* (literally "Better-Westy," a sarcastic description of people from the former West Germany who believe they know everything better than the people from the former East Germany). While this language reveals an author steeped in contemporary German discourse, the perspective is still that of an outsider looking in. Lander herself sums it up as follows: "I am not a part of this. I can laugh at it" (Goozé and Kagel 19).

[7] Lander was born in 1931 and grew up in a Yiddish-speaking family in Atlanta. After marrying a German man, she followed him to Germany, where she completed her education with a doctorate from the *Freie Universität* in Berlin. Despite the dissolution of her first marriage, she returned to Berlin where, not including a year in Sri Lanka in 1984/85, she has lived ever since.

[8] The term life-writing has been proposed by feminist critics like Shari Benstock. It challenges the traditional limits of autobiography by including other forms of self-revelatory writing like autobiographical fiction.

[9] "Wir sind noch nicht auf asiatischem Kochniveau. Wir sind gerade mal auf dem italienischen" (46).

[10] It is also interesting that Lander includes herself in the German "we."

[11] "Sie lächeln wirklich. Sie setzen nicht, wie Europäer meist meinen, das Lächeln auf" (77). Because of this article's focus on food, I cannot discuss the implications of these cultural differences. For a detailed discussion of the role of geographical displacement in Lander's work, see Goozé. Goozé analyzes Lander's geographical "elsewhereness" by situating her texts within a context of discussions regarding Germans and Jews. While she also employs some structuralist and feminist studies of food to decipher Lander's culinary project, she uses only texts published up to 1992. My article thus complements Goozé's work by incorporating newer perspectives from the evolving field of Food Studies, and also by providing a stronger focus on some gendered issues connected to food.

¹² "Man hatte Zeit im alten Süden. Im alten Süden, wo die, die aßen, alle weiß waren, und die, die servierten, alle schwarz" (108-09).

¹³ "Man ist was man ißt." The origin of this saying can be traced to an aphorism by Jean Anthelme Brillat-Savarin, who remarked, "Tell me what thou eatest, and I will tell thee what thou art" (xxxiii). Especially in Germany, because of the homophony between *ist* ("is") and *ißt* ("eats"), it is one of the best-known and often repeated truisms about food.

¹⁴ "Die irrationalen Ver- und Gebote der frühen Kindheit sind sehr schwer zu tilgen. [...] Man kann sie, wenn überhaupt, nur mit dem Kopf verwinden, nicht mit dem Gefühl" (42).

¹⁵ "Dennoch: Schwierigkeiten mit dem Schweinebraten hatte ich von Anfang an, habe ich noch überhaupt mit Schwein. Ganz habe ich das Verbot, Schweinefleisch zu essen, nie verwunden" (42).

¹⁶ "Aber gerade Schweinebraten im Sinne von Mama verwerten zu wollen, bereitet mir stets ein zwiespältiges Gefühl" (42).

¹⁷ "himmlisch unkoscher" (110).

¹⁸ "[I]ch mochte es nur zu gern, andere auf ihre Widersprüche hinzuweisen. Die biblischen Gesetze zum Kaschrot boten dazu immer Gelegenheit, denn sie sind herrlich unlogisch" (110).

¹⁹ "Nein, Mamas koschere Seele hatte im Restaurant keine Macht über Tatte und mich" (111).

²⁰ "Man kann nicht nur immer Tiefgefrorenes essen. Das ist ungesund. [...] Außerdem schmeckt es nicht" (147).

²¹ While Blend's remark refers to the writings of Pat Mora, Louise Ehrdrich, and Gloria Anzaldúa, I think it applies to Lander's text as well.

²² "[S]oll ich jetzt in die Küche gehen? Sollte ich mich nicht lieber an den Schreibtisch setzen und arbeiten? Wenigstens eine Seite schreiben" (93-94).

²³ "'Aber, Mama, ich schreibe', erkläre ich, um ihr Verständnis ringend: 'Wenn ich gleich jede Haushaltslappalie erledigen wollte, würde ich nur noch am Putzen und Aufräumen sein. Damit wird man doch nie fertig'" (144).

²⁴ "Eigentlich wollte ich abnehmen, aber ich hatte diese Zeitschrift abonniert. Ich will immer abnehmen. Was ist das für ein Leben?" (7).

²⁵ "Warum nur ist Lust nicht vernünftig?" (7).

²⁶ "Selten hat mich eine Lektüre so angeregt" (15).

²⁷ "Aha: dein Pornoheft ist wieder da" (21).

²⁸ For a further discussion of this topic, see Lupton, "Gendered Foods."

²⁹ "Ich weiß, wie gut sie schmecken, ich brauche sie doch nicht zu essen! Ich kann sie einfach servieren, nicht wahr? Damit die Gäste schwärmen" (98).

[30] Although fast food, in the way we know it today, was not available in the 1940s, Lander uses this term to describe the daily hamburger her protagonist buys at Krystall's burger stand at the bus station on her way to school (30).

[31] "Ich beschloß, Disziplin und Qualität in mein Leben zu bringen. Es ziemt sich doch nicht für eine angehende Dichterin, die eigenen Widersprüche zu dulden, schlecht zu essen, dick zu sein" (32).

[32] "Es war eine Paradoxie [...] zwischen Abnehmen und Gut-Essen" (66).

[33] "Wie haben die das denn hingekriegt?" (22).

[34] "Moment des Wahnsinns" (106).

[35] "Jetzt darf nichts, aber auch nicht das geringste mehr schiefgehen, sonst ist es wie bei Stoßstange-an-Stoßstange-Dichte auf der Autobahn: ein einziges kleines Hindernis und alles bricht zusammen" (145).

[36] "Innig wünsche ich mir die Charakterstärke, zu einer einfachen Küche zurückkehren zu können, obschon meine Gäste inzwischen diese 'Gourmet'-Menus von mir erwarten" (146).

[37] Anthony Bourdain, in his popular memoir/exposé *Kitchen Confidential: Adventures in the Culinary Underbelly,* expresses this sentiment even more strongly: "Life without stock is barely worth living" (82).

[38] "[W]as als Verwertung von Resten begann, ist längst zum Vorhaben geworden, Reste übrigzuhaben" (35).

[39] "Wenn sie gegangen sind, schenken wir uns einen Whisky ein: 'Mmmm', wird er sagen, und morgen, morgen haben wir Überbleibsel" (158).

[40] "Meine Kochambitionen haben ihren Ursprung in Mamas guter Küche, und diese war deshalb so gut, weil sie niemals etwas wegwerfen konnte" (11).

[41] "Mit ihrer Kochkunst überwand meine Mutter die engen Grenzen ihrer Herkunft. Aber ihre Kochkunst verband sie auf eine tiefere Weise mit ihrer Herkunft, denn der Stolz ihres Mannes zu sein, seine Würdigung täglich herauszufordern und zu erleben, das strebten die jiddischen Mamas immer schon an" (13).

[42] "Mein ganzes Leben lang suchte ich sehnlich eine solche Würdigung, wie ich sie zwischen Tatte und Mama erlebt habe. Ich denke, ihr Fehlen war der wahre Grund für das Scheitern meiner ersten Ehe, und ich bin sicher, ihr Dasein ist der tiefere Grund für das Glück meiner zweiten" (14).

[43] "Und nun sitze ich da mit meinen Heften, koche aufwendig, manchmal aufopfernd [...] werde immer dicker, und alles, was ich will, ist, es Mama gleichzutun. Ich will Tattes satten und glücklichen Blick" (14).

[44] In *Feeding the Family,* Marjorie L. DeVault has revealed how the often invisible work of planning, shopping, cooking, and serving meals can

become oppressive as well as rewarding for women. While many women express pride in their contributions, in literally *producing* family, this satisfaction is often mixed with frustration and exasperation.

[45] "Lamm ist doch ganz einfach" (118).

[46] "'Ich finde es einfach unredlich,' sagte Tony beharrlich, 'wenn du "ganz einfach" sagst und dabei alles wegläßt, was für dich selbstverständlich zum Handwerk gehört, wovon aber ein anderer keine Ahnung hat.... Dann versucht man. Man macht es genau, wie du gesagt hast. Es wird aber natürlich nicht so gut wie bei dir, und du bist die Größte'" (120-21).

[47] Susan J. Leonardi has pointed out that even the root of "recipe," the Latin *recipere*, implies an exchange: a giver and a receiver (340).

Works Cited

Adelson, Leslie A. "Imagining Migrants' Literature: Intercultural Alterity in Jeannette Lander's *Jahrhundert der Herren*." *The Imperialist Imagination: German Colonialism and Its Legacy*. Ed. Sara Friedrichsmeyer, Sara Lennox, and Susanne Zantop. Ann Arbor: The U of Michigan P, 1998. 265-80.

──────. "Interkulturelle Alterität: Migration, Mythos und Geschichte in Jeannette Landers 'postkolonialem' Roman *Jahrhundert der Herren*." Trans. Barbara Mennel. *Denn du tanzt auf einem Seil: Positionen deutschsprachiger MigrantInnenliteratur*. Ed. Sabine Fischer and Moray McGowan. Tübingen: Stauffenburg, 1997. 35-52.

──────. "Jeannette Lander's *Ein Sommer in der Woche der Itke K.*: Jews and Other 'Others': On Representations and Enactments." *Making Bodies, Making Histories: Feminism and German Identity*. Lincoln: U of Nebraska P, 1993. 87-124.

──────. "There's No Place Like Home: Jeannette Lander and Ronnith Neumann's Utopian Quest for Jewish Identity in the Contemporary West German Context." *New German Critique* 50 (Spring/Summer 1990): 113-34.

Benstock, Shari. "Authorizing the Autobiographical." *The Private Self: Theory and Practice of Women's Autobiographical Writings*. Ed. Shari Benstock. Chapel Hill: U of North Carolina P, 1988. 10-33.

Blend, Benay. "In the Kitchen Family Bread Is Always Rising: Women's Culture and the Politics of Food." *Pilaf, Pozole, and Pad Thai: American Women and Ethnic Food*. Ed. Sherrie A. Inness. Amherst: U of Massachusetts P, 2001. 145-64.

Bloom, Lynn Z. "Writing and Cooking, Cooking and Writing." *Pilaf, Pozole, and Pad Thai: American Women and Ethnic Food*. Ed. Sherrie A. Inness. Amherst: U of Massachusetts P, 2001. 69–83.

Bourdain, Anthony. *Kitchen Confidential: Adventures in the Culinary Underbelly*. New York: Bloomsbury, 2000.

Bourdieu, Pierre. *Distinction: A Social Critique of the Judgement of Taste*. Trans. Richard Nice. Cambridge: Harvard UP, 1984.

Brillat-Savarin, Jean Anthelme. *The Physiology of Taste*. Trans. M.F.K. Fischer. New York: Liveright Publishing Corporation, 1948.

Counihan, Carole M. "Introduction—Food and Gender: Identity and Power." *Food and Gender: Identity and Power*. Ed. Carole M. Counihan and Steven L. Kaplan. Amsterdam: OPA, 1998. 1–10.

Coward, Rosalind. *Female Desire*. London: Paladin, 1984.

DeVault, Marjorie L. *Feeding the Family: The Social Organization of Caring as Gendered Work*. Chicago: The U of Chicago P, 1991.

Donati, Kelly. "The Pleasure of Diversity in Slow Food's Ethics of Taste." *Food, Culture & Society* 8.2 (Fall 2005): 227–42.

Goldman, Anne. "'I Yam What I Yam': Cooking, Culture, and Colonialism." *De/Colonizing the Subject: The Politics of Gender in Women's Autobiography*. Ed. Sidonie Smith and Julia Watson. Minneapolis: U of Minnesota P, 1992. 169–95.

Goozé, Marjanne E. "The Interlocution of Geographical Displacement, Cultural Identity, and Cuisine in Works by Jeannette Lander." *Monatshefte* 91.1 (1999): 101–20.

Goozé, Marjanne, and Martin Kagel. "'I am not a part of this. I can laugh at it. But I know it.' A Conversation with Jeannette Lander." *Women in German Yearbook 15*. Ed. Patricia Herminghouse and Susanne Zantop. Lincoln: U of Nebraska P, 2000. 17–31.

Iggers, Jeremy. *The Garden of Eating: Food, Sex, and the Hunger for Meaning*. New York: BasicBooks, 1996.

Inness, Sherrie A. "Introduction: Eating Ethnic." *Pilaf, Pozole, and Pad Thai: American Women and Ethnic Food*. Ed. Sherrie A. Inness. Amherst: U of Massachusetts P, 2001. 1–13.

Korsmeyer, Carolyn. *Making Sense of Taste: Food and Philosophy*. Ithaca: Cornell UP, 1999.

Kraft, Helga, and Dagmar Lorenz. "Interview with Jeannette Lander." *The German Quarterly* 73.2 (Spring 2000): 129–44.

Lander, Jeannette. *Überbleibsel: Eine kleine Erotik der Küche*. Berlin: Aufbau, 1995.

———. "Unsicherheit ist Freiheit." *Fremd im eigenen Land: Juden in der Bundesrepublik*. Ed. Henryk M. Broder and Michel R. Lang. Frankfurt a.M.: Fischer, 1979. 258–64.

Leonardi, Susan J. "Recipes for Reading: Summer Pasta, Lobster a la Riseholme, and Key Lime Pie." *PMLA: Publications of the Modern Language Association of America* 104.3 (1989): 340–47.

Lupton, Deborah. *Food, the Body and the Self.* London: Sage, 1996.

MacClancy, Jeremy. *Consuming Culture: Why You Eat What You Eat.* New York: Henry Holt, 1992.

Rappoport, Leon. *How We Eat: Appetite, Culture, and the Psychology of Food.* Toronto: ECW P, 2003.

Shafi, Monika. "'Between Worlds': Reading Jeannette Lander's *Jahrhundert der Herren* as a Postcolonial Novel." *Women In German Yearbook 13.* Ed. Sara Friedrichsmeyer and Patricia Herminghouse. Lincoln: U of Nebraska P, 1997. 205–24.

———. "Point of No Return: Conflicting Desires in Jeannette Lander's Novel *Eine unterbrochene Reise.*" *Women in German Yearbook 15.* Ed. Patricia Herminghouse and Susanne Zantop. Lincoln: U of Nebraska P, 2000. 33–48.

Smith, Sidonie and Julia Watson. "Autobiographical Subjects." *Reading Autobiography: A Guide for Interpreting Life Narratives.* Minneapolis: U of Minnesota P, 2001. 15–48.

Stern, Lisë. *How to Keep Kosher: A Comprehensive Guide to Understanding Jewish Dietary Laws.* New York: Harper Collins, 2004.

Tisdale, Sallie. *The Best Thing I Ever Tasted: The Secret of Food.* New York: Riverhead Books, 2000.

Watson, Julia and Sidonie Smith. "Introduction: Mapping Women's Self-Representation at Visual/Textual Interfaces." *Interfaces: Women, Autobiography, Image, Performance.* Ed. Sidonie Smith and Julia Watson. Ann Arbor: The U of Michigan P, 2002. 1–46.

ABOUT THE CONTRIBUTORS

Heather Merle Benbow is Lecturer in German Studies at the University of Melbourne. She has written feminist articles and book chapters on Kleist, Goethe, Kant, and others.

Kelly Comfort received her PhD in Comparative Literature from the University of California, Davis in 2005. She is Assistant Professor of Spanish in the School of Modern Languages at the Georgia Institute of Technology. Her research focuses on European and Latin American literature of the modern period and her current book project explores the relationship between the ideal of art for art's sake and the reality of art for capital's sake in narrative works from both sides of the Atlantic. She is also editing a collection of essays on the dehumanizing and rehumanizing aims of aestheticism.

Catherine Dollard is Assistant Professor of History at Denison University. She received her PhD in History from the University of North Carolina at Chapel Hill. She has published articles on the history of German female education and on the sexual iconography of German single women and recently completed a book manuscript, *The Surplus Woman: Constructions of the Unmarried in Imperial Germany, 1871–1914*.

Sara Eigen received her PhD in 2001 from Harvard University and is Assistant Professor in the Department of Germanic and Slavic Languages at Vanderbilt University. She is co-editor of *The German Invention of Race*, a collection of essays on eighteenth-century science, philosophy, political theory, and literature, published in 2006 with SUNY Press. This year she received the Max Kade Award for her article entitled, "Self, Race, and Species: J.F. Blumenbach's Atlas Experiment," which appeared in 2005 in the *German Quarterly*. She has finished a manuscript entitled, *The Requirements of Kinship: German Enlightenment and the Nature of Community*, and has published essays and given talks on eighteenth- and twentieth-century literature, science, film, and law.

Angelica Fenner is Assistant Professor in Cinema Studies and a member of the graduate faculty in the Program in German Literature, Culture, and Theory at the University of Toronto. With historian Eric Weitz she co-edited the volume *Fascism and Neo-Fascism: Critical Writings on the Radical Right* (2004) and has published critical essays on the role of migration in German, Turkish, and French cinemas. Her current research investigates how documentary films mediate discourses of memory, migration, and auto/biography.

Heike Henderson is Associate Professor of German and German Section Head at Boise State University, where she has taught a wide variety of upper-division literature and culture classes since 1997. Her research expertise is in contemporary German literature. She has published on non-native authors, especially Turkish-German women writers, on representations of food in literature, and on finding balance between family and career. She is currently working on a book manuscript about the role of food in contemporary German literature and society.

Helga Kraft is Professor of Germanic Studies in the Department of Germanic Studies at the University of Illinois at Chicago. Her areas of research include nineteenth- and twentieth-century literary and cultural studies with a focus on gender and drama. Her book publications include *Writing against Boundaries: Nationality, Ethnicity and Gender in the German-speaking Context*, co-editor (2003); *Ein Haus aus Sprache: Dramatikerinnen und das andere Theater* (1996); *Mütter—Töchter—Frauen: Weiblichkeitsbilder in der Literatur*, co-editor (1993); and *Die Welt des Klanges: Musikalische Zeichen in Heinrich von Kleists Werken* (1976).

Richard Langston is Assistant Professor of German at the University of North Carolina at Chapel Hill. His research focuses primarily on literary and visual cultures in the postwar and contemporary periods. His forthcoming book, *Visions of Violence: German Avant-Gardes after Fascism*, examines the steady reconfiguration of avant-garde aesthetics into the twenty-first century. Langston has served as Director of the language program at UNC since the fall of 2002. He also trains and supervises graduate teaching assistants for all levels of language instruction.

Dagmar C.G. Lorenz is Professor of Germanic Studies at the University of Illinois at Chicago. Her research focuses on Austrian and nineteenth and twentieth-century German and German-Jewish literary and cultural issues and Holocaust Studies, with an emphasis on history, social thought, and minority discourses. She was the editor of *The German Quarterly* (1997–2003) and held offices in MLA, GSA, MALCA, and AATG. Book publications include *Keepers of the Motherland: German Texts by Jewish Women Writers* (1997), and *Verfolgung bis zum Massenmord: Diskurse zum Holocaust in deutscher Sprache* (1992) and the following edited volumes: *A Companion to the Works of Elias Canetti* (2004), *A Companion to the Works of Arthur Schnitzler* (2003), *Contemporary Jewish Writing in Austria (1999), Transforming the Center,* with co-editor Renate S. Posthofen *Eroding the Margins: Essays on Ethnic and Cultural Boundaries in German-Speaking Countries* (1998), and *Insiders and Outsiders: Jewish and Gentile Culture in Germany and Austria* (1994).

Margaret McCarthy is Associate Professor of German at Davidson College, where she also teaches Film Studies. Her research interests include twentieth-century German literature and film, film adaptation, and German popular culture. She has published essays on Ingeborg Bachmann, Jutta Brückner, Wim Wenders, Doris Dörrie, G.W. Pabst and Anna Duden, among others. She co-edited *Light Motives: German Popular Film in Perspective* (2003).

Beth Muellner is Assistant Professor at the College of Wooster in German and Women's Studies, where she teaches a variety of courses on the nineteenth and twentieth centuries, including the Weimar Republic, Travel Writing, and German Film. Her dissertation explores German women's travel writing from 1850 to 1930 that details women's experiences with trains, bicycles, and automobiles. She has published most recently on Malwida von Meysenbug. Her current research explores the friendship between Meysenbug and Swiss writer Meta von Salis and probes the influence of exiled women's intellectual communities on emancipation and the German women's movement.

Andrew Piper is Assistant Professor in the Department of German Studies at McGill University. He is the author of "Rethinking the Print Object: Goethe and the Book of Everything," which appeared in a special issue of *PMLA* called "Book History and the Idea of Literature." He is currently completing a book on the mobility of literature in the early nineteenth century entitled *Bibliocosmos*.

Gabriela Stoicea, a native of Romania, earned an MA in German from the University of Illinois at Urbana-Champaign in 2005 and is currently working toward a PhD in German Studies at Yale University. Her research focuses on the intersection of gender, politics, and aesthetics in Weimar literature and film, but she is also interested in Germany's intellectual history, German drama, and Balkan cinema, as well as various literary and cinematic representations of the Holocaust.

Marlene Streeruwitz is an Austrian writer who lives in Vienna. She also spends part of the year in New York, London, and Berlin. She started her career writing for the theater, and most of her plays are collected in *Waikiki-Beach. Und andere Orte. Die Theaterstücke.* (1999). This volume includes *Waikiki-Beach., Sloane Square., New York New York., Elysian Park., Ocean Drive., Tolmezzo., Brahmsplatz., Bagnacavallo., Dentro.,* and *Boccaleone*. In the mid-1990s Streeruwitz shifted her creative focus to prose fiction. She has published the following novels: *Verführungen. 3. Folge. Frauenjahre.* (1994); *Lisa's Liebe.* (1997); *Nachwelt.* (1999); *Majakowskiring.* (2000); *Partygirl.* (2002); *Norma Desmond. A Gothic SF-Novel* (2002); *Morire in levitate.* (2004); *Jessica, 30.* (2004); *Entfernung.* (2006). The writer holds a PhD in Germanic Studies, proudly calls herself a feminist, and has lectured and published widely on cultural issues, especially on gender topics. Book publications in this area include: *Sein. Und Schein. Und Erscheinen. Tübinger Poetikvorlesungen.* (1997); *Können. Müssen. Dürfen. Sollen. Wollen. Müssen. Lassen. Frankfurter Poetikvorlesungen.* (1998); *Und. Überhaupt. Stop. Collagen. 1996-2000* (2000); *Und. Sonst. Noch. Aber., Texte II. 1996-1998* (2002); *Gegen die tägliche Beleidigung. Vorlesungen.* (2004).

NOTICE TO CONTRIBUTORS

The *Women in German Yearbook* is a refereed journal. Its publication is supported by the Coalition of Women in German. Contributions to the *Women in German Yearbook* are welcome at any time. The editors are interested in feminist approaches to all aspects of German literary, cultural, and language studies, including pedagogy, as well as in topics that involve the study of gender in different contexts: for example, work on colonialism and postcolonial theory, performance and performance theory, film and film theory, or on the contemporary cultural and political scene in German-speaking countries.

While the *Yearbook* accepts manuscripts for anonymous review in either English or German, binding commitment to publish will be contingent on submission of a final manuscript in English. The editors prefer that manuscripts not exceed 25 pages (typed, double-spaced), including notes. Please prepare manuscripts for anonymous review and follow the sixth edition (2003) of the *MLA Handbook* (separate notes from works cited). Also use our special manuscript preparation guidelines posted on the WIG website. Send the manuscript as an email attachment in Microsoft Word to each editor:

Helga Kraft
Department of Germanic
 Studies
(M/C 189) 601 Morgan Street
University of Illinois
Chicago, IL 60607-7115

Phone: 312-996-3205
E-mail: kraft@uic.edu

Maggie McCarthy
Department of German and
 Russian
(Campus Box 6991) 209 Ridge Rd
Davidson College
Davidson, NC 28036

Phone: 704-894-2266
E-mail: mamcarthy@davidson.edu

For membership/subscription information, contact Vibs Petersen, (Studies of Culture and Society, Howard Hall, Drake University, Des Moines, IA 50311; e-mail: vibs.petersen@drake.edu).